# CRISIS AND TRANSITION IN ITALIAN POLITICS

# CRISIS AND TRANSITION IN ITALIAN POLITICS

Edited by

## Martin Bull

and

## Martin Rhodes

## FRANK CASS

LONDON • PORTLAND, OR

*First published 1997 in Great Britain by*
FRANK CASS & COMPANY LTD
Newbury House, 900 Eastern Avenue
London IG2 7HH

*and in the United States of America by*
FRANK CASS
c/o ISBS
5804 N.E. Hassalo Street, Portland, Oregon 97213-3644

Transferred to Digital Printing 2004

**Library of Congress Cataloging-in-Publication Data**
A catalog record of this book is available from the Library of Congress

**British Library Cataloguing in Publication Data**

Crisis and transition in Italian politics
  1. Italy – Politics and government – 1976–
  I. Bull, Martin J.  II. Rhodes, Martin  III. West European
  politics
  320.9'45

  ISBN 0-7146-4816-7 (cloth)
  ISBN 0-7146-4366-1 (paper)

This group of studies first appeared in a Special Issue on
'Crisis and Transition in Italian Politics' in
*West European Politics*, Vol.20, No.1, January 1997
published by Frank Cass & Co. Ltd.

Typeset by
Vitaset, Paddock Wood, Kent TN12 6HF

# Contents

# Between Crisis and Transition: Italian Politics in the 1990s

## MARTIN BULL and MARTIN RHODES

The last special issue of *West European Politics* devoted to Italian politics was published in 1979.[1] The timing of that issue was apposite. It came at the end of a decade of social, economic and political crisis in which Italy was portrayed as the 'sick man of Europe'. Yet, the originality of that issue lay in its challenge to much of the existing literature which sought to portray Italy as an 'anomaly' among west European democracies. It showed that, despite its unique features, the politics of Italy were, in many ways, comparable to those of other nations.

Fifteen years on, few would question the need for a further special issue on Italian politics. This is not just because much has changed since 1979, but more specifically, because so much has appeared to change since 1989. Indeed, it could be argued that, despite the significance of the 1979 issue and of the social science research on Italy it helped to generate, something analogous to a 'popular portrayal' of Italy is happening in many of the analyses of Italy today. The dramatic developments since 1989 and the crisis which has resulted have generated a new focus on the country, yet this has to a large extent been dominated by the idea, particularly prevalent in the early 1990s, that Italy has been undergoing a 'revolution', and that, once again, there is something unique about democracy *all'Italiana*.

Any analysis of political change which focuses only on this period is bound to be reductive and incomplete. This new special issue on Italian politics seeks to analyse the last decade and a half of Italian political development through the prism of the changes of the 1990s. The 1990s will, inevitably, be seen as a watershed decade in Italian political development. Yet, contrary to the popular portrayal of these changes as revolutionary, these years have witnessed considerable continuity beneath the surface change, making the contemporary period one of ongoing transition rather than rupture with the past. This is not to deny the significance of recent changes. On the contrary, by exploring developments over the past 15 years across a range of sectors and areas, the authors in this collection seek to identify the deep trends of political change in Italy's transition beneath the ephemera of day-to-day political life – the focus of much current analysis. They reveal a political system that is both dynamic and sclerotic, adaptable and blocked, and with a surprising degree of institutional inertia. Thus while some aspects of the system are adjusting to the new challenges of the decade, other areas are adapting much more slowly, despite the headline-grabbing political upheavals of recent years. Indeed, paradoxically, it is those areas which appear to have witnessed the most dramatic changes (and specifically the political parties) which are proving to be most dilatory in driving Italy's transition forward. This combination of vigour and stagnation lies at the heart of the Italian paradox; and while the transition remains incomplete, so the 'crisis' will continue. The aim of this introduction is to explore briefly the nature of this paradox.

THE ITALIAN MODEL

Although all of the articles in this collection focus uniquely on the Italian situation, a number of preliminary points should be made about the comparative dimension. For despite the fact that Italy, like other European countries, has been made the subject of comparative research – which has countered, as already noted, the idea that Italy was an anomalous case among western democracies – something may have been lost by the tendency to search for the comparable at the expense of the particular. This point was already made in the 1980s by those who argued for the existence of a 'southern model' of democracy against those who argued that, in broad comparative terms, no such model existed.[2] Yet if there was nothing 'special' about Italian democracy – let alone that of the other countries of southern Europe which underwent a process of political and economic 'modernisation' much later – then how do we make sense of the upheavals of the last few years? Why is the transition towards what is popularly called the 'Second Republic' – presented by many Italian commentators as a 'normalisation' of Italian politics and a progressive move into the European mainstream – proving so difficult? This raises a second question: if Italy is in transition, what is it moving away from and where, precisely, is it heading?

To argue that the Italian situation has more in common with that of the newly democratising countries of central and eastern Europe than with other western democracies is clearly to overstate the case. In terms of foreign politics, Italy is hardly an outsider in the western democratic camp. Italy is a founder member of the European Union (EU) and an ardent promoter of greater European integration; it is a long-standing and committed member of the western alliance; its economy is deeply integrated with those of its EU partners and it is a signatory of the international agreements that regulate trade, labour and human rights in the west. In domestic political terms, it would be a mistake to underestimate Italy's democratic credentials: it has a set of well-established and respected constitutional norms, a strong party system, a high level of political participation (party membership and voter turnout) and vibrant associational and political sub-cultures.

Yet, by the same token, it would be misleading to assert that there was nothing distinctive, or, dare one say, 'defective', about Italian democracy. First, there are the features of a 'southern type' of politics that it shares with other countries of the region, including the problem of inadequate political institutionalisation and what Sapelli has called an 'anomic division of political labour' – the result of a 'balkanisation' and exploitation of the state by particular sectors of the political and economic élite and the absence of an administrative technocracy. For Sapelli, Italy is a significant example of the weaknesses to be found in southern European democracy, based, as it is, on 'collusion, a lack of sense of state and the ubiquity of clannish parties', a problem compounded by its weak embrace of the Weberian concept of 'belief in law'.[3] Second, alongside the positive aspects of its democracy there are numerous – and interconnected – *sui generis* defects, some of which are the specifically Italian expressions of the 'southern type': the political dualism between north/centre and south that parallels the economic disparities between these regions; the dominance of the Christian Democratic Party (DC) and its satellites, its tactical exclusion of the second largest political party (and culture) – the Italian Communist Party (PCI) – from national power until the 1990s, and its systematic colonisation of the state machine; and the routinisation of what we can call 'illicit governance', based on extensive networks of exchange (*scambi occulti* – hidden exchanges)[4] spanning the public administration, public sector and political parties, creating a 'hidden power' structure behind the already tarnished democratic facade of a 'blocked' and incomplete democracy.

STRUCTURAL CRISIS

If we accept this characterisation of Italy as 'normal' democracy in outward appearance, but one 'handicapped' by the legacy of 'modernisation without development', then we can begin to understand the structural roots of the Italian crisis. In many senses, the developments of the last few years represent a struggle between traditional and modernising forces and the norms of political behaviour and social organisation they each promote and defend. While the traditional forces have been responsible for the impasse reached by the political system by the end of the 1980s, their modernising counterparts have been seeking a way out of the morass. The Italian impasse can be expressed in terms of its incapacity for internally generated political reform and inescapable drift towards 'systemic crisis' – an expression used by Maurizio Ferrera in this volume to describe the Italian welfare system, but applicable, in fact, to the entire polity.

Glib assertions to the contrary, Italy by the late 1980s/early 1990s could no longer be characterised as a country whose many problems could be disregarded on the basis of *eppur se muove* (nevertheless it works).[5] As the experience of the 1990s has shown, the tensions within the system had been building up with cumulative and debilitating effect. The *pentapartito* (five-party coalition) government under the self-interested control of the so-called CAF – the strategic and cynical alliance of Bettino Craxi, Giulio Andreotti and Arnaldo Forlani – had taken to its logical extreme a form of government based on the permanent exclusion from power of the main party of the left (representing consistently more than a quarter of the electorate) and on the distribution of spoils and patronage. The squalid pursuit of not just party but individual aggrandisement reached its apogee in the Socialist Party and the quite ostentatious display on the part of some of its members of potentate power. The political class was manifestly ethically bankrupt and incapable of reforming either itself or the institutions it had neglected or turned to its own, particularistic, usage via the 'privatisation of the public sphere'.[6] As discussed in the analysis by Martin Rhodes, 'blocked democracy' had helped to spawn a system that was not just corrupt but systematically *corrupted*, to the extent that 'illicit governance' had become the norm. The economic problems of the country were in part connected to this process, facilitated by the absence of an administrative technocracy and a 'rational' and 'functional' capacity for decision making – all negative features of what della Sala calls a 'weak' or 'non-state', one exploited not just by its political masters, but captured, in a self-perpetuating cycle of clientelistic exchange, by a broad range of societal interests. Again, the welfare system exemplifies the more general 'functional crisis' of the state. By the late 1980s, recurrent public-sector deficits had generated an enormous public-sector debt that was constraining Italian fiscal and monetary policy and beginning to generate important political strains. By the early 1990s, these strains began to manifest themselves in the 'tax revolt' which underpinned the success of Umberto Bossi's secessionist *Lega Nord* (Northern League) and now pose a serious challenge to national identity.

Broadly speaking, then, Italy has been undergoing a growing crisis with four dimensions:[7]

(1) a crisis of the political parties, which had gradually moved away from being organisations devoted to the mobilisation of the electorate and the expression of ideological and policy preferences, to being machines for mobilising, distributing and exchanging resources;

(2) a crisis of the political class, which had become more and more degenerate and degraded by the logic of *partitocrazia* and *scambi occulti*

and which, with the collapse of the Soviet Union, and the final laying to rest of the supposed 'Communist threat', had lost their only rationale for clinging to power, except for the continued 'privatisation' of the public sphere;

(3) a crisis of institutions, which the political class, incapable of anything other than clannish, party 'fetishism', was unable or unwilling to reform, and which, as in the case of Parliament, helped contribute to the inefficiency and incapacity of the state as a decision-making body and compounded the crisis of public finances (witness the chaos of budgetary politics, beset until recent years by secret voting and the exertion of clientelistic pressures on members of the Chamber of Deputies and Senate);

(4) and a crisis of the state, more broadly conceived, as a legitimate system of governance, protecting and sustaining the identity of the nation. While one can debate the origins of the state's lack of legitimacy in Italy, it is clear that the politicians in Rome had done much to discredit themselves over the previous 30 years or so, and that their unpopularity preceded the revelations of the *Tangentopoli* ('Bribesville') scandals. Yet these revelations fuelled a rejection of politicians that now threatens not just the revitalisation of democratic government but the unity and stability of the country.

In short, the *structural* crisis invests the political class, the political parties, institutions and, more generally, the state and national identity. It is, therefore, fundamentally a political crisis, but one with distinct economic and social implications. This should be distinguished from the conjunctural crisis, even though, as will be argued below, the two are inextricably linked.[8]

CONJUNCTURAL CRISIS

The conjunctural crisis refers to the crisis ostensibly triggered by *Tangentopoli* and the collapse of support for the traditional parties between 1992 and 1994. The structural and conjunctural crises are inevitably linked but, at the same time, of a different order. The structural crisis is deeply rooted in the institutional arrangements of the country and in the norms of political behaviour. The conjunctural crisis is the expression of the sudden breakdown of political parties, alliances and networks that were, on the one hand, partly responsible for the systemic problems of the country, and, on the other, partly its victims. For the logic of the political system and its underpinning power structure simultaneously undermined the system's institutional foundations and precluded the emergence of forces capable of reforming them. In many respects, collapse was the inevitable consequence of the systematic abuse of power. If, by the late 1980s, the system was rotten, its very nature also hindered the key political actors from behaving much differently if they wished to stay in power.

The unfolding of the conjunctural crisis is documented by James Newell and Martin Bull and Roberto D'Alimonte and Stefano Bartolini. The meltdown of the old configuration of parties was, by comparative standards, extraordinarily rapid, so rapid, in fact, that it created a vacuum which new and recycled parties and movements attempted to fill. This vacuum allowed the creation and successful electoral launch of a truly new and original phenomenon in *Forza Italia*, described by one commentator as a 'virtual party'.[9] The Berlusconi experience – his rise to power only four months after launching *Forza Italia*, and his subsequent turbulent eight months as Prime Minister – was, with the fall of politicians like Craxi and Andreotti, a symbol of the completely unpredictable nature of the crisis which could produce unexpected and ephemeral outcomes and multiply the dimensions of the crisis. In the case of Berlusconi, his rise to the premiership prompted a major debate on both his 'conflict of interests' and, more broadly, on the use and abuse of the media in Italian politics, as outlined by Luca Ricolfi.

Why precisely the collapse of the traditional parties occurred *when* it did has been the subject of much speculation but, as yet, little systematic exploration.[10] In the popular imagination, it was caused by the collapse of communism and the exposure by Italian magistrates of a massive system of corruption operated for years by the political parties. These factors are important but they are inadequate by themselves in explaining why the Italian polity, specifically in the 1990s, should have witnessed the effective removal of its former political class and the dramatic reconfiguration of its party system. As already discussed, there are deeper historical and structural reasons which relate to the nature of the post-war Italian political system. There are also changes in society and in the nature of the economy to take into account, as well as the transformation of the international political and economic context.

Of the domestic factors, three are worthy of note. First, there was a growing disjuncture between a modernising and highly successful private-sector economy, composed of both dynamic small- and large-sized firms, and a decrepit state machine and public sector. Additional domestic pressure was exerted by the internationalisation of this economy in the 1980s (see below). Second, there was the emergence of social and reform movements, accompanied by a new type of politician no longer willing to accept 'illicit governance' and its implications for society. The most powerful expressions of this were the emergence of the *Rete* (the Network), led by former DC politician, Leoluca Orlando, and the associated anti-

Mafia movement in the south, the referendum movement led by Mario Segni, and the Northern League led by Umberto Bossi. Third, the expropriation of the state by political parties began to meet its physical limits, given the inflationary dynamic in the *mercato occulto* (black market economy) and the ever more ferocious intra- and inter-party struggle for resources to which this gave rise. Once the exposure of illicit governance had begun in Milan, the proliferation of the *Tangentopoli* investigation, and its attraction of widespread support from the populace, owed much to the independence and politicisation of the Italian judiciary – as examined by Carlo Guarnieri – and the peculiar nature of Italian criminal procedure. In the absence of the role played by the Italian magistrates (and their powers of investigation), it is doubtful that the crisis of the political establishment would have been so extensive. This role in itself triggered a crisis in judicial–political relations, but this, again, was an inevitable product of the nature of the development of these relations in the post-war period.

At the same time, there are international factors that should be taken into account, two of which are particularly noteworthy. The collapse of communism in eastern Europe obviously had a significant impact in a country which was home to the largest communist party in the West. It marked the drying up of US aid to the traditional parties of government, (the decline in which had long proceeded the fall of the Berlin Wall), and – with the transformation of the PCI into the Democratic Party of the Left (PDS) – the end of the communist threat in Italy, whether symbolic or real. True, the Italian Communists had ceased to be a real 'threat' many years earlier, and such arguments had been increasingly used in a purely instrumental manner by many leading Christian Democrats and Socialists to keep the Communists excluded from power. Yet, the effect of an unequivocal renunciation of the party's teleological nature, in the broader context of the collapse of the international Communist regimes and fraternity, on the social bases of the governing parties should not be underestimated. Voters hostile to left-wing extremism who had long learned to 'hold their noses' and vote Christian Democrat, were effectively released to fish in other pools, an effect unanticipated by the Christian Democrats (and Socialists) themselves, whose initial response to the PCI's transformation was muted, when not cynical and apparently disbelieving.

The second, and ultimately more important, international factor was the burgeoning influence of the European Community and the impact within Italy of economic internationalisation. In essence, the European Community has introduced a new style of politics into southern Europe, based more on northern 'Protestant' or 'technocratic' norms which fit ill alongside the personalised, clientelistic politics of the south. While the latter have often subverted the former, the battle between these norms began to expose the endemic weaknesses of Italy's 'anomic' division of political labour already in the 1980s with the troubled transfer into Italian law of Community directives and their inadequate implementation, as well as the widespread fraudulent abuse of EC aid. At the same time, the deficiencies of the economy were being exposed to new scrutiny by international capital markets. Moreover, the traditional collusive practices that had informally regulated investment, the stock exchange and corporate governance were being undermined by the need to conform to new regulations, as signalled by the manifest lack of confidence in the Italian system expressed by foreign investors. The signing of the Maastricht Treaty, in a country famed for its pro-EC populace, immeasurably increased the pressure on Italian political elites who had only slowly and reluctantly responded to the need to begin long-term financial and economic reform. That they were incapable of doing so effectively was perhaps symptomatic of the extent to which the governing parties' power bases had become dependent on levels of patronage and corruption which the country could no longer afford if it wished to remain in the club of advanced European nations.

The extent to which the above factors actually precipitated the crisis is open to question, but they were certainly important in creating a context ripe for change and in promoting a modernising élite – in both the political and economic spheres – which was increasingly dissatisfied with the status quo. At this juncture, crisis and transition, became inseparable, the former closely shaping the course of the latter.

TRANSITION

Viewed together, the studies in this special issue show how, despite the dramatic changes of the 1990s in various aspects of the system, the changes in the style of Italian governance have been affected far more by external, outside forces than by the goals and strategies of political actors inside the *palazzo*. Della Sala shows how the role of the state and governance in Italy is undergoing considerable change as a result of the demands arising from European integration on the performance of the economy. On the one hand, the state has been ceding authority upwards ('hollowing out') to the EU in terms of the broader objectives of macro-economic policy. On the other, responding to these demands has required a 'hardening' of the state towards the groups and interests traditionally used to exercising influence over economic policy inside the state and society. Consequently, Italy's traditional state model, one based on the penetration of the state and economic policy-making by a multitude of interests, rendering policy making fragmented and inefficient, is being undermined.

This has occurred, moreover, at a time when the political parties and party system have been undergoing a deep crisis. The consequence, as Pasquino argues, has been the effective suspension of party government in the 1990s, and an increasing dominance of technicians (and notably ex-central bankers) over key decision-making positions.[11] And even with the resurrection of party government under Romano Prodi, it is notable that the central characteristic of the government is a curtailing of its decision-making autonomy by the demands of the Maastricht Treaty – a government, moreover, whose main component part, for the first time in Italian history, is the ex-Communist party (PDS), and which is supported in Parliament by the current Communist party (Communist Refoundation). The consequence of a 'technocratic' response to economic problems, legitimised by the need to respond to external pressures, has delivered notable successes, including recent advances in tackling the public sector deficit (producing a surplus net of interest payments), reducing inflation and lowering interest rates – a virtuous circle which cannot be broken if Italy is to join the club EMU countries.

At the same time, significant changes to welfare provision were achieved in 1992, 1993 and 1995, as outlined in the article by Maurizio Ferrera. These reforms are significant breakthroughs with respect to the institutional legacies of the past, and are aimed at responding to the system's in-built growth pressures as well as the legacy of debt under new economic and monetary constraints. Similarly, as noted in the contribution by Marino Regini and Ida Regalia, changes in relations between the state, employers and trade unions – as well as in the behaviour and organisation of the social partners themselves – have been driven to a large extent by the external context, specifically the constraints of the 'Maastricht parameters', the globalisation of markets and the intensification of international competition: all three place a premium on the search for greater consensus in industrial relations and its institutionalisation in the form of an incomes policy, although recent threats to undermine this consensus from various parts of the union movement underline the fragility of both the arrangements and the legitimacy of the policies underpinning them. In short, the 'hardening' of the state should not necessarily be equated with the denial of any influence to organised groups, but the adaptation of those groups to a more informal (and usually decentralised) mode of exercising influence.

These quite impressive changes in the nature of economic governance contrast strongly with the current lack of progress in institutional reform, as explored in the pieces by Gianfranco Pasquino, Bruno Dente and Giacinto della Cananea. If one believed the rhetoric of the parties and many commentators, Italy, in the 1990s, is on the cusp of fundamental constitutional reform. Yet, thus far, only one fundamental institutional reform has been achieved – the electoral system – and this has not had, until now, the consequences expected. The most far-reaching reform of the state would be the dismantling of Italy's unitary–decentralised state and its replacement with a genuine federal structure. The political prominence of the Northern League, and its secessionist demands, when combined with the federalist proposals of virtually all the political parties, would appear to suggest that this is likely. Yet, not only do deep disagreements prevail over the type of federalism deemed useful and over the procedure by which it could be achieved, but the debate reveals scant awareness of any of the complex and fundamental questions which would need to be resolved in any such constitutional change. The situation is, in Pasquino's words, one of 'confrontational stalemate'.

Moreover, changes in central–local relations, as documented by Dente, are likely to hinder radical reform of the state in a federalist direction. While the likely recipients of new federal powers (regional governments) have generally languished in the late 1980s and early 1990s, the communal levels of government have undergone a significant renovation in structure and personnel, the first a product of the reform which introduced the direct election of local mayors, and the second a consequence of the need to replace personnel implicated in the corruption scandals. The revived communes, whose new-found influence is perhaps best expressed in the cross-party 'Mayor's Movement' are unlikely to cede happily powers to a regional or new federal level of government.

The contrast drawn by della Cananea between the transformation of finance and the stasis in the administrative sphere is telling. The importance of external pressures on public finances is visible and direct, including Italian membership of the EMS, the discipline of financial markets and compliance with the criteria for EMU membership. But none of this directly affects public administration (although, as in the case of welfare, the indirect relationship is an important one) and cannot, therefore, act as a major driving force to change. Consequently, reform of the administration, and further reform of the welfare state, is impeded by the strength of vested interests and the problems that still afflict the effective wielding of governmental power in Italy, including the constraints of coalitions built on a wide range of parties, and the habitual clannish and often selfish behaviour of politicians. Many of the latter have yet to learn that the pay-offs for party 'fetishism' are not what they were, and this is creating a yawning divide between an old world of personalised and clientelistic political behaviour and a new world characterised by an increasingly technocratic, or 'rational', approach to decision making.

It could be argued, in short, that the Italian state is undergoing change in various areas, but it is change which is largely divorced from progress on fundamental constitutional issues which might amount to a genuine regime transformation. For change is clearly slowest in materialising precisely where it is dependent on the political parties, despite the fact that the political parties and party system appear, prima facie, to have changed and renovated themselves more than any other parts of the system. A closer analysis of the parties and party system shows why this so. There is no doubt that the configuration of parties which characterised the post-war Republic has been swept away. As documented in the study by James Newell and Martin Bull, the 1990s have witnessed a transformation in the number and type of parties and the nature of the alliances they have formed. This transformation has been a tortuous and complex affair, one which has seen the complete demise of the party which dominated Italian politics for over 50 years, the Christian Democrats. Nevertheless, the scope and significance of this transformation should not, at this stage, be overestimated. Not only is the transformation incomplete, but it remains unclear how permanent many of the new party organisations and alliances will be, untested as they are by time, and still dominated by individuals with competing notions of what types of parties and alliances are necessary to create a stable party system.

This caution is confirmed by an analysis of the party system itself. Roberto D'Alimonte and Stefano Bartolini show that, beneath the turmoil of the changes in parties and alliances, the party system's essential characteristics (in terms of fragmentation, degree of bipolarity and voting behaviour) have not changed to the degree which might be presumed. The party system has become more competitive (mainly on the 'supply side' of political parties) and there is a clear bipolar tendency. Moreover, as Martin Rhodes and Luca Ricolfi demonstrate, new rules on party financing and media access have begun to induce a change in the behaviour of parties and the nature of political campaigns. But both parties and the party system are a long way from achieving a stable dynamic, whereby two stable coalitions alternate in government. In the meantime, the continuing conflict produced by the parties' tactical manoeuvring has its effects throughout the political and economic system. The parties, therefore, remain agents of paralysis and instability rather than unambiguous forces for change. The collapse of the old configuration has not improved the opportunities for change in those areas of the system dependent on the co-ordinated action of parties as the key representatives of societal demands. Ideological polarisation may be less than it was in the 1960s and 1970s, but the levels of tactical and strategic conflict remain as high. And, as the work of Giovanni Sartori and others has long shown, the stability of a party system has considerable implications for the nature of the political system and quality of democracy as a whole.

FUTURE PROSPECTS

This brings us back to the question of where Italian democracy might be headed. Three broad scenarios can be sketched out. The first is the achievement of fundamental constitutional change and the birth of a new regime. The idea of regime change has been prominent in much of the literature, and has been shaped, to a large extent, by a line of thought which views the first half of the 1990s in Italy as a 'revolution' which needs explaining *tout court*.[12] Our view is that the decade has, thus far, witnessed the unfolding of a long-term structural crisis which is overlaid and inextricably intertwined with a conjunctural crisis. The dramatic nature of the conjunctural crisis should not hide both the limitations of the change achieved at that level, nor the extent to which changes at other levels have been continuing regardless. The removal of the 'regime party' after 50 years and the consequent end of many features associated with the 'party regime' may, in popular parlance, amount to a symbolic shift from the 'First' to the 'Second' Republic. Yet, without fundamental constitutional innovation, it is difficult to consider seriously the notion of a regime change.

The second scenario is one in which, due to the continued failure of party government, there is further recourse to solutions of a technical nature. This might be important for Italy's economic future and, therefore, for the future containment of extremist political solutions. A failure to enter EMU, for example, could have significant repercussions on Italian politics, and particularly the type of political platforms (secessionist or otherwise) which large sectors of the Italian population might be prepared to support. Yet, as Pasquino makes clear, recourse to technicians is not healthy, if feasible, for an apparently mature democracy. Dependence on bankers and economists to run the nation sets a dangerous precedent and is unlikely to cultivate a maturing of politics. Post-Prodi, therefore, it is more likely that such a solution will be avoided as far as possible.

The third scenario is the gradual 'normalisation' of Italian politics without either significant constitutional reform or a resort to technicians. This will depend, to a great extent, on the actions of the Prodi government. Yet, while it is true that what this government does in terms of economic policy and reform of government will be critical, just as important will be developments in the parties and the party system before the next elections. The need for greater policy responsiveness and political accountability, referred to by Pasquino, will, to a large extent, depend on the emergence of a party system based on stable bipolarity between a reduced number of political forces. Achieving this will depend, in turn, on the manoeuvring of both political élites and the larger party organisations such as the PDS. The decisions they make about their existence, nature and alliance strategy will be critical to Italy's future governance; and they will need to act much more responsibly than their defunct predecessors.

## NOTES

1. Sidney Tarrow and Peter Lange (eds.) 'Special Issue on Italy in Transition: Conflict and Consensus', *West European Politics* 2/3 (Oct. 1979). It was published as a book by Frank Cass & Co. Ltd. in 1980.
2. For opposing side of this debate, see G. Pridham, 'Comparative Perspectives on the New Mediterranean Democracies: A Model of Regime Transition', ibid. 2/7 (April 1984) pp.1–29 and A. Lijphart, T.C. Bruneau, P. Nikiforos Diamandourous and R. Gunther, 'A Mediterranean Model of Democracy? The Southern European Democracies in Comparative Perspective', ibid. 11/1 (Jan. 1988) pp.7–25.
3. See G. Sapelli, *Southern Europe Since 1945: Tradition and Modernity in Portugal, Spain, Italy, Greece and Turkey* (London and NY: Longman 1995).
4. See D. Della Porta, *Lo scambio occulto. Casi di corruzione politica in Italia* (Bologna: Il Mulino 1992).
5. The best academic version of this argument is Joseph LaPalombara, *Democracy Italian Style* (New Haven CT: Yale UP 1987), a book which was highly controversial, particularly amongst Italians, from the date of its publication.
6. See M. Magatti, 'La modernizzazione fallita della società italiana: Tra fiducia personale e fiducia istituzionale', *Quaderni di Sociologia* 38–39/8 (1994–5) pp.33–53.
7. This categorisation was suggested by Roberto D'Alimonte and Stefano Bartolini.
8. This structural-conjunctural approach can be contrasted with more structural approaches found in Massimo Salvadori, *Storia d'Italia e crisi di regime. Alle radici della politica italiana* (Bologna: Il Mulino 1994) and some of the contributions to M. Caciagli, F. Cazzola, L. Morlino and S. Passigli (eds.) *Italia fra crisi e transizione* (Roma-Bari: Editori Laterza 1994).
9. P. McCarthy, 'Forza Italia: nascita e sviluppo di un partito virtuale', in P. Ignazi and R. S. Katz (eds) *Politica in Italia. I fatti dell' anno e le interpretazioni. Edizione 95* (Bologna: Mulino 1995) pp.139–60.
10. See M.J. Bull, 'The Roots of the Italian Crisis', *South European Society and Politics* 1/1(Summer 1996) pp.131–7 for a review of some of the literature. Gianfranco Pasquino, 'Le coalizione di pentapartito (1980–91): quale governo dei partiti?' and Alfio Mastropaolo, 'Perché è entrata in crisi la democrazia italiana? Un'ipotesi sugli anni Ottanta', both in Caciagli *et al.* (note 8) are noteworthy in this respect.
11. For an in-depth study of the role of the banking technocracy in Italian economic policy making, see Kenneth Dyson and Kevin Featherstone, 'Italy and EMU as a *'Vincolo Esterno'*: Empowering the Technocrats, Transforming the State', *South European Society and Politics* 1/2 (Autumn 1996) pp.273–300.
12. For an expression of this view see, for example, Mark Gilbert, *The Italian Revolution: The End of Politics, Italian Style?* (Boulder, CO and Oxford: Westview Press 1995).

# Hollowing Out and Hardening the State: European Integration and the Italian Economy

## VINCENT DELLA SALA

*This account uses the case of budgetary politics to argue that European integration and economic interdependence have contributed to the 'hollowing out' and hardening of the Italian state. It argues that there has been a displacement of national state authority to other levels of government and to parts of civil society. This requires state structures that are less permeable to penetration and demands from civil society. In turn, a 'hollowed out' state becomes a less likely target for societal interests as state authority is displaced. Italian budgetary politics, characterised recently by the quest to achieve the convergence criteria set out in the Treaty on European Union, illustrate both these processes; that is, state authority being displaced and decreasing access for societal demands.*

It is somewhat ironic that shortly after scholars were calling for the state to be 'brought back in' as a central focus of inquiry, various publications have emerged that have contemplated its demise and possible disappearance. At the heart of works with titles such as, 'What Future for the State?' and 'The Crisis of the State', is the question of whether national states continue to have the capacity to organise collective responses to social and political demands.[1] Two broad, and not exclusive, themes have emerged in the discussion of the state in advanced industrialised societies. The first concentrates on the 'hollowing out' of state authority and capacity. While not denying that the state will remain an important political and discursive arena, these arguments emphasise the displacement of national state authority away from national states towards other levels of governance and to parts of civil society. A second approach highlights the attempts to strengthen certain decision-making institutions within state structures, especially the executive and its agencies. In this instance, it is not the future of the national state that is in question but the balance of powers between state institutions, so that system effectiveness is given priority over representation.[2] As a consequence, it is much more difficult for societal interests to find access points and to penetrate decision-making structures.

The aim of this analysis is to bring together these two sets of concerns to argue that the 'hollowing out' of the state and the 'hardening of its shell' are complementary processes; that is, the displacement of national state authority requires state structures that are less permeable to penetration from interests and demands emanating from civil society. In turn, a 'hollow' national state leads to claims for less inclusive representation in decision making and for a reduced space for policy-making discourse. Italy has been called a 'weak' and permeable' state. The following analysis will focus on budgetary politics in Italy in light of the convergence criteria for entry into the single currency established by the Treaty on European Union (TEU) to assess the extent to which the Italian state is becoming a hollow entity coated by a hard shell.

Budgetary politics centre on making choices that represent the values, priorities and structures that are prized in a particular society. How these choices are made and the relative authority of the structures that make them may tell us something about state capacity for economic management. Increasingly, these choices are made by national states whose economies are highly integrated into international financial markets, and therefore, sensitive to the capital movements. National governments must operate on two fronts in making public policy decisions: first, they must create the conditions to maximise access to this financial world; second, they must provide rapid, coherent and decisive policy responses once they have opened themselves up to this environment.

This raises the question of how a national state, not known for its rapid and coherent decision making, makes budgetary choices in the inter-dependent global economy. As we will see shortly, Italy is often described as a 'weak' state, lacking the capacity to aggregate demands into coherent policy programmes. Moreover, it is highly integrated into the global economy; and more specifically, it now operates within a regional economy whose borders have been almost entirely removed for capital mobility. In the case of budgeting, it has one of the highest debt-to-GDP ratios amongst OECD countries; and it faces great challenges to meet the convergence criteria set out in the TEU. The aim of our discussion is to examine how Italian policy makers have responded to these challenges, and to what extent pressures to weaken state capacity for economic management have affected states that are known to be already 'weak' in this respect.

The discussion will be divided into two main sections. The first will explore some of the arguments about the future of the national state and make the case for hollow, hard states. It will illustrate that Italy has been characterised as a 'weak', 'permeable' state, captured by sectional interests. The second section will provide some background to the Italian case, and will focus on budgetary politics in light of the criteria for entry into a European single currency set out in the TEU. It will demonstrate that budgetary politics in Italy reveal both a 'hollowing out', as further authority is assumed by EU commitments or by market forces and principles; and a 'hardening' of the state as pressures to create more timely, coherent policy making have made it more difficult for societal interests to penetrate state structures.

## HOLLOW STATES WITH HARD SHELLS

A number of challenges have led to a displacement of national state authority in decision making: economic interdependence, financial deregulation, technological change, greater capital mobility, greater consolidation of regional economic and trading blocs. Not surprisingly, increased economic interdependence and globalisation have contributed to the generation of an intense argument about the future of the national state. On the one hand, arguments about the continued importance of the role of national states in the global economy persist, pointing out that states continue to be the only vehicle that can make authoritative decisions at the transnational level. Moreover, their role is enhanced by capital mobility as they are the only form of regulation of economic and social life that may deal effectively with the demands generated by an interdependent global economy. The emphasis on 'national competitiveness' enhances states rather than diminishes their authority.[3] In addition, while the state may be losing its capacity in some areas, such as control of capital movements, it is trying to enhance its powers in others such as the control of the movement of people, immigration and law and order.[4]

On the other hand, at least four works have begun to suggest that we are witnessing a 'disarming' or hollowing out of the state.[5] As Susan Strange argues, 'State authority has leaked away, upwards, sideways and downwards. In some matters, it seems to have gone nowhere, just evaporated.'[6] The sources of this displacement are traced back to processes that have encouraged or created greater capital mobility and economic interdependence. This has led, in part, to the shifting of political authority upwards to supranational organisations; downwards to regional and local governments seen as better situated to provide responses in areas such as training and education; sideways to new polities such as the European Union (EU) whose emerging federal processes have taken on many of the responsibilities assigned to national states. In addition, state authority has disappeared as elements of civil society have undertaken (or re-assumed) the capacity to make decisions in several areas. The most obvious instance in this respect has been the emphasis on markets as a means of economic and social regulation; but it also includes attempts to have the 'third sector' or non-governmental structures replace both markets and states in the delivery of many services. The result is that national states have become 'defective' or 'like old trees, hollow in the middle, showing signs of weakness and vulnerability to storm, drought, or disease, yet continuing to grow leaves, new shoots, and branches'.[7]

The 'hollowing out' analogy provides at least two useful insights. First, it suggests that changing state capacity is a process that takes place at different levels; and can lead to a focus on what state capacities remain within the core, and what has been transferred or eroded. It highlights a close relationship between pressures to change the balance of powers between national states and sub-national governments, and those to change boundaries between states and other forms of social regulation such as markets. Second, Strange's description reveals that even as states are being 'hollowed out', they may assume new responsibilities and may try to respond to emerging political demands.

The literature has paid less attention to the political and institutional features of the 'hollowed out' state. Although some mention is made about the continuing importance of executive authority, the link between displacement of state authority and the type of state structures that will emerge has not been addressed. Some arguments have dwelt on elements of executive authority, leading partly to notions of 'weak' and 'strong' states. Weak states may be described as those that lack the capacity to 'achieve the kinds of changes in society that their leaders sought to achieve through state planning, policies and actions'.[8] The capacity of executives to make and implement policy decisions is seen as the key variable that places states at particular points on the weak–strong state spectrum.[9] 'Strong' states were seen to be those that had clear distinctions between state and civil society, while those closer to the weak end of the spectrum tended to have a blurring of the lines between the two.[10]

However, the link between the boundaries of executive authority and the 'hollowing out' of the state has not been addressed entirely. As Vivien Schmidt points out, one response of the national state to international pressures has been, a 'strengthening of executive authority vis-à-vis societal interests'.[11] This is not simply because many of the consequences of economic interdependence and globalisation fall within areas that are normally under the executive's jurisdiction. It also is the case that inclusive, representative decision making requires a broader consensus among a wide range of societal interests than that left simply to the executive and its agencies. Pressures for a 'hollowing out' would directly affect many of those interests; and any attempt to displace state authority would find obstacles in those institutions and structures that had been permeated by societal interests. Therefore, the paradoxical situation arises in that 'weak' states would face greater problems in being 'hollowed out', while in 'strong' states, where clear boundaries have been established between the state and civil society, it is much easier to displace state authority and harder to mobilise resistance to 'hollowing' out.

Several works have argued that the displacement of state authority is not inevitable but the result of state actions, implying that not all states may be able to make and implement decisions that give greater space to, for instance, markets in regulating social and economic life.[12] Andrew Gamble argues that a 'free economy' requires a strong state to, among other things, limit the power of trade unions and quell resistance to changes to the welfare state.[13] Gamble's argument is a useful one but perhaps describing the state as 'strong' may be a bit misleading. It suggests that state capacity to affect outcomes in civil society is enhanced. This may be the case in some instances but the overall effect of displacing state authority is that state capacity will be limited. It may seem that the state is 'stronger' in that its impermeability to penetration from some societal groups has been enhanced. On the other hand, a 'hollowed out' state has less capacity to penetrate civil society and regulate social and economic life. It is more useful to speak of a state that is being 'hollowed out' while its shell is being hardened. For instance, seeking consensus from a broad range of groups that includes trade unions, students and social movements on fiscal restraint and austerity will be difficult if decision-making structures are permeable and provide access and veto points. In turn, displacing state authority will help to establish clear lines between the state and society, making it harder for societal interests to gain access to decision making.

The 'hardening' of the shell takes on forms that go beyond the strengthening of the executive with respect to more inclusive institutions. It also refers to arguments which suggest that certain realms of decision making are purely technical exercises with no feasible political alternatives. For instance, the discourse in the EU about market liberalisation, fiscal restraint and meeting the convergence criteria is presented as the only feasible choice for economic policy. In this instance, policy making becomes a 'technical', not a political, exercise that is to be rendered immune from civil society, or at least certain interests; and structures that are seen to be independent of direct political control, such as the Bundesbank, are the models to set policy. The result is that decisions are made far from sites that provide access for representational claims.

HOLLOWING OUT AND HARDENING THE ITALIAN STATE

Italy is a good example of the complementary processes of hollowing out and hardening the shell of the state. As in other advanced industrialised states in the post-war period, the Italian state played an active and extensive part in the regulation of economic and social life. Moreover, beginning in the late 1960s and early 1970s, pressure from trade unions and other social movements led to a wide range of social and labour market policies that ensured state protection of social and economic benefits.[14] This reflected another important change: the increasing penetration of decision-making structures by a wide range of social and economic interests. Italy was seen as the classic 'weak' state in which the political authority of the executive was limited so that it could not achieve its policy objectives.[15] The result was a state that has been described as a 'non-state' state; that is, having state structures that had been 'captured' by such a broad range of societal interests that its authority was seriously curtailed.[16] This is especially the case in economic policy making since the early 1970s as it is characterised as incremental, serving micro-sectional interests, and without any clarity or coherence. It is not that major policy decisions are not taken in as much as these decisions are not the product of processes and structures that can set clear objectives, establish procedures and instruments to achieve them and then use the instruments of government to implement them. Rather, they are incremental, reactive policies that do little to enhance the government's ability to anticipate and deal with socio-economic demands.[17]

From the late 1960s decision making became more open and accessible to a wide range of social and political forces, including the opposition parties.[18] Pressures for greater political participation and the continuing anomaly of Italian democracy – the lack of alternation in power – led to the full implementation of the Constitution, the dispersion of power and strict limits on the use of executive power. The open, consensual decision-making process allowed a broad range of interests and micro-sectional demands to affect policy choices. In many cases, parts of the state were parcelled out to these interests and the political parties that represented them. The dispersion of power meant that it was difficult to locate the centre of political and policy decision making. The result is that policy making in Italy demonstrates many of the characteristics of what may be described as 'weak states'; that is, those states that, 'lack the ability to provide strong direction in steering the nation-state through troubled economic waters'.[19]

### The Italian Road to Europe

A state with weak economic management capacity should be susceptible to the transforming forces of markets and supranational authority such as the European Union. This leads the discussion to a brief examination of the impact of European integration. The aim of this section is not to debate whether European integration is an economic or political project, or whether a federal European structure will eventually replace national state authority. Rather, it will simply provide a short description of some of the key developments in the last decade that have placed policy-making pressures on state authorities in Italy, as elsewhere in the European Union.

The recession of the early 1980s contributed to a consensus amongst member states and business elites in the European Community (EC) that centred on two key points about the role of national states in economic management. [20] First, no single government could hope to pursue autonomous industrial and economic policies without raising serious doubts in financial markets, especially if those states were part of arrangements such as the European Monetary System (EMS).[21] Second, a consensus began to form on limited government intervention in the economy, as the primary objective should be promoting productivity and competitiveness through the control of inflation.[22] The emphasis was on a policy of 'sound money', with the German Bundesbank as the model for removing politics from the making of monetary policy. The event that symbolised the new consensus was the U-turn in economic policy by the Socialist government in France in 1983. The Mitterrand experience with an expansionary policy in the face of recession was rejected by international financial markets and the Socialists were faced with the choice of abandoning either their policy or participation in the EMS; the Socialists relinquished the former.

The recession of the early 1980s, the policy shift in France, conservative governments in Germany and Britain, and mobilisation by European business élites helped generate support for the completion of the internal market in the mid-1980s. It galvanised efforts to liberalise the movement of goods, capital, and to a lesser extent, people, not only across EC borders but also within the member states. Many member states had to take policy measures to prepare their own internal markets for the greater competition that the Single European Act (SEA) would bring, and to conform to European directives. The liberalisation of economic activity within and across European borders helped generate momentum to go further and aim for full economic and monetary convergence. There is an economic debate as to whether the completion of the internal market required or resulted in monetary union. It certainly created the political conditions that made it easier for political leaders in the late 1980s to consider economic and monetary union by the end of the century.

The negotiations that led to the commitment to achieve economic and monetary union enshrined in the Maastricht Treaty were long and intense, but they were based on a few widely shared assumptions. First, that the room for manoeuvre for national governments in monetary policy was limited and that their commitment to policies of 'sound money' (low inflation, low government debt, control of public finances, market efficiencies) was tested almost daily by the international financial markets. In practice, this meant that countries suspected of wavering in their policy of sound money were targets of frequent speculation as to whether they could maintain their position within the EMS. Second, the negotiations leading to economic and monetary union in the Maastricht Treaty assumed that there would be structures to ensure the convergence of economic policies in the transition to a single currency, and long after.

Both these assumptions led to two fundamental features of economic and monetary union that would accelerate the transformation of economic management in national states: the so-called convergence criteria, which reflect the consensus on 'sound money', and multilateral surveillance.[23] Any member state that wishes to be part of the single currency must have public deficits at three per cent of GDP (or making significant progress in that direction); public debt at 60 per cent of GDP; and inflation at no higher than 1.5 per cent of the three best performing countries. In preparation for monetary union, the central banks in member states must be made independent of direct government control, with the German Bundesbank serving as the model. The Commission and the Council will be charged with implementing a series of procedures to monitor closely the policies and their outcomes in the member states so that these may be moving closer to convergence. All member states must submit multi-year convergence programmes that detail budgetary and policy expectations and objectives that are scrutinised by the Commission along with other member states through the Council. The convergence programmes are supplemented by annual reports by each country. Member states that are not performing well in terms of economic convergence are issued recommendations by the Council, the Commission and, after 1994, the European Monetary Institute. In addition, in preparation for monetary union, there is an annual publication of a list of countries that are deemed to have 'excessive deficits'. These close surveillance mechanisms of government economic management will be even more acute if and when monetary union is achieved. They have become signals that international markets respond to, and the threat of sanction here is in the form of capital flight.

Although the Maastricht Treaty did provide for a social chapter, the essence of economic and monetary union is to enshrine the consensus that was formed in the mid-1980s around limited government intervention in the economy and limited policy autonomy for member states. It may be described as an economic constitution for Europe that closely binds its members to pursuing a clearly defined course of economic management. There is nothing in the Treaty that forces governments to adhere to its economic and monetary criteria. However, given the close interdependence of European economies and their integration in world financial markets, few governments could risk the sanctions that might accrue for being 'unconstitutional' in their economic policies.[24]

*Italian Budgetary Politics*

Italy has been struggling to bring its public finances under control for about 20 years but it has met with little success. Its level of public debt has grown at a significant rate due to the annual accumulation of deficits throughout the 1980s.[25] The figures in Table 1 reveal that there was a significant jump in public deficit levels between 1970 and 1975, and that it is not until 1992 that there is a noticeable drop to below the 10 per cent figure. The jump in the early 1970s may be traced to two developments. The first was economic slowdown in the wake of the first oil shock after nearly a quarter of a century of significant economic growth. The second, and related source, was that the economic slowdown highlighted some of the social policies that were won by the labour movement in the unrest of the late 1960s and early 1970s. Student and labour movements secured at least four concessions that included the protection of incomes, a generous pension scheme for wage earners, health services and university access.[26] The result was numerous structural demands on public expenditure, many of which, such as income-maintenance programmes, were particularly sensitive to economic slowdowns.

It is not surprising, given the consistently high levels of public deficits, that Italy would eventually have high levels of public debt. The second column in Table 1 reveals that by the time Italy agreed to the convergence criteria in the TEU, its public debt to GDP ratio was at about 100 per cent, with little sign of significant decrease on the horizon. In fact, even after the level of public deficit began to show a consistent decline after 1992, debt levels continue to rise (albeit at a slower rate). This reflects the fact that the size of the deficit is greater than the rate of economic growth, making it difficult to begin to pay down the debt.

Tables 2 and 3 provide an indication of where spending priorities have been placed, and of the spending sources of deficits and debt. Interest payments have taken over as the largest area of spending, and there is a significant decrease in the percentage allocated to social policy (broadly defined to include health, pensions and income maintenance), transfers to regional and local governments, and direct state intervention in industry (including regional assistance to southern Italy). There also has been a noticeable cut in the percentage assumed by spending on education. The extent to which spending on programmes has been cut to make up for the larger role assumed by interest payments on the debt is demonstrated by the final column in Table 1. By 1991, revenues covered all current spending; and beginning the following year, governments continued to cut away at current spending so that there would have been surpluses in the absence of interest payments.

TABLE 1
PUBLIC DEBT AND DEFICIT
(PERCENTAGE OF GDP)[1]

| Year | Public Deficit | Public Debt | Primary Balance[2] |
|------|------|------|------|
| 1970 | 3.7 | 38.0 | 2.1 |
| 1975 | 11.6 | 57.6 | 8.1 |
| 1980 | 8.5 | 57.7 | 3.2 |
| 1981 | 11.4 | 59.9 | 5.2 |
| 1982 | 11.3 | 64.9 | 4.2 |
| 1983 | 10.6 | 70.0 | 3.1 |
| 1984 | 11.6 | 75.2 | 3.6 |
| 1985 | 12.6 | 82.3 | 4.6 |
| 1986 | 11.6 | 86.3 | 3.1 |
| 1987 | 11.0 | 90.5 | 3.1 |
| 1988 | 10.7 | 92.6 | 2.6 |
| 1989 | 9.9 | 95.6 | 1.0 |
| 1990 | 10.9 | 97.8 | 1.3 |
| 1991 | 10.2 | 101.4 | 0.0 |
| 1992 | 9.5 | 108.0 | −1.9 |
| 1993 | 9.6 | 117.3 | −2.6 |
| 1994 | 9.0 | 121.4 | −1.7 |
| 1995 | 7.5 | 122.9 | −3.5 |
| 1996[3] | 5.9 | 122.7 | −4.3 |
| 1997[3] | 4.4 | 121.1 | −5.4 |
| 1998[3] | 2.6 | 117.9 | −6.4 |

1. The figures include central, regional, provincial and local governments, along with all state public agencies and enterprises.
2. Primary balance removes interest payments from calculation of expenditure and revenue.
3. Bank of Italy estimates.

*Source*: Data collected from annual reports to parliament by the Treasury and Budget ministries; and from data presented by the Governor of the Bank of Italy, Antonio Fazio to the Interministerial Committee on Economic Planning in Banca d'Italia, *Bollettino Economico*, no. 25 (Oct. 1995) pp.152–5.

TABLE 2
ALLOCATION OF PUBLIC EXPENDITURES
(PERCENTAGE OF TOTAL)

|  | 1979 | 1981 | 1983 | 1985 | 1987 | 1989 | 1991 | 1993 |
|---|---|---|---|---|---|---|---|---|
| Total Spending (billion lire) | 103,947 | 178,744 | 259,890 | 353,456 | 439,762 | 488,213 | 579,966 | 634,690 |
| General Administration | 3.5 | 3.0 | 3.3 | 2.7 | 3.0 | 3.1 | 3.4 | 3.3 |
| Defence | 4.6 | 3.8 | 4.0 | 4.1 | 3.9 | 4.0 | 3.6 | 3.2 |
| Justice | 0.9 | 1.0 | 1.0 | 1.0 | 0.9 | 0.8 | 1.0 | 1.0 |
| Internal Security and Civil Protection | 2.4 | 2.1 | 2.0 | 2.0 | 2.1 | 2.4 | 2.4 | 2.8 |
| International Affairs | 2.3 | 2.2 | 2.1 | 2.5 | 2.7 | 3.1 | 3.0 | 3.4 |
| Education and Culture | 12.2 | 10.6 | 10.2 | 9.1 | 9.4 | 10.1 | 10.3 | 9.9 |
| Housing | 1.0 | 1.4 | 1.4 | 1.0 | 1.4 | 0.8 | 0.9 | 0.5 |
| Social Policy | 22.1 | 22.6 | 21.7 | 22.8 | 27.6 | 24.1 | 24.3 | 17.8 |
| Transport and Communication | 7.8 | 7.7 | 8.0 | 8.6 | 7.5 | 6.5 | 5.8 | 5.2 |
| Agriculture | 0.9 | 1.4 | 1.3 | 1.0 | 1.4 | 1.5 | 1.1 | 0.7 |
| Industry, Trade and State Intervention | 9.2 | 11.3 | 10.5 | 8.8 | 6.3 | 5.7 | 3.1 | 4.2 |
| Regional and Local Government Transfers | 20.7 | 16.8 | 13.4 | 13.6 | 12.9 | 12.7 | 12.6 | 12.3 |
| Interest Charges on Public Debt | 7.9 | 11.2 | 15.6 | 16.4 | 15.9 | 19.2 | 23.1 | 28.1 |
| Other Financial Commitments | 4.4 | 4.9 | 5.4 | 6.3 | 5.1 | 6.0 | 5.4 | 7.7 |

*Source*: Data collected from annual report on the state of the economy presented to Parliament by the Budget and Treasury ministers.

The evidence suggests that 1992 was a major turning point in the evolution of Italian public finances and budgetary processes. Processes already underway, such as changing budgetary priorities, were accelerated, and major reversals in terms of deficit levels were signalled for the first time and have continued since then. Two factors help to understand the changes that took place in 1992. First, the convergence criteria in the TEU established clear reference points and a timetable for budgetary targets. Governments could choose to ignore the criteria, and risk being accused of jeopardising Italy's chances of being part of the single currency. Conversely, governments could now use the criteria as the reason for bringing about changes to public expenditure, affecting the role of the state in economic and social life. The introduction of clear reference points was particularly important in a budgetary process where debt and deficit targets were met only in 1986 in the period between 1983 and 1992.

TABLE 3

INCREASES IN GOVERNMENT SPENDING
(PERCENTAGE INCREASE FROM TWO YEARS EARLIER)

|  | 1981 | 1983 | 1985 | 1987 | 1989 | 1991 | 1993 |
|---|---|---|---|---|---|---|---|
| Total Spending | 71.9 | 45.4 | 36.0 | 24.1 | 11.0 | 18.8 | 8.6 |
| General Administration | 43.9 | 62.0 | 12.6 | 35.3 | 15.0 | 29.9 | 6.7 |
| Defence | 43.8 | 52.8 | 39.3 | 17.4 | 13.9 | 6.1 | -1.3 |
| Justice | 49.4 | 45.7 | 27.5 | 17.5 | -8.1 | 52.3 | 15.2 |
| National Security | 49.7 | 42.3 | 36.7 | 28.9 | 24.3 | 22.6 | 24.2 |
| International Affairs | 57.5 | 43.4 | 58.1 | 33.9 | 31.0 | 14.9 | 22.2 |
| Education and Culture | 48.7 | 40.8 | 21.3 | 27.8 | 20.0 | 20.5 | 5.1 |
| Housing | 142.5 | 44.6 | -5.8 | 74.1 | -33.3 | 23.7 | -32.9 |
| Social Policy | 75.8 | 39.8 | 42.8 | 50.5 | -3.1 | 20.0 | -19.9 |
| Transport and Communication | 70.5 | 49.9 | 45.9 | 8.4 | -3.4 | 6.0 | -2.6 |
| Agriculture | 167.3 | 34.2 | 9.3 | 72.0 | 17.0 | -17.4 | -29.2 |
| Industry, Trade and State Intervention | 111.5 | 35.1 | 14.6 | -11.1 | - .1 | -34.0 | 46.9 |
| Regional and Local Government Transfers | 39.7 | 15.7 | 37.8 | 18.5 | 9.2 | 17.4 | 7.1 |
| Interest Charges on Public Debt | 143.0 | 101.4 | 43.3 | 17.0 | 34.3 | 43.2 | 32.8 |
| Other Financial Commitments | 91.6 | 61.6 | 59.4 | .13 | 31.1 | 7.4 | 54.3 |

*Source*: See Table 2.

Second, pressures from international currency markets that forced the Italian government to pull out of the exchange rate mechanism (ERM) in September 1992 immobilised opposition to spending cuts, and, to a lesser extent, tax increases. The newly formed government led by Giuliano Amato, composed largely of non-political technocrats in key economic ministries, not only introduced a mini-budget that combined tax increases and spending cuts for 38,800 billion lire (approx. $25 billion US) but also announced major privatisation programmes. Moreover, the currency crisis paved the way for the approval of a government bill that delegated to the government the authority to change four areas considered to be structural sources of deficits: health, pensions, public sector employment and local government finance. The legislation was an important development not simply because it introduced structural changes that brought immediate savings of about 13,000 billion lire ($8.6 billion), and long-term savings. For instance, changes introduced to pensions gave the government flexibility in limiting early retirement packages; and in health services, it introduced income brackets for families which would determine prescription and doctors' fees.[27] Moreover, the delegated legislation gave the executive a virtual free hand to introduce changes in the four areas with little possibility for Parliament to obstruct or amend the reforms. Given the relatively weak position of government legislation in the parliamentary process, delegating to the government the powers to reform four areas of major public expenditures was seen by political and economic observers as an 'historic' turning point.[28]

The Amato government put through a series of measures in its first six months, beginning in July 1992. In addition to the mini-budget and the delegated legislation, it introduced further savings of 41,700 billion lire ($27.8 billion) in the 1993 budget approved in December 1992, including 7,000 billion lire to be raised through privatisation. In total, the Amato government's action led to cutting the size of the budget deficit by about $60 billion in a single year. It was followed by subsequent budgets brought forward by governments led by Carlo Ciampi (1994) and Lamberto Dini (1996), and to a lesser extent Silvio Berlusconi (1995), that continued the trend of reducing the deficit. What makes the reversal since mid-1992 even more impressive is that it took place during a period of recession and later sluggish economic growth.

While Italy will not, in all likelihood, meet the convergence criteria for deficit levels in 1997, the Prodi government expects to be within the three per cent range by 1998. More importantly, political discourse on economic policy has been taken over by the objectives which the Italian government set for itself in signing the TEU.[29] Amato, in a speech before the Senate vote to confer confidence in his government, said there was no alternative to the European commitments. The choice was not whether Italy would leave the EU, but whether it would be relegated to its second division and become its 'Disneyland', or whether it would choose to concentrate its efforts on meeting the convergence criteria.[30] Budgetary politics, which include privatisation plans, now have a focal point that mobilises a broad range of political and social forces: employers' organisations, the Bank of Italy, all the parties on the centre-left with the exception of the die-hard Communist Refoundation, most of the parties on the centre-right, with the ex-Fascist National Alliance ambivalent on major spending cuts, and the trade unions giving only reluctant support.

What is striking about this broad consensus is that the reversal in budgetary politics has been carried out largely through cuts in spending, at a ratio of two to one with respect to tax increases. Increases in expenditure in the 1970s and 1980s were not matched by increases in revenue raised through taxation – which led some economists to argue that if Italy had increased taxes at rates similar to the OECD averages for the period, debt and deficit levels would have been at more manageable levels.[31] The most significant measures on the revenue side in the 1990s include the privatisation of state-held enterprises which brought close to 30,000 billion lire ($20 billion) to the state coffers between 1992 and 1995.[32] Another revenue measure has been to be more aggressive in reducing levels of tax evasion; this includes simplifying the tax code and enhancing the powers of tax inspectors. Alesina and Mare argue that tax evasion in 1991 amounted to 15 per cent of GDP, higher than the deficit level. They argue that if tax evasion in Italy since the 1970s had been at United States levels, the debt to GDP ratio in the 1990s would be about 80 per cent, if tax evasion had been at UK levels, the debt ratio would be 60 per cent. However, tax evasion was part of a political compromise that would have been difficult to abandon without causing major problems for the fragile governing coalitions.[33] Concessions made to industrial workers in the form of pensions and incomes policies, to students in the form of low university tuition fees, and regional aid to southern Italy were countered by a relaxed approach to tax collection, especially from shopkeepers, professionals, and small to medium enterprises.

Interestingly, it has been the ex-Communist, Democratic Party of the Left (PDS), that has provided the most consistent public and parliamentary support for reversing the trend in public finances through privatisation and major changes to key areas of social policy and public expenditure. This reflects a change in the terms of political discourse. In effect, whether or not Italy will be part of a single currency at its inauguration, it has begun to implement the objectives of 'sound money' policies that were at the heart of the Maastricht criteria; and by the time the process is over, the boundaries of state intervention will have changed drastically in key areas such as health, pensions and state ownership of firms and key industries.

## Hollowing, Hardening and the Displacement of State Authority

The evolution of budgetary politics in Italy reveals both the hollowing out of the Italian state and the hardening of its shell. The state's authority is being displaced in at least two directions. First, although ultimate responsibility for budgetary decisions continues to rest with the national state, Italian governments throughout the 1990s have pointed to Europe as the source of fiscal restraint and rigour. In political discourse, not only Europe but international financial markets are presented as an external force dictating budgetary policy. For instance, the assessment of budgetary plans by the Bundesbank, the Commission, and bond rating agencies are given precedence over that of trade unions or even political parties.[34] In accepting the convergence criteria, Italian governments accepted not only further limits on monetary policy but, implicitly, also on levels of spending and taxation.

These and other European commitments also have contributed to a second source of hollowing out: the retreat of the state from many areas of social and economic life, and the primacy of market principles and forces. Italy embarked on major plans for privatisation and restructuring of the welfare state relatively later than other industrialised states. It is only now in the 1990s, with the blunt instrument of the convergence criteria to marginalise resistance, that governments have put through major reforms that have introduced greater market forces to many parts of the economy, and put into private hands major state holdings. For instance, Italian governments tried at least on two occasions in the 1980s, with little success, to introduce or increase user fees for medical and health services. In the 1980s, not only did governments not deal with the large financial problems of the pension system, they made many pensions even more generous. In the period since 1992, changes increasing user fees in health and university education have been implemented relatively easily, and not only was the pension system reformed in 1995, the government has also started to crack down on fraudulent claims.[35]

Political contingencies may help to explain the recent reversals in Italian economic policy. First, the collapse of all the traditional parties has radically changed the political landscape. None of the parties that ran for office in the 1994 elections were present under the same banner just seven years earlier. More importantly, judicial investigations, leading to one-third of the members of the Chamber of Deputies being under investigation or facing corruption charges in 1994, unmasked an extensive patronage network that, directly or indirectly, drained public resources. Second, the emergence of new political forces, such as the Northern League, put fiscal responsibility and tax reduction firmly on the political agenda. The new political forces were able to combine anti-tax sentiments with public reaction to the corruption scandals of the 1990s, which led to greater questioning of the utility of public expenditure and state intervention in the economy.

The political conditions, while helping to create a political opportunity structure for change, do not provide a complete account. First, the commitments made at Maastricht were agreed to by Prime Minister, Giulio Andreotti (facing charges for collusion with the Mafia) and Foreign Minister, Gianni De Michelis (convicted of accepting illegal political contributions), well before the corruption crisis broke; Amato's changes in 1992 were introduced prior to the wave of major investigations and indictments of major political figures. Second, the primary balance in 1991 was already indicating that a reversal in budgetary politics was underway. Third, the extent of change in the parliamentary class should not be overestimated; over 100 ex-Christian Democrats were re-elected in 1996 along with a number of ex-Socialists and ex-Liberals. Finally, there is no reason to assume that simply changing party labels or even the members of the parliamentary class will lead to a change in approach to budgetary politics and economic policy making. The question remains of why so little resistance was offered by most political and social forces.

The hollowing out that has taken place could not be carried out without the complementary process of making the state less permeable to societal interests. Paradoxically, the objectives set in the Treaty that weakened national state capacity were accepted by the Italian government precisely because they would strengthen the decision-making capacities within the state.[36] In order for the state to give way to market forces and supranational authorities, the boundaries within its own borders between state and society must be redrawn. As we saw earlier, the conventional view is that the Italian state was 'captured' or 'expropriated'. Decision making required extensive cumbersome negotiations to produce a consensus across a broad range of social and political forces. Quite often, that consensus was forged by using finances to trade benefits between different groups or perhaps providing state protection for parts of the economy. It was easier to appease different social interests through public expenditures than it was to mobilise social and political forces to cut government spending, liberalise the economy or cut the size of the public sector.

The Maastricht Treaty ensured that the boundaries of state-society relations in the economy could no longer ignore outside pressures. It introduced a new set of binding rules that forced upon all social and political interests serious questions not unlike those posed by the French Socialists in 1983. If Italy wants to be part of the economic and monetary union, it needs to change the terms of state intervention in the economy, and in order to do that, national state structures must have the capacity to set policy objectives and pursue them autonomous from social and political con-straints. Moreover, the convergence criteria have helped to remove partisan, ideological and political considerations from the discussion of drastic measures. A consensus has emerged across political boundaries that goes from centre-left to centre-right that claims that there are no alternative policies available if Italy wants to be at the centre of economic and monetary union.

It is not surprising, then, that between 1992 and 1996 Italy's Prime Ministers were: Giuliano Amato, who made his mark as Minister of the Treasury in the late 1980s; Carlo Azeglio Ciampi, a former Governor of the Bank of Italy, who led a government of 'technocrats'; Silvio Berlusconi, whose claim to fame prior to entering politics four months before leading his coalition to victory in the 1994 elections was as one of Italy's leading entrepreneurs; Lamberto Dini, a former director-general of the Bank of Italy, who also led a government of technocrats that assumed power when the Berlusconi government fell in late 1994; and Romano Prodi, an economics professor, who formed a centre-left government after the 1996 elections that included Dini as Foreign Minister and Ciampi as the new minister for both the Budget and Treasury portfolios. Italians were not happy just to have an independent central bank; they wanted to have the bank officials leading the country.

In addition to attempts to 'remove' politics from the budgetary process, thereby making it less open to challenge by societal interests, there has been a growing consensus that the permeability of the process itself needs to be addressed. A series of measures has been taken to strengthen the executive, and within that, the role of key economic ministries such as the Treasury.[37] Changes to the electoral law in 1993 have helped to mobilise political groups into two coalitions, and focused attention on candidates to lead a government. This is in marked contrast to the previous practice where any number of factions and groups could influence the choice of the head of the executive. More importantly, changes to parliamentary rules and procedures have given the government greater control of the budgetary process in the legislature. There is now a clear timetable for the budget, and the executive can set budgetary targets early on in the process. While governments still have few guarantees that the budget that emerges from Parliament will look exactly how it was presented, they do have greater assurance that at least the broad objectives, such as deficit and spending levels, will not be breached. [38] Within Parliament, the Budget Committee of the Chamber of Deputies (to a lesser extent in the Senate) has emerged as a champion of fiscal restraint, and has become a gateway for all spending decisions in Parliament. Interests seeking budgetary concessions no longer have the broad array of access points to achieve their objectives. Many commentators claim that restricting this access is necessary if the budget targets of the TEU are to be met.[39] Finally, a 'super' ministry responsible for economic affairs (combining the Treasury and Budget portfolios) was created in 1996, after a long discussion throughout the 1990s about concentrating powers. By assigning Ciampi to the position, the Prodi government was sending a clear signal that it wanted to create a powerful structure, seen to be above the partisan fray, to make the most important economic decisions relatively immune from social and political demands.

CONCLUSION

The hollowing out of states is a process with little prospect of being reversed in the near future; and it will have consequences for state structures. The Italian case demonstrates that even 'permeable' states will face the pressure to displace state authority, and as a consequence, will begin to address questions about the penetration of societal interests within state structures. The political arena becomes a shrinking one in which the space for societal interest to represent claims continues to be narrowed. In turn, as the space for the articulation of claims diminishes, it becomes easier to make decisions to continue to displace authority.

Italy embarked on the road to reverse the direction of its public finances before bringing about institutional changes. The introduction of a new electoral law and the gradual process of strengthening the executive have made it easier to mobilise support for fiscal restraint. Conversely, the convergence criteria have made it easier for the executive to claim greater authority in the decision making process. The result is a process of hollowing out of the Italian state as the capacity to penetrate its structures is being decreased. The question remains, however, of whether a hollow state with a hard shell can mobilise support and maintain social cohesion in a period of economic and political transition. The Italian state was 'penetrated' partly as a means of consolidating democracy and maintaining social peace. The gamble is that a hollow, hard state can do the same.

## NOTES

Vincent della Sala would like to thank the Social Sciences and Humanities Research Council of Canada for financial assistance.

1. P. Evans, D. Rueschemeyer and T. Skocpol (eds.) *Bringing the State Back In* (Cambridge UP); Special Issue of *Daedalus* 124/2 (Summer 1995) on 'What Future for the Nation State?'; Special Issue of *Political Studies* 42 (1994) on 'Contemporary Crisis of the Nation State'; P. McCarthy and E. Jones (eds.) *Disintegration or Transformation? The Crisis of the State in Industrialised Societies* (NY: St Martin's Press 1995).
2. Robert Dahl, 'A Democratic Dilemma: System Effectiveness and Citizen Participation', *Political Science Quarterly* 109/1 (Spring 1994) pp.23–34.
3. Vincent Gable, 'The Diminished State: A Study in the Loss of Economic Power', *Daedalus* 124/2 (Spring 1995) p.24; Philip Cerny, 'The Limits of Deregulation', *European Journal of Political Research* 19 (1991) pp.181–4.
4. Michael Mann refers to state capacity as, 'The capacity of state to actually penetrate civil society, and to implement logistically political decisions throughout the realm'. See Michael Mann, 'The Autonomous Power of the State: Its Origins, Mechanisms and Results', *Archives Européenes de Sociologie* 25 (1984) p.189.
5. Manfred Bienefeld, 'Financial Deregulation: Disarming the Nation State', *Studies in Political Economy* 37 (Spring 1992) pp.31–58; Susan Strange, 'The Defective State', *Daedalus* 124/2 (Spring 1995) pp.55–75; Bob Jessop, 'Towards a Schumpeterian Workfare State?' *Studies in Political Economy* 40 (Spring 1993) pp.7–39; R.A.W. Rhodes, 'The Hollowing Out of the British State', *Political Quarterly* 65/2 (April 1994) pp.138–51.
6. Strange, ibid. p.56.
7. Ibid. p.57.
8. J. Migdal, *Strong Societies and Weak States* (Princeton UP 1988) pp.4–5.
9. John Zysman, *Governments, Markets and Growth* (Ithaca, NY: Cornell UP 1983) pp.295–6.
10. Peter Katzenstein, 'Conclusion: Domestic Structures and Strategies of Foreign Economic Policy', in idem (ed.) *Between Power and Plenty* (Madison: U. of Wisconsin Press 1978) p.322.
11. Vivien Schmidt, 'The New World Order, Incorporated: The Rise of Business and the Decline of the Nation State', *Daedalus* 124/2 (Spring 1995) p.86.
12. For instance, see L. Pauly, *Opening Financial Markets* (Ithaca, NY: Cornell UP 1988) and

T. Porter, *States, Markets and Regimes in Global Finance* (Basingstoke: Macmillan 1993).

13. Andrew Gamble, *The Free Economy and the Strong State* (London: Macmillan 1988).
14. Giancarlo Morcaldo, *La finanza pubblica in Italia* (Bologna: Il Mulino 1993) pp.65–73.
15. Alan Posner, 'Italy: Dependence and Political Fragmentation', in Peter Katzenstein (ed.) *Between Power and Plenty* (Madison: U. of Wisconsin Press 1978); Pippo Ranci, 'Italy: the weak state', in F. Duchêne and G. Shepherd (eds.) *Managing Industrial Change in Western Europe* (London: Frances Pinter 1987).
16. Gianfranco Pasquino, 'Rappresentanza degli interessi, attività dei lobby e processi decisonali: il caso italiano di istituzioni permeabili', *Stato e Mercato* 21 (Dec. 1987) pp. 403–29; Sergio Fabbrini, 'Lo stato 'nonstato': L'Italia tra disaggregazione e federalismo', Paper presented to the *Convegno Annuale della Società Italiana di Scienza Politica*, Urbino, 13–15 June 1996.
17. See John Ikenberry, 'The Irony of State Strength: Comparative Responses to the Oil Shocks in the 1970s', *International Organization* 40/1 (Winter 1986) p.136.
18. Bruno Dente, 'Le politiche pubbliche in Italia', in idem (ed.) *Le politiche pubbliche in Italia* (Bologna: Il Mulino 1990).
19. William Chandler and Herman Bakvis, 'Federalism and the Strong-state/Weak-state Conundrum', *Publius* 19 (Winter 1989) p.60.
20. David Cameron, 'The 1992 Initiative: Causes and Consequences', in A. Sbragia (ed.) *Europolitics* (Washington: Brookings 1992); Wayne Sandholtz and John Zysman, 'Recasting the European Bargain', *World Politics* 42/1 (Oct.–July 1990) pp.95–128; Andrew Moravcsik, 'Negotiating the Single European Act', in R. Keohane and S. Hoffman (eds.) *The New European Community* (Boulder, CO: Westview Press 1991).
21. Bernard Connelly and Jurgen Kroger, 'Economic Convergence in the Integrating Community Economy and the Role of Economic Policies', *Recherches Économiques de Louvain* 59/1–2 (1993) pp.37–40.
22. Tommaso Padoa-Schioppa, *L'Europa verso l'unione monetaria* (Torino: Einaudi 1992) pp.xiv–xv.
23. Alexander Italianer 'Convergence in Europe: State of Affairs', in A. Wildavsky and E. Zapico-Goni (eds.) *National Budgeting for Economic and Monetary Union* (Dordecht: Martinus Nijhoff 1993).
24. Stephen Gill, 'The Emerging World Order and European Change: The Political Economy of European Union', in Ralph Miliband and Leo Panitch (eds.) *Socialist Register 1992* (London: Merlin Press 1992).
25. Camera dei Deputati. Servizio Studi. 'Debito pubblico e fabbisogno; Evoluzione e politiche di rientro (1983–1994)', *Documentazione e ricerche,* XII Legislatura, n.35 (Sept. 1994) pp.3–6.
26. Daniele Franco, *L'espansione della spesa pubblica in Italia (1960–1990)* (Bologna: Il Mulino 1993) pp.35–50.
27 D.L. 382, 1992.
28. Marco Rinforzi, 'Con la fiducia del Senato la legge delega va in porto', *Il Sole 24 Ore,* 23 Oct. 1992.
29. An interesting example of this was an editorial that appeared in the newspaper *La Repubblica*. The author, trying to recall attention to the perennial problem of many parts of Sicily and southern Italy lacking running water, gas and electricity, called for the delivery of these basic services as criteria for entry into the single currency. The assumption is that only policy objectives seen as gateways to the single currency will gain attention from policy makers. Antonio Ramenghi, 'Acqua, luce e gas per Maastricht', *La Repubblica*, 17 July 1996.
30. Senato della Repubblica, XI Legislatura, *Resoconto Stenografico,* 30 June 1992, p.12.
31. Vito Tanzi, 'Il Sistema Tributario Italiano: Una Prospettiva Internazionale', in Andrea Monorchio (ed.) *La finanza pubblica italiana dopo la svolta del 1992* (Bologna: Il Mulino 1996) p.23.
32. These include major banks, insurance companies and almost the entire state holdings in steel. See Alfredo Macchiato, *Privatizzazioni: tra economia e politica* (Roma: Donzelli, 1996) p.43.

33. Alberto Alesina and Mauro Mare, 'Evasione e Debito', in Andrea Monorchio (ed.) *La finanza pubblica italiana dopo la svolta del 1992*, p.70.
34  Elena Polidori, 'Brava Italia, manovra ok: L'Europa e l'FMI promuovono Prodi', *La Repubblica*, 29 June 1996.
35. Maurizio Ferrera, 'The Rise and Fall of Democratic Universalism: Health Care Reform in Italy, 1978–1994', *Journal of Health Politics, Policy and Law* 20/3 (Summer 1995) pp.275–302; Giuliano Cazzola, *Le nuove pensioni degli italiani* (Bologna: Il Mulino 1996).
36. Kenneth Dyson and Kevin Featherstone, 'Italy and EMU as a *'Vincolo Esterno'*: Empowering the Technocrats, Transforming the State', *South European Society and Politics* 1/2 (1996) pp.273–300.
37. David Hine and Renato Finocchi, 'The Italian Prime Minister', *West European Politics* 14/2 (April 1991) pp.79–86.
38. Camera dei Deputati, XI Legislatura, *Ciclo annuale di bilancio* (Rome 1993); see also the contribution of Giacinto della Cananea in this volume.
39. Andrea Manzella, 'Interventi istituzionali: la logica di coordinamento tra politica ed istituzioni', in CNEL (ed.) *Continuità e Rinnovamento della Politica Economica* (Roma: CNEL 1992); the Dini government introduced a bill to 'rationalise' public finances that would see the executive strengthened in its capacity to determine spending levels D.L., n.3438, 1995.

# No Longer A 'Party State'?
# Institutions, Power and the Problems of
# Italian Reform

## GIANFRANCO PASQUINO

*Italy's transition has been characterised by governments based on some or several non-political components. Ciampi's and even more Dini's government stressed their technical and non-parliamentary quality. Berlusconi's short-lived governmental experience was deliberately intended to challenge not only the Italian 'partitocrazia', but also any version of party government. The Italian transition cannot reach a successful completion until and unless new forms of policy responsiveness and political accountability are created. The Olive Tree coalition's electoral victory of April 1996 has produced the preconditions for a renewed party government. It remains to be seen whether Prime Minister Prodi will consider institutional and constitutional reforms a priority. Until new institutional structures are shaped and new constitutional rules are drafted, the Italian transition will continue.*

A transition is a transition is a transition ... There is no doubt that the Italian political system has been undergoing a transition for some time, at least since 1992. It is a peculiar transition from a democratic regime, correctly defined as a *partitocrazia* (one dominated by political parties), to another regime, more or less equally democratic. The old regime was dominated, for better or for worse, by the political parties. Its demise was the cause and the effect of the growing weakness and corruption of the party system and, with due distinctions, of all political parties,[1] and several socio-economic actors. The new regime will almost certainly be democratic though, of course, the outcome of all transitions is bound to remain uncertain. But it will definitely be a different kind of democracy less grounded on political parties and more oriented to bestow power on institutions and institutional leaderships.

It is not just that the starting date of the Italian transition cannot be identified precisely;[2] even its causes are largely controversial.[3] Small wonder, then, that the outcome remains difficult to forecast. The crisis of transition has yet fully to unfold and its various possible solutions have yet to become clear. My argument is that the nature of the next regime and the quality of its democracy will be to a large extent conditioned by the type of reforms made to Italian institutions. At stake are both the *form of government* – whether it should be presidential, semi-presidential, neo-parliamentary, or classical parliamentary – and the *form of state*, that is, whether federalism, (and in what form) should be implemented. Understandably, then, the various proposals so far are based on very different conceptions of the state and executive power and indicate preferences for very different types of regime.

In this analysis, I will first describe the process leading to the only institutional reform thus far implemented during the transition – that of the electoral law – and briefly assess its impact on the party system. Then, I will analyse the dynamics of government formation over the last three years. Finally, I will conclude by evaluating the proposals for institutional and constitutional reforms and their likely consequences for the completion of the transition.

THE REFORM OF THE ELECTORAL LAW

In Italy institutional and constitutional reform have been discussed intensely for more than ten years. Parliament appointed two special Committees to formulate proposals: the first, the Commission chaired by the Liberal MP, Aldo Bozzi, functioned from November 1983 to January 1985; the second, the Commission chaired by the Christian Democrat MP, Ciriaco De Mita, functioned from September 1992 to January 1994 (when De Mita was obliged to resign and was replaced by Nilde Iotti). Both Committees produced lengthy and significant reports which were duly put aside, because of lack of agreement and fear of change on the part of the political groups represented in Parliament. Moreover, some parliamentary sessions were specifically devoted to the discussion of proposals for institutional and constitutional reforms: May 1988; July 1991, following a solemn message to Parliament by the President of the Republic, Francesco Cossiga; and August 1995. Finally, one must recall that in the 1980s Bettino Craxi, first when secretary of the Socialist Party, then when Prime Minister, stressed – though, perhaps, in a manipulative way – the need for major reform of the Italian political system, its institutions and constitution, but to no avail. To cut a very long and confusing story short, mutual vetoes, and perhaps a massive dose of bad faith, paralysed the Italian Parliament and made any reform whatsoever impossible.

Nevertheless, and precisely because Parliament proved unable to enact any reform, the initiative was undertaken from the outside by an Electoral Referendum Movement.[4] Due to the nature of the Italian referendum, the mechanism can be applied only to repeal entire laws or specific portions of some laws. Therefore, the Referendum Movement targeted the law on proportional representation as responsible for the political and governmental stalemate and succeeded in promoting two referendums aimed to repeal the proportional components of those laws. The success of the first one held in June 1991 on a minor clause of the electoral law, the reduction of the number of preference votes to be cast by the voters, opposed by all the governing political class, was widely interpreted as a mandate for a major electoral reform.[5] As a matter of fact, the consequence of the second referendum held in April 1993 amounted almost to a major electoral reform. The Italian electoral system was drastically reformulated: from a proportional electoral formula applied in relatively large constituencies to a mixed system, three-quarters of the seats to be attributed by a plurality system in single-member constituencies, one-quarter to be attributed through a proportional formula.[6]

In the meantime, threatened by another referendum, the Italian Parliament had succeeded in formulating an electoral reform for all municipal governments largely based on plurality criteria and entailing the popular election of the mayor plus a seat majority bonus. Thereafter, when the issue of electoral and institutional reforms returned into the hands of the political class, there was a stalemate once again. Even though the revision and modifications of Italian institutions and mechanisms now appear to be absolutely indispensable both for the sheer functioning of the political system and for the overall construction of a new democratic regime based on majority criteria, at the time of writing, the political stalemate has not been broken. As a consequence, the issue of institutional and constitutional reform is being brandished as the distinguishing feature of the two major political alignments: the centre-left *Ulivo* (Olive Tree coalition) and the right-wing *Polo della Libertà* (Freedom Alliance).

It has to be said that the many politicians opposed to any electoral reform whatsoever and the few politicians who favoured electoral reform were both right. For different reasons some of them feared and some of them hoped for significant realignments. The impact of the new electoral law on the parties and the party system has been devastating. It is, of course, true that most parties were already undergoing a process of change and decline and that the party system was, as a consequence, entering a phase of de-alignment. It is also true, however, that the new electoral law precipitated and magnified some of these changes. Leaving a more complete treatment of these changes respectively to the analyses by Newell and Bull and Bartolini and D'Alimonte, here it will suffice to remark that, generally speaking, not a single party holding governmental offices in the so-called First Republic participated as such in the Berlusconi government which was created after the first use of the new electoral law. In practice, the new situation is slightly more complicated than this. For instance, some surviving Christian Democrats and Liberals, though under different labels, were part of the 1994 winning coalition. In any case, the new electoral law produced an unprecedented and largely unexpected political transformation and dynamic.

Only a few points can be raised and discussed here. What is important to stress is first of all the appearance of a strong political constraint on even the major parties against the creation of electoral coalitions. Second, the inevitable composite nature of these coalitions both on the left and on the right and their inherently unstable quality; and third, a widespread sense of precariousness in the new politics. It is probably too early to tell whether one will see the emergence of a 'cartel party' in Italy.[7] Indeed, at least three parties, National Alliance (AN), the Democratic Party of the Left (PDS) and Communist Refoundation (RC), do not appear to be willing to renounce their organisational identity. However, some cartel electoral competition is made compulsory by the new electoral system and even some cartel parliamentary aggregation may be considered useful. While most changes are still in the making and will be affected by a possible revision of the electoral law, either in the French direction of a run-off majority system, or in the British direction, of a simple plurality system applied in single-member constituencies, what has not yet emerged is candidate-centred politics.

Traditionally feared and criticised by both the Christian Democrats and the Communists, the personalisation of politics has made inroads at the national level, as the case of Berlusconi convincingly shows, as the negative impact of the utter inability of the Progressives to choose a candidate of their own for the office of Prime Minister and their poor March 1994 electoral results confirms, and as Lamberto Dini's added value in the April 1996 elections suggests. However, the personalisation of politics has not yet in any visible and measurable way affected either the selection of candidates for single-member constituencies or the behaviour of Italian voters. All this is meant to underline that while a dealignment of the old party system, facilitated by the new electoral law, has certainly taken place, a realignment is inevitably in the making. At this point, though, it is impossible to forecast when and how, if ever, such a realignment will occur.

Probably, the electoral victory of the Ulivo coalition led by Romano Prodi has accelerated the process. Nevertheless, a stable realignment will depend as much on the enactment of revisions of the electoral law or its drastic overhaul as on changes in the mechanisms for the formation of Italian governments. It is, therefore, necessary to turn our attention to these mechanisms, their application and their consequences.

GOVERNMENT FORMATION

One common feature of most political transitions has been a rather frequent turnover of government coalitions as well as a frequent resort to general elections. In Spain it took three general elections as well as three different governments, though supported by the same parliamentary majority, before the transition ended in a successful democratic consolidation. The case of Greece is similar. Three general elections and three different governments, though relying on the same parliamentary majority, were needed to bring the transition to its end. The situation was slightly more complicated in Portugal: six general elections, ten governments supported by changing parliamentary majorities, a revision of the post-revolutionary constitution. No surprise, then, that Portuguese democracy had to wait a longer time before becoming consolidated.[8] To take another case, for several reasons often considered comparable to the Italian experience, in the Polish transition there have already been two Presidents of the Republic, three general elections and four governments based on different parliamentary majorities. If one takes the date of the second electoral referendum, April 1993, as the institutional beginning of the Italian transition, in less than three years there have been three extremely different governments: one before and two after a general election, three different Prime ministers as well as three completely different parliamentary majorities. Once again, the Olive Tree coalition's victory in April 1996 and the formation of Romano Prodi's government have at least the potential of changing all this and of ushering in a new phase of political stability. I will argue, however, that a successful completion of the Italian transition needs substantial institutional and constitutional reforms.

*Ciampi*

The government led by Carlo Azeglio Ciampi lasted 353 days[9] and was supported by a parliamentary majority made up from the Christian Democrats (DC), the Socialists (PSI) the Social Democrats (PSDI) and the Liberals (PLI); selective, but solid support was also provided by the PDS. The government led by the former Governor of the Bank of Italy was the product of the first real attempt really to abide by Art. 92 of the Constitution in the nomination by the Prime Minister himself of ministers, a task the Prime Minister ought to perform, not the secretaries of the parties. Indeed, at least ostensibly, Ciampi chose his own ministers without explicitly proceeding to a bargain with the parties and without accepting the dictates of the so-called parliamentary delegations. Italian parties thus began to lose some of their most significant powers. Moreover, Ciampi also appointed three ministers belonging to the former Communist Party (PCI), now the PDS,[10] and so ended a political discrimination that had existed since May 1947.

Even in its functioning, Ciampi's government introduced significant and positive innovations.[11] The Prime Minister spoke only to the issues on the government and parliamentary agenda – avoiding all political chit-chat – and the ministers were remarkably silent in implementing the Cabinet's decisions, without revealing any internal dissent and without avoiding collective and individual responsibility. Finally, Ciampi's government also gave a lesson in substance and style. When its time to resign arrived, as agreed upon with the President of the Republic and solemnly declared in Parliament – that is once the new electoral laws had been approved, the new constituencies had been designed and the financial law had been passed by Parliament – Ciampi did resign. His government lasted almost exactly one year, though it had enjoyed full powers for no more than nine months. The Prime Minister appeared to have ended his short-lived and unexpected political career at that point, but he has returned in style as Minister of the Treasury in Prodi's government. His abrupt, though planned and never publicly regretted, end depended fundamentally more on the inability, rather than on the unwillingness, of the left-wing alignment (the Progressives) to draft him as their candidate for Palazzo Chigi.[12]

*Berlusconi*

The March 1994 elections were not simply fought with new and profoundly different electoral rules. The very existence of these new rules as well as the decline and fragmentation of the old governing parties encouraged the formation and the participation of new political actors. Again, other articles in this volume explore in detail these changes and their impact on the party system. As to the government, there was an almost complete overhaul in comparison with the past. Silvio Berlusconi's masterpiece – the formation of two very different coalitions between his newly founded political movement *Forza Italia* (FI)[13] and, respectively, the *Lega Nord* (Northern League) in northern constituencies and the *Alleanza Nazionale* (National Alliance) in several central and most southern constituencies – was rewarded by the voters. After some political jockeying by Umberto Bossi, the leader of the Northern League, the two electoral coalitions transformed themselves into a governing coalition and on 10 May Berlusconi formally informed the President of the Republic that he accepted the appointment as Prime Minister. On 18 and 20 May he received a vote of confidence respectively from the Senate (159 yes, 153 no, 2 abstentions) and from the Chamber of Deputies (336 yes, 245 no). With the exception of two former

Liberals and one former Christian Democrat, Berlusconi's ministers were all newcomers to their offices, and most of them were undergoing their first ever parliamentary experience.

Berlusconi's governmental team represented a curious mixture of old (former Liberals, Christian Democrats, Socialists) and new (FI as well as National Alliance) politicians. However, what is more important is that the governmental team constantly tried to credit itself for being in sharp discontinuity with all previous governments, especially with its immediate predecessor, Ciampi's government. Indeed, it suffered from the comparison and the competition with Ciampi's government so much so that Berlusconi and his collaborator repeatedly accused that government of being simply the last embodiment of Italian *partitocrazia*. What is relevant for any analysis of the Italian transition is not the public policy productivity of Berlusconi's government, but its overall institutional dynamics.[14] In particular, Berlusconi's experience in government was characterised by three sets of major inter-institutional conflicts: the government against the President of the Republic, the government against Parliament, and the government against the judiciary.

For several reasons, above all the enormous, untackled and unsolved conflict between his private interests as an entrepreneur and TV tycoon and his public duties as Prime Minister, Berlusconi declared war on the judges, especially those of '*Mani Pulite*' ('Clean Hands' inquiry) in Milan, who have recently indicted him, and vice-versa. In spite of its numerical size, his parliamentary majority in the Chamber of Deputies was always fluctuating and, in the Senate, it remained numerically very thin. As a consequence, Berlusconi often and eagerly entered into a political collision with Parliament and with parliamentary prerogatives, rules and regulations. In order to bypass Parliament, the Prime Minister very often resorted to decree legislation (see Table 1 in which a comparison is provided of the performance by the three governments discussed here. It is worth noting that Prodi's government inherited 90 decrees that had been enacted and re-enacted by Dini and not approved by Parliament). Finally, Berlusconi and his majority entertained a very conflictual relationship with the President of the Republic, Oscar Luigi Scalfaro, whom they identified and criticised as the spokesman and representative of the 'First Republic.' In particular, some first-rank deputies of National Alliance (as well as Giuliano Ferrara, Minister for Relations with Parliament) in more – though sometimes less – veiled declarations asked for Scalfaro's resignation in order to open the way to a 'Second Republic' unencumbered by the weight of the past. Scalfaro was considered to be part and parcel of that allegedly disreputable past, both because he had been elected by the 1992 Parliament and because he interpreted the Constitution in a very strict sense.

The denouement of all these inter-institutional conflicts came about when the Northern League decided to withdraw its parliamentary support from Berlusconi's government. Several parliamentarians jointly elected, thanks to the coalition between the Northern League and FI, preferred to leave the League and side with Berlusconi. To no avail. On 22 December 1994 Berlusconi decided to resign in order to avoid a parlia-mentary vote of no confidence that would have gone against him. His government had lasted only 225 days, rather less than the Italian average of about 300 days. By resigning before a vote was taken, Berlusconi hoped to obtain from the President of the Republic the dissolution of Parliament and immediate early elections. In any case, he claimed his right to be reappointed on the grounds of a curious mandate theory. More precisely, his argument was that, thanks to the new electoral law, the voters had chosen not only a parliamentary majority, but had also given a mandate to a leader of that parliamentary majority, that is himself. Therefore, the dissolution of the parliamentary majority automatically entailed the dissolution of Parliament. If an attempt could be made to prevent this outcome, only the leader of that parliamentary majority was entitled to it.

Clearly, Berlusconi tried to transform a purely political issue, the breakdown of his parliamentary majority, into a constitutional issue. His main argument was that the new, three-quarters plurality/one-quarter proportional electoral law had substantially transformed the nature of the political system. What was admissible in the so-called 'First Republic', was no longer possible or acceptable under the new rules. Obviously, Berlusconi was challenging the very nature of a parliamentary form of government, aiming at a presidential system and, as all his critics remarked, at a sort of 'tele-plebiscitary' democracy. Here it is impossible to develop all the points raised by Berlusconi and his opponents and to disentangle the various arguments.[15] It will suffice to point out that the President of the Republic declared that the argument articulated by Berlusconi was worthy of the utmost consideration together with the constitutional implications.

Recognising that, following the new electoral rules and their implementation in the March 1994 elections, something important had changed, Scalfaro indicated that he had decided to act taking two constraining factors into serious consideration. The first factor was the series of articles of the Constitution concerning the formation of Italian governments and the dissolution of Italian parliaments. The second factor was the outcome of the March 1994 elections. Therefore, Scalfaro declared himself unable to sanction the formation of a new government majority made up of the Northern League plus other groups, such as the Progressives and the *Popolari*, which had lost the 1994 elections. He maintained his firm opposition to the solution that Berlusconi had immediately chastised as a *ribaltone* (an overhaul of majorities). As a consequence, he asked Berlusconi to suggest a person not unacceptable to him who was capable of forming and leading a government for a relatively short, perhaps pre-defined, period of time. Moreover, the President of the Republic took the unprecedented step of asking the appointed Prime Minister to choose as ministers and under-secretaries only persons not holding elective offices.

## Dini

From this context, characterised by political-constitutional constraints and by the cautions made necessary by a difficult transition, the name of Lamberto Dini emerged for the premiership to lead a government of non-parliamentarians (*tecnici*, defined by *The International Herald Tribune* as 'low-profile professionals'). Never a member of Parliament himself, Dini had previously been the Treasury Minister in Berlusconi's government. The political colour of his ministers and under-secretaries was largely unknown, though most of them belonged to the Roman politico-bureaucratic land-scape, easily associated with moderate Christian Democrats. Finally, as it was repeatedly proved in all the votes of confidence requested by the Prime Minister himself,[16] his parliamentary majority was provided by the centre-left: Northern League, *Popolari*, Progressives and, occasionally, Communist Refoundation, that later suffered a split on the most contro-versial of the issues, that is reform of the pension system. Even though the centre-left parliamentary majority was supportive of the government, Dini produced the highest number of decrees among the three governments here analysed in more or less the same amount of time (as shown in Table 1) and, in fact, of all Italian governments. This is a clear indication that Dini's government sought to avoid and bypass most parliamentary checks and balances.

TABLE 1

DECREES ENACTED BY GOVERNMENTS

|  | Governments | | |
|---|---|---|---|
|  | Ciampi | Berlusconi | Dini |
| *Decrees* |  |  |  |
| Enacted | 98 | 193 | 223 |
| Approved | 5 | 54 | 38 |
| Modified | – | (42) | (27) |
| Not modified | – | (12) | (11) |
| Expired | 92 | 133 | 135 |
| Rejected | 1 | 5 | 3 |
| Returned to the government | 11 | 24 | 8 |
| Pending approval |  |  | 47 |

*Source*: Adapted from data provided by the *Ufficio Informazioni Parlamentari e Archivio Legislativo del Senato*, Nov. 1995, pp.8–10.

What kind of task did Dini's government perform and what kind of contribution did it make to the Italian transition? For many obvious reasons the role of Dini's government was, first of all, to lower the temperature of political conflict. To some extent, and with ups and downs, this task was accomplished in a satisfactory way, so much so that, when Dini resigned as promised, at the end of December 1995, his re-appointment became a distinct possibility. In any case, when a renewed Dini government proved impossible, the overall climate appeared so much changed that even Berlusconi seemed inclined to accept the formation of a government of *larghe intese* (broad agreements), something he would have scorned just a few months before. Second, precisely because his government was non-political, the trade unions and the centre-left were willing to grant Dini enough discretion and support the implementation of the reform of the pension system. Third, though less positively, Dini's government had not been especially interested in encouraging and supervising the formulation of those rules indispensable for streamlining the new democratic game. For instance, the government did not push through the norms concerning fairness in access to TV during electoral campaigns and did not support the bill intended to discipline the conflict of interests. Dini himself had only indicated his preference for a few and not particularly incisive and effective measures and mechanisms to stabilise executive power. The Minister for Institutional Reforms never introduced any bill for this purpose nor did he play a very active role in a lively debate.

More important than anything else, however, is the overall image of the government which the Prime Minister deliberately and constantly projected. The easing of exaggerated political tensions was paid for by an exaggerated emphasis on the non-political, purely 'technical' nature of the government. This had two major drawbacks. On the one hand, this emphasis nourished and strengthened a traditional Italian belief that so-called professional politicians pursue partisan interests only and, as a consequence, non-political leaders are better and more capable of pursuing general interests. The disdain for politics and the anti-politic sentiment of large portions of the Italian electorate appeared to be vindicated by Dini's experience. The Prime Minister and his collaborators did nothing to dispel this interpretation. The search for 'a man of Providence' outside the political arena went, of course, beyond the person of Dini and focused especially on the famous public prosecutor, Antonio Di Pietro. On the other hand, exactly because of its non-political nature, Dini's government appeared fatally unequipped to facilitate the Italian transition. It could not bring the transition to a successful completion. On the contrary, it was bound to prolong the transition, and thereby increase the political risks of some restoration and backlash.

The risks of restoration were visible in the attempts to reintroduce massive doses of proportional elements into the electoral laws as, for instance, in the new law drafted for the election of regional councils in April 1995. There were also visible, though less successful, attempts to recreate a centrist political alignment in a position to bargain both with the right and left, thus destroying any possibility of a democratic regime based on the principle of rotation in government of two clearly distinct coalitions. Incidentally, rotation in government had been defined as the major goal of the Electoral Reform Movement. As to the risks of backlash, the experience and the continuation of Dini's government were seen as a distortion of the democratic game by many voters of the centre-right and decried as a suspension of democracy by Berlusconi and his collaborators. Their resentment could easily have been transformed into political vendettas had they won the April 1996 elections. Therefore, instead of having structurally relieved the political climate, it appears that Dini's government may have just temporarily suppressed continuing and irrepressible political tensions.

Finally, put in perspective, the accomplishments of Dini's government appear somewhat ephemeral. The political climate runs the risk of deteriorating again, the issue of institutional reforms has not been tackled and no significant step has been made towards the completion of the Italian political transition. Some analysts would add that the reform of the pension system will soon have to be revised. On the basis of available comparative knowledge drawn from cases as diverse as Greece and Spain, Portugal and Poland, one feels safe in noting that a transition can be brought to a successful completion exclusively by a political government representing the views of an electoral majority. But Dini's experience did not enable any substantial progress in terms of political or institutional transformations leading towards the creation of a better Republic. On the contrary, as long as the project, attributed to Dini, of creating a political centre is not defeated, a major political component of the transition will not be successfully solved. Moreover, the very idea of party government has been seriously damaged by Dini's experience and so far nothing has been formulated to replace it. Finally, the overall issue of institutional and constitutional reform looms large over the future of any government – and in the immediate future that of Romano Prodi.

WHICH, IF ANY, PARTY GOVERNMENT?

The last Italian government (before the Prodi administration) to exhibit all the characteristics associated with party government was the seventh, and last, government led by Giulio Andreotti (April 1991–April 1992). As in all previous Italian governments, decisions were made by elected party officials or by those under their control; policy was decided within parties which then acted cohesively to enact it; and officials were recruited and held accountable through parties.[17] Notwithstanding a few and feeble criticisms[18] – which go against the accumulated evidence and the experience of Italian voters and being useful only because they address their attention to some limiting factors – Italian political parties had completely dominated the policy-making process and had staffed all the political, socio-cultural and economic offices they wanted. Even in April 1992, when the crisis of the political system was imminent, the Christian Democrats and the Socialists reached an agreement on how to distribute the most important offices: Palazzo Chigi (the headquarters of the Prime Minister) and the Quirinale (the seat of the Presidency of the Republic). Italian party politicians in government did not shy away from pretentiously displaying their ability to expand the control of their parties not only over the State, but also over society. They dangerously underestimated the ensuing reaction, especially in some northern areas where a few sectors of Italian society felt confident of their ability to survive and thrive without the support, and against the interference, of the parties.

This self-confidence, however, should by no means be equated with the willingness and inclination of all sectors of Italian society to get rid of 'their' political parties and party government entirely for self-government. An aspiration cannot be mistaken for reality. Also, because of the weakness of the institutional arrangements, party government in Italy had probably been inaugurated by default and never sustained by explicit theories[19] and consistent practice. Up to 1992 the alternatives to party government had been neither visible nor viable. In 1995, following three governments whose 'party governmentness' was certainly and deliberately curtailed, the alternatives to party government Italian-style remained neither particularly feasible nor especially appealing.

The three governments whose experience has been analysed from the perspective of their institutional position and political contribution *did* represent an attempt to go beyond the party government phase. Ciampi's government purposefully attempted to lighten the weight of parties and *partitocrazia* in the Italian politico-economic system and to introduce some technocratic criteria into the governance of the Republic in order to promote the public interest. Unfortunately, Ciampi's experience in government was too short to produce incisive and lasting results. Berlusconi's team of aggressive newcomers wanted completely to discredit all previous experiences of party government and to show that the Italian political system could be effectively managed according to corporate-like criteria. Forza Italia the *partito-azienda* (party-corporation), wanted to run the Italian political system as if it were just a mega-corporation and to show that the entrepreneurial class is definitely superior to the political class, at least to that class composed of traditional politicians of the centre-left alignment. Finally, more or less willingly and consciously, Dini's government represented the highest stage in this process of delegitimation of party government in Italy. A government staffed by 'low-profile professionals' not only outlasted Ciampi's team of good politicians and esteemed professors, it also beat Berlusconi's *governo-azienda* (government-corporation) on its own ground – technical capabilities.

It may be just one more irony of the political history of Italy that the transition began with the fall of the last party government in a long series of governments led by Andreotti and culminated in a government without parties led by Lamberto Dini (who owes a lot to Andreotti – e.g., the suggestion of several, not necessarily the best, ministerial office-holders.) In peculiar ways, there are two features common to both governmental experiences. The first is that, by intentionally opposing and consistently rejecting any institutional reform, Andreotti paved the way for the political transition, whereas, by consciously *not* attacking the politics-laden issue of institutional reform, Dini simply prolonged it. The second is that both the Andreotti and Dini governments evaded the central principle of party government: political accountability. Throughout the 1980s and still in the early 1990s, Andreotti felt so confident in his ability to reproduce the necessary electoral consensus that he, the dominant majority of Christian Democrats and Craxi's Socialists, operated without giving any attention to the problem of political accountability. They thought they could still maintain control over all the vital political and economic processes regardless of the changing distribution of electoral consensus. Coming from the opposite extreme, that is without enjoying the support of well-oiled power networks, and over-stressing the non-political nature of his government, Dini obtained a similar result. Not having a predetermined political majority, he exploited his scope for governmental manoeuvre and evaded the problem of accountability.

With all its drawbacks, party government Italian-style had provided substantial policy responsiveness and was sufficiently grounded in political accountability.[20] The Italian political transition started when individual parties began to decline as organisations and proved themselves no longer capable of providing enough policy responsiveness, and when the party system as a whole – as well as governments – could no longer be considered politically accountable. For different reasons, Ciampi, Berlusconi and Dini further reduced the ability of the Italian variant of party government to supply policy responsiveness and political accountability. The destructive component of the transition has been substantially completed. It remains to be seen whether the various political actors are aware of the stage now reached and are capable of making real their proposals for the reconstruction of a viable system of policy responsiveness and political accountability.[21]

## INSTITUTIONAL AND CONSTITUTIONAL PROPOSALS

Should party government be revived and, if so, in what form? These are the questions that are raised and have to be answered by proposals for institutional and constitutional reform. The word 'proposal' is preferable to 'project' because Italian political actors have so far been largely unwilling, and on the whole unable, to formulate full-blown projects. Since in Italy party government is often, though wrongly, equated with *partitocrazia*, and sharply criticised, it is no wonder that almost all the proposals for reform give very little explicit attention to the revival of party government. Only lip service is paid to the need to revive viable political parties as structures for the mobilisation of voters, for policy responsiveness to citizens' demands and for the political accountability of office-holders. Even lip service is quite rarely paid and mostly provided only by the Progressives and the *Popolari*. All the other relevant actors, who have carefully shunned the term party for their political organisations, have other considerations and other goals in mind. For example, the former neo-fascists are now members of the National Alliance; Berlusconi has called his political movement Forza Italia; the Northern League has purposefully avoided any identification with traditional party organisations, and even most former Christian Democrats have either joined the Christian Democratic Centre (CCD), or become members of the Christian Democratic Union (CDU), and so on. Understandably so, because the so-called, First Republic remains almost completely identified with *partitocrazia*, a system dominated by political parties. A large sector of public opinion believes that, if the 'Second Republic' is to be a better Republic, then it should be founded on different principles and organisations. Therefore, the establishment or re-establishment of party government is not the paramount goal of most reformers. On the contrary, the dominant goal seems to be the transcendence of party government.

If that is the case, then the content of the proposals for institutional and constitutional reforms so far formulated become more comprehensible. The greatest contrast is between the proposals of National Alliance, in favour of a unitary state in the form of a presidential republic, and those of the Northern League, in favour of a federal state constructed in the form of a neo-parliamentary republic. The term neo-parliamentary is used in the Italian constitutional debate to refer to a strengthened role for the Prime Minister, not just as a *primus inter pares*, but as the leader of the winning coalition and of the governmental team. Behind the Northern League's request for a federal state, there lies the idea that northern areas will be in a better position to govern themselves if unencumbered by the so-called Roman bureaucracy. As for the governing of the South, it will be a problem for its inhabitants and, in particular, for the southern ruling classes to resolve. According to the League's spokesmen, a federal state would function better not just with less bureaucracy, but also with less politics. Obviously, the federal institutional arrangements are meant to introduce a major difference with the unitary past, but their role will also be to free societal forces.

This recipe, and the reasoning behind it, has, up to very recent times, gone largely unchallenged by the other political actors, with the exception of the National Alliance, because the Northern League still occupies, or was believed to occupy, a pivotal position in the political alignment. What is more important for our analysis is that the Northern League seems to be available to support only those institutional and constitutional proposals making room for its paramount goal of a federal state. The re-establishment of party government is well beyond the League's interests, preoccupations, and goals. Neither the National Alliance nor FI is interested in the question of how to reintroduce party government into the Italian political system. After a brief flirtation with different ideas, it now appears that both political allies share a strong preference for a presidential republic. To put it more precisely, both the leader of FI, Silvio Berlusconi, and the president of National Alliance, Gianfranco Fini, are in favour of the direct election of the President of the Republic who would play the role, simultaneously, of chief executive. The institutional model to be imitated seems to be that of the United States of America, even though neither Berlusconi nor Fini show much interest in the institutional checks and balances indispensable for a presidential republic.

Their preference for a presidential republic can be explained with reference to two main motives. The first is purely partisan. They are both well aware that the centre-left has always had great difficulty in finding a popular, appealing leader. In fact, in all surveys, the leaders of the centre-left always trail behind Berlusconi and Fini, and even behind Dini and Di Pietro. Therefore, the direct election of the chief executive promises to be a bonus for the centre-right, as well as for Berlusconi and Fini themselves. Second, both Fini and, especially, Berlusconi show some impatience with the slow working of the Italian Parliament and for the complex negotiations necessary to convince not only the opposition, but also the often litigious majorities of all colours. They believe it desirable and functional to bypass parliamentary intermediation and create a direct relationship with the voters. Obviously, thanks to Berlusconi's ownership of three national TV stations, they start with a significant advantage over their opponents. It must be added that they have shown themselves able to 'telecommunicate' their messages in a technical and political manner which is far superior to that of their centre-left opponents. Indeed, their opponents have decried the overall situation as leading to 'telecracy', and in any case requiring anti-trust legislation (see the contribution by Luca Ricolfi in this volume).

That said, the general point remains that the centre-right *Polo* argues the case for a presidential republic in which the President will have the upper hand, a dominant role, in which politics will be highly personalised and parties will, at most, be simply vehicles for gathering some electoral consensus, not instruments for maintaining a working relationship with the electorate during the executive tenure. If the centre-right *Polo* has its way, party government will never again emerge in the Italian political system. On the contrary, Italian citizens will witness the appearance and consolidation of a no-party State concentrating power in the hands of directly elected political leaders. Though it may understandably remain a moot point one can hypothesise that there will be fluctuating policy responsiveness, depending on the results of public opinion polls, and less overall political accountability.

Ostensibly, at least, the institutional and constitutional proposals of the centre-left are quite different. The leaders, and supporters, of the centre-left oppose the direct election of the chief executive not only because they believe, in a partisan way, that both Berlusconi and Fini enjoy easier access to televised political communication and are more adroit in utilising that medium. It is also because, in both the Catholic-Christian Democratic and Communist political traditions and conceptions of democracy, there has been less space and praise for personal leadership and more for organisations, be they social and/or political. There has also been more general diffidence regarding the political role of television. In any case, within the centre-left there are divisions and rifts concerning the role of personalities in politics, the reconstruction of party organisations and the creation of institutional leadership. For these reasons, the institutional and constitutional proposals of the centre-left – for instance, the programme presented by Romano Prodi's Olive Tree alliance – appear to be less precisely defined, less incisive and less capable of being persuasively communicated to the voters.

The different souls of the centre-left oscillate between two extremes: those who would like to revive a political system in which the government could be constantly required to bargain with (a relatively fragmented) parliament and in which government leadership would be the expression of party leadership; and those in favour of a system in which the voters would have more influence in the selection of government leadership, a leadership which would also steer the course of its quite disciplined and supportive parliamentary majority. A fair amount of personalisation is made necessary by the second option. However, it is susceptible to two significantly different institutional solutions. The first one is the so-called Westminster model in which the designated Prime Minister is the leader of the winning party or, in the Italian political system, of the coalition, and this is understandably an element bound to weaken the model. In any case, this solution requires a reform of the electoral system in the direction of plurality or majority formulae.

The second solution, that should be more appealing to the centre-right *Polo* and might be considered a meeting ground for some of its leaders, is a semi-presidential system: the model of the Fifth French Republic. In this case, some satisfaction would be granted to those who desire the direct election of the President of the Republic and some satisfaction would also be granted to those who desire to establish strong ties between the Prime Minister and his parliamentary majority. Naturally, the French-style semi-presidential model offers some possibility for the revival of parties and of party government.[22] Paradoxically, even the often criticised likelihood of cohabitation between a President of the Republic elected by one popular majority and a Prime Minister enjoying the confidence of a different parliamentary majority may transform itself into a sobering factor capable of carrying through the Italian political transition without producing excessive and unmanageable conflicts and tensions.

It goes without saying that the solution proposed by Berlusconi and Fini will still make possible the formation of government teams made up of professionals, managers and of non-parliamentarians much like the US administration. It will also allow non-professional politicians to win the highest office without necessarily having to create and rely on a stable and structured political organisation. Political outsiders may, in fact, carry the day and then be quickly replaced. Because it may create precarious coalitions, governments and leaders, this is not exactly the most ideal solution for bringing the Italian transition to a successful completion. On the other hand, the solution proposed, albeit tentatively and hesitatingly, by the centre-left appears to be better equipped to encourage the formation of political groups and to mobilise and revive political organisations. It would also help lead the transition towards a satisfactory conclusion. It remains to be seen whether the Olive Tree coalition will consider as a real priority the enactment of incisive institutional and constitutional reforms, more or less bargained with the *Polo*. What is certainly true is that the electoral victory of the Olive Tree coalition has created the political preconditions for completing the transition. However, only the reform of the institutions and the Constitution will create a new, well functioning and even more democratic political system.

## CONCLUSION: TOWARDS A NO-PARTY STATE?

At this point, any reconciliation of the different institutional and constitutional proposals seems rather unlikely. On the contrary, there is now a situation of confrontational stalemate. This kind of stalemate may be broken by a technical agreement, for instance, to give birth to a Constituent Assembly empowered with the task of reformulating those parts of the Constitution concerning the structure of the state and the form of government. Or it may be broken by a resort to referendums. However, the Italian Constitution explicitly prevents referendums from dealing with the form of government and, in any case, it will be for Parliament to decide whether a referendum should be called on the form of state. Constitutional referendums can only defeat a reform once it has been enacted by Parliament.

No precise indicators and/or measures of the completion of a transition have been formulated and applied. However, it can be convincingly argued that transitions end and democratic consolidation, or reconsolidation, is achieved once all the relevant political actors accept the (new) rules of the institutional and constitutional game and work through those rules in order to change them. There may, of course, be an extensive period of ambiguity in which transition and consolidation overlap. But without the widespread acceptance of the (new) rules, there clearly will be no consolidation.

If this hypothesis is correct, the Italian transition is still mid-stream and all its political actors and institutions are under stress. In any case, judging from the most important institutional and constitutional proposals, there are very few chances that *partitocrazia* will re-emerge. Because of the composite nature of the two major competing coalitions, it is also unlikely that party government will reappear. On the contrary, there is the risk that something resembling a no-party state will be the product of some constitutional reforms. If that is the case, the relevant question to ask will concern the quantity and quality of Italian democracy. Nostalgia for *partitocrazia* is largely misplaced. Moderate preoccupations for some of the alternatives which might appear in the future are more justified.

## NOTES

1. A stark defence of the old regime and its parties can be found in Mauro Calise, *Dopo la partitocrazia* (Turin: Einaudi 1994).
2. Briefly, there are those who believe that the starting date was the collapse of the Berlin Wall in Nov. 1989, the first electoral referendum in June 1991, the great leap forward of

the Northern League in the general elections of April 1992 or Berlusconi's victory in the general elections of March 1994.

3. The causes are alternatively identified as: the transformation of the PCI into the PDS; the consequent loss of identity of a Christian Democratic Party no longer considered necessary by the voters as an anti-Communist bulwark; the emergence of the Northern League as an anti-party movement; or 'Mani Pulite' (Clean Hands) investigation and the subsequent exposure of systemic corruption. On several of these points see Mark Gilbert, *The Italian Revolution. The End of Politics Italian Style?* (Boulder, CO: Westview Press 1995) and Patrick McCarthy, *The Crisis of the Italian State. From the Origins of the Cold War to the Fall of Berlusconi* (NY: St Martin's Press 1995).

4. The details can be found in my 'The electoral reform referendums' in Robert Leonardi and Fausto Anderlini (eds.) *Italian Politics. A Review Volume 6* (London: Frances Pinter 1992) pp.9–24.

5. On this point, see Patrick McCarthy 'The Referendum of 9 June' in Stephen Hellman and Gianfranco Pasquino (eds.) *Italian Politics. A Review Volume 7* (ibid. 1992) pp.11–28.

6. The legislative outcome is too complex to be discussed and assessed in a few sentences. The best short description of the details can be found in Richard S. Katz, 'The 1993 Parliamentary Electoral Reform' in Carol Mershon and Gianfranco Pasquino (eds.) *Italian Politics. Ending The First Republic* (Boulder, CO: Westview Press 1995) pp.93–112.

7. Richard S. Katz and Peter Mair, 'Changing Models of Party Organisation and Party Democracy: The Emergence of the Cartel Party', *Party Politics* 1/1 (Jan. 1995) pp.5–2l.

8. Data and analyses supporting my point can be found in some of the contributions to the book edited by Richard Gunther, Nikiforos Diamandouros and Hans-Jurgen Puhle, *The Politics of Democratic Consolidation. Southern Europe in Comparative Perspective* (Baltimore and London: Johns Hopkins UP 1995).

9. It is important to remark that Ciampi resigned on 13 Jan. 1994 and remained in office, therefore, only to look after current affairs and to supervise the electoral process until Berlusconi was appointed Prime Minister on 28 April 1994.

10. The governmental experience of Augusto Barbera (Relations with Parliament), Luigi Berlinguer (University), and Vincenzo Visco (Finance) lasted a few hours only. They were obliged to resign in the wake of a Chamber vote rejecting the request by the judges of Milan to put the Socialist leader, Bettino Craxi, on trial.

11. On Ciampi's experience, see the inside story accurately and sympathetically told by Carlo Chimenti, *Il governo dei professori* (Florence: Passigli Editore 1994).

12. Perhaps taking all too seriously the new electoral laws as designing a sort of Westminster model for Italy, the PDS secretary Achille Occhetto did not explicitly disavow the possibility that in the case of electoral victory, the leader of the largest party of the Progressive coalition might become the Prime Minister. This declaration scared many voters and, in any case, made it impossible for the Progressives officially to declare their support for Ciampi who, for some of them, seemed to offer too little in the way of novelty. On these various points, see Martin Rhodes, 'Reinventing the Left: The Origins of Italy's Progressive Alliance' in Carol Mershon and Gianfranco Pasquino (eds.) *Italian Politic: Ending the First Republic* (Boulder, CO: Westview Press 1995) pp.113–34 and Martin J. Bull, 'The Failure of the Progressive Alliance ' in Richard S. Katz and Piero Ignazi (eds.) *Italian Politics: The Year of the Tycoon* (ibid. 1996) pp.79–96.

13. See Patrick McCarthy, 'Forza Italia: the Overwhelming Success and the Consequent Problems of a Virtual Party' in Richard S. Katz and Piero Ignazi (eds.) *Italian Politics. The Year of the Tycoon* (Boulder, CO: Westview Press 1996) pp.3l–55 and Marco Maraffi 'Forza Italia' in Gianfranco Pasquino (ed.) *La politica italiana. Dizionario critico 1945–1995* (Roma-Bari: Laterza 1995) pp.247–59.

14. See Stefano Ceccanti and Sergio Fabbrini, 'Transizione verso Westminster? Ambiguità e discontinuità nella formazione del Governo Berlusconi' in Gianfranco Pasquino (ed.) *L'alternanza inattesa. Le elezioni del 27 marzo 1994 e le loro conseguenze* (Soveria Mannelli: Rubbettino 1995) pp.256–84.

15. I have done this in my *Mandato popolare e governo* (Bologna: Il Mulino 1995).

16. Having no pre-defined parliamentary majority, Dini's government was obliged to request

several votes of confidence, or more precisely seven: five in the Chamber of Deputies, two in the Senate, both in order to cut short lengthy debates and to consolidate the support of the centre-left. Eventually, as in the Chamber of Deputies in Dec. 1995, the request for a confidence vote served the purpose of calling the bluff of the centre-right and showing that Berlusconi's alignment was neither cohesive nor disciplined.

17. I am quoting the requirements of party government as formulated by Richard S. Katz, 'Party Government. A Rationalistic Conception' in Francis G. Castles and Rudolf Wildenmann (eds.) *Visions and Realities of Party Government* (Berlin-New York: de Gruyter 1986) pp.30–71 and 'Party Government and Its Alternatives' in Richard S. Katz (ed.) *Party Governments: European and American Experiences* (ibid. 1981), esp. p.7.
18. For the best of these statements see Bruno Dente and Gloria Regonini 'Politics and Policies in Italy' in Peter Lange and Marino Regini (eds.) *State, Market, and Social Regulation. New Perspectives on Italy* (NY: Cambridge UP 1989) pp.51–79.
19. I have argued this point at length in my 'Party Government in Italy: Achievements and Prospects' in Richard S. Katz (ed.) *Party Governments: European and American Experiences* (Berlin-New York: de Gruyter 1987), pp.202–42.
20. The necessary evidence is presented, hopefully in a convincing manner, in my 'Party Government in Italy' (note 19).
21. A thorough discussion of these aspects is provided by Sergio Fabbrini, *Quale democrazia. L'Italia e gli altri* (Roma-Bari: Laterza 1994) pp.105–64.
22. Karlheinz Reif, 'Party Government in the Fifth French Republic' in Katz (note 17) pp.27–37.

# Financing Party Politics in Italy:
# A Case of Systemic Corruption

## MARTIN RHODES

*Party finance in Italy has been regulated by law since 1974. But the introduction of regulation did little to restrain the expansion of well established practices of financing from bribes and kickbacks. Indeed, there are good reasons to suggest that the form of regulation actually fuelled the rapid growth of corruption throughout the Italian political system in the 1970s and 1980s which led, eventually, to the collapse of the traditional parties in the early 1990s. This collapse, and the ground-swell of popular anti-party sentiment that accompanied it, provided an opportunity for reform, but only after a referendum banned all public subvention of parties and political campaigns. A new law on party finance introduced at the end of 1993 breaks with 20 years of tradition and public funding is now restricted to reimbursement of candidates and lists of candidates – rather than parties – for campaign expenditure only. Whether this will prevent the re-emergence of widespread illicit party financing has yet to be seen.*

In many countries, public funding of political parties has been the preferred option for minimising the undue influence that private contributors can have over politicians. For public money, at least in principle, provides an alternative to special interest money that is susceptible to regulation and control. It is one of the key elements of a fair and legitimate electoral system. But as Alexander and Shiratori have pointed out, not every political culture provides fertile ground for the implementation of political reforms and there is always the chance that reforms may produce unintended or unforeseen consequences.[1] Italy is a case *par excellence* of this problem. Party finance and campaign funding was totally unregulated before 1974 when the discovery of extensive corruption produced hastily drafted legislation. Given the nature of the 'political culture' – a blocked democratic process, dedicated to excluding the large Italian Communist Party (PCI) from power, and extensive interpenetration between parties and public agencies and corporations – the 1974 law had perverse effects which, arguably, contributed to the corruption and – in the 1980s – degeneration of the main Italian political parties. The collapse of these parties in the wake of the widespread *Tangentopoli* ('Bribe City') scandals was accompanied by a citizenship revolt against the political system, and one manifestation of this revolt was the vote by referendum to abolish public funding for political parties in April 1993. This created the opportunity for a new and rather innovative law on party financing later that year, the impact of which has still to be assessed.

It is impossible in the Italian case – and perhaps also in that of many other countries – to consider the issue of political financing in only its most visible aspects. For in Italy for many years there have been 'two dimensions of power': one in which the rules of law and formalities of democracy prevail; an another in which they are ignored and which has been likened to a Hobbesian state of nature.[2] Both have been inextricably interlinked, for the survival and *modus operandi* of Italian political parties – the primary source of the democratic legitimacy of the state – has depended closely on their activities in a dimension of power whose rules of operation were not just undemocratic but subversive of democracy and illegal. This has been true of most areas of political life in Italy, due to the extensive influence of political parties in public administration at all levels, as well as in the large-scale Italian public sector. The funding of political party activities has thus drawn deeply on a process of *scambio occulto* (hidden exchange)[3] in the second, illegal arena of power, as well as on the legitimate means provided by the state.

For these reasons, while concentrating on the attempts of the Italian state to regulate political financing, the following analysis will make frequent reference to *lo stato sommerso* (the submerged state) and to the decaying system of parties and party organisation which accelerates after the introduction of the first political finance law. Part one looks briefly at the introduction of political finance regulation in the mid-1970s as a hasty response to revelations of political corruption involving the major political parties. Part two examines the role played by the 1974 regulations over the following two decades and explores the perverse effects that such regulation can have in a system with a poorly institutionalised governing class, a weak technocratic tradition and, with the exception of the Communist Party (PCI), fragile party organisations beset by clientelism and personality cults. These are characteristic of all southern European countries, but what makes the Italian case especially interesting is its position between the new democracies of the region and the older, more strongly institutionalised democracies of northern and continental Europe.[4] Part three looks at the recent period of popular revolt against the political establishment and the opportunity this has provided for reform. The abolition of state subsidies to parties and their replacement with a new set of regulations on 'electoral discipline' and reimbursements for campaign expenditure has been simultaneous with the emergence of new parties and the mutation of those parties which survived from the *ancien régime*. But they have also emerged in a context marked by a profound change in the nature of political marketing and manipulation of the media by politicians. This raises the issue of the relevance of conventional forms of regulation in an era of 'mediatisation'.

### 1974: POLITICAL SCANDAL AND THE LAW ON STATE CONTRIBUTIONS TO POLITICAL PARTIES

Between 1948 and 1974 there was no regulation of party funding in Italy and the private system of multiple channels of finance that had emerged in the pre-Fascist period continued to prevail. These channels included membership subscriptions; contributions from private organisations (including 'kickbacks' or bribes on contracts and supplies to central and local party administrations paid by private and public sector companies); the diversion of public money into party accounts; so-called 'black' (i.e. unofficial and illegal) contracts and interest on the accounts of state and quasi-state economic agencies; income from the economic activities of the parties themselves (including businesses controlled via co-operatives and other financial and trading companies) and donations from the party's 'flanking organisations' (e.g. trade unions) or from abroad.[5] Clearly, an extensive, unregulated system of this type will provide ample opportunities for dubious – although not necessarily illegal – financial practices.

### *The 1973 Oil Scandal*

Corruption offences were to increase significantly in Italy from the mid-1970s,[6] but corruption was a constant of the Italian system in the 1950s and 1960s and led to calls for a reform of party finance in Italy from the early 1960s onwards. In 1963 there were official proposals by the Christian Democrats (DC) and the Socialists (PSI) for the public funding of parties. But it was not until the so-called 'oil scandal' of the early 1970s that 'high-level' corruption involving political parties was brought to the attention of the media and public: previous scandals had been under-reported by a supine media and more easily buried by the Christian Democrats and their governing partners.[7] The context for the revelations of the early 1970s was created by the first oil price shock which led the government to introduce drastic energy saving policies and measures to restrict the price increases generated by supply restrictions. Investigations of market cornering and illegal price fixing revealed an extensive system of *tangenti* (bribes) involving the association of oil derivatives producers – the *Unione Petrolifera* – and based on direct linkages between the association's former president, Vincenzo Cazzaniga, and the four administrative secretaries of the parties of the governing coalition. The aim of the businessmen was to exert policy influence in a number of specific areas, including, for example, obtaining licences for the construction of oil plants and influencing the direction of government energy policy priorities (primarily to prevent a switch from oil-based to nuclear-based electricity production). The state electricity production company, ENEL, was also heavily involved.[8]

The attitude of leading politicians to the revelations at the time was dismissive. In a revealing interview with the newspaper *Corriera della Sera*, Ciriaco De Mita – then Minister for Industry and future Christian Democrat general secretary and Prime-Minister – stated that 'they are creating a scandal without foundation simply to excite public opinion and gratify it with tales of speculation and corruption. ENEL finances parties but this is among the, shall we say, 'sub-institutional' obligations of ENEL (...) the real problem is that only around a fifth of the money requested by the parties in the name of the parties actually arrives and is retrieved. The Italian political class is not corrupt but within it there is a small group of conspirators that discredits the entire system'.[9] This comment reflected the fact that the political party 'colonisation' of Italy's public administration and burgeoning public sector – especially by the Christian Democrats – had made such transactions unremarkable and routine. From the business side, public and private-sector enterprises had long manipulated political parties via close clientelistic relations – in order to shape the policy process, as illustrated by the role of the Unione Petrolifera.[10] Indeed, it is the routinised and institutionalised nature of corrupt political funding that is the distinguishing feature of the Italian system.

But while leading politicians wondered publicly at the fuss being made in the media, the 'dark side' of the system of invisible power revealed by the oil scandal was being made manifest in external interference in the investigations and threats against the magistrates involved. It should not be forgotten that the mid-to-late 1970s were the years of 'the opening to the left' which culminated in the so-called *compromesso storico* (historic compromise) of 1976–79 in which the PCI began to receive a degree of legitimation as a *de facto* participant in 'governance', through its abstentions in favour of the DC-led coalition. In response, 'subterranean' forces – spanning the major political parties, the judiciary, the armed forces and police and big business – began to build an alternative 'government in waiting' in preparation for the day when the threat of a genuine Communist participation in government became real. The mysterious death of the DC Prime Minister, Aldo Moro – ostensibly at the hands of the Red Brigades – who backed the 'historic compromise' may, in retrospect, have been connected with these machinations which, as revealed by the P2 Masonic Lodge investigations of the 1980s, had already assumed the role of a 'counter-state'.[11] But this was yet to come. In 1974, despite the fact that the leader of the Republicans and then Treasury Minister, Ugo La Malfa admitted receiving money from ENEL for his party, proceedings against other leading figures – including the leading DC politician and then Defence Minister, Giulio Andreotti (who in the 1990s was indicted on charges of 'Mafia association') were dropped and the governmental crisis triggered by the revelations resolved. At that point, the scandal disappeared from the headlines and public opinion was diverted by the referendum on divorce.

### Law No. 195 – A Screen for Corruption?

The culpability of the political class and those business managers involved was consequently diminished by obfuscation and delay and an apparent solution to the problem was found in the new law on public financing of parties that was passed in record time by the Italian Parliament. Law no. 195 of 2 May 1974 on 'State Contributions to the Financing of Political Parties' established a system of public subventions for parties receiving more than 2 per cent of the valid votes in general elections, outlawed contributions to parties from public sector companies, required the declaration of contributions from private sources in publicised party balance sheets (private individuals contributing more than 1 million lire were to be named) and introduced sanctions against those who contributed and received funds illegally and against parties for violating the rules on the publication of annual accounts (see Table 1 for details). But, importantly, it also maintained the system of parliamentary immunity against prosecution (this would only be overturned in the early 1990s in the midst of the *Tangentopoli* scandals). It can be argued, in fact, that the law's principal and immediate effect was to absolve those implicated in the 'oil scandal' and provide a screen behind which corrupt financing could proceed, and indeed proliferate. Chiesi goes so far as to argue that, resulting in part from a deal struck between the Christian Democrats and Socialists, the 1974 law actually contributed to the expansion of the 'invisible dimension of power' and the progressive degeneration of the parties.[12] By penalising forms of financing that had previously been legal, maintaining the status of political immunity from prosecution of members of Parliament, introducing a procedure for the publication of party accounts that provided for neither transparency nor an effective scrutiny of party finances, the law on party finance did nothing to constrain competition between the parties in their struggle to exploit public resources for their own political ends. Thus, the 1974 law emerged at the intersection of the 'visible' and 'invisible' states. While providing a cloak of legality for party activities – primarily by sanctifying unverifiable and fraudulent party financial accounting – the law also encouraged an expansion of illicit funding while protecting politicians and parties from the magistracy.

## The 1974 Law on Party Finance

The perverse effects of the 1974 law require further investigation against the background of changes in the party system and party organisation during the 1970s and 1980s. All parties agreed to the law 195 except the Liberals who were afraid of losing their autonomy under a state controlled system. Under the law, 15 per cent of public funding for election campaigns was distributed in equal shares to all parties which had a candidate in two-thirds of the constituencies and won at least one seat by direct votes and not less than two per cent of total votes; 85 per cent was distributed in proportion to election results. Basic finance for party organisation was distributed as follows: 2 per cent in equal shares to all parties, 23 per cent through a 'mixed system' and 75 per cent in proportion to election results. Donations above 1 million lire had to be declared but there were no limits placed on the size of these and no tax concessions. Companies with more than a 20 per cent government stake were forbidden to give gifts to parties. Public subsidies were to be published on 31 March of each year in the parties' financial balance sheets, and any real estate, shareholdings in commercial companies, ownership of companies and other forms of economic activity were to be declared in a separate report.[13]

In the 1980s, this gamut of rules was extended in several stages. In 1981 these restrictions were extended to Italian or European MPs, regional, provincial or municipal council members, to candidates standing for election to such offices, to groups inside political parties and persons holding offices in the parties. Law no. 441 of July 1982 required that MPs declare their personal financial situations and positions as directors or auditors of companies, present their annual income tax returns and provide details of election campaign spending. Similar laws cover regional and provincial councillors, councillors of municipalities which are provincial capitals as well as people holding positions in public agencies, economic agencies, and private companies in which the state has more than a 20 per cent stake. In law no. 413 of August 1985, parties were required to publish an account of party expenditure for electoral campaigns that clearly reported itemised costs (e.g. expenses for media access, publications, posters, etc.) and the distribution of state subventions between the central party organisation and its periphery. The details of these regulations are set out in Table 1 below.

TABLE 1

REGULATIONS ON PARTY FINANCE, 1974–93

| Parliamentary Party | Law No. 195 2 May 1974 | (1) An annual contribution is provided for any parliamentary group. Its president is entitled to keep a fixed sum and pay the rest to the party.<br>(2) The annual global fund is fixed at 45 billion lire and ⅔ is distributed through the Chamber and ⅓ through the Senate.<br>(3) Each chamber allots its own fund according to the following rules:<br>(a) 2% is shared equally among all parliamentary groups.<br>(b) 23% is divided as follows:<br>– a fixed sum to all national parties (whether represented by their own parliamentary group or by MPs belonging to the chamber mixed group);<br>– ⅒ of the sum due to national parties is given both to linguistic minority parties with at least 2 seats, and to any parliamentary group (except the mixed group) that does not represent any organised political party but participated in the last general election under its own symbol;<br>– ⅟₂₀ of the sum allotted to national parties is due to individual MPs representing linguistic minority groups or parties.<br>(c) The remaining 75% is distributed proportionally to all parliamentary groups on the basis of their membership.<br>(4) The president of any parliamentary group must pay not less than 95% of the total sum received (points a, b and c) to his own party. The Presidency of the parliamentary mixed groups must pay proportionally to all parties represented within the group not less than 95% of the sum received on the basis of the group membership (point c above).<br>(5) The President of any chamber allots subventions on the basis of a plan approved by the Presidency of the Assembly and upon request of the President of the parliamentary group. |
| | Law No. 659 18 Nov. 1981 | (1) The 1980 global fund is fixed at 72,630 million lire. It is fixed at 82,886 million lire from 1 January 1981. The fund is no longer divided between the two Houses of Parliament.<br>(2) 90% (not 95%) of the sums must be paid to the parties (both by the President of any parliamentary group and by the Presidency of the mixed groups). |
| To Central Party for Regular Expenses | Law No. 195 2 May 1974 | (1) Parties receive subventions through parliamentary groups.<br>(2) Party budgets must be drawn up according to a draft budget provided by the law and must be published in the party official newspaper and in 1 independent national newspaper by the 31st of January every year. |
| | Law No. 659 18 Nov. 1981 | Party budgets must be drawn up on the basis of a draft budget approved by the president of the Chamber in agreement with the president of the Senate. Party budgets |

are also published in a special supplement of the Gazzetta Ufficiale della Repubblica Italiana.

| | |
|---|---|
| Law No. 413<br>8 Aug. 1985 | Party budgets must be published between the 31st of January and the 31st of March of every year. The President of the Chamber, consulting the President of the Senate, may exempt from publication in newspapers if it is proved that expenditures exceed the state subvention by 20%. An account of party expenditure for electoral campaign must be included in the party budget. It must clearly report costs by item (e.g. expenses for media access, publications, posters, etc.) and the distribution of state subvention for electoral campaigns between the central party and the periphery. |

| | | |
|---|---|---|
| Campaign<br>Subsidies | Law No. 1952<br>2 May 1974 | (1) State contributions for national elections amount to 15 billion lire.<br>(2) Financial aid is allotted to any party that contests, under the same symbol, at least ⅔ of the constituencies for the Chamber of Deputies and either gets at least 1 quotient and (at least) 300,000 votes at national level, or wins at least 2% of the valid votes at the national level (national parties); any political group or party that participates in the election for the Chamber of Deputies and gets at least 1 quotient in any region whose special status provides protection for linguistic minorities.<br>(3) 15% of the total fund is distributed equally to all national parties. The remaining 85% is divided proportionally to all parties (both national and linguistic minority parties) according to the election results for the Chamber of Deputies.<br>(4) The sums are paid upon request of party secretaries to the President of the Chamber. |
| | Law No. 422<br>8 Aug. 1980 | For regional elections:<br>(1) A global fund of 15 billion lire is allotted as partial reimbursement for the June 1980 regional elections.<br>(2) 20% of the sum is distributed to all parties with at least 1 representative on any regional council. The rest (80%) is divided proportionally according to the election result (still among parties with at least 1 seat on any regional council).<br>(3) The sums are paid upon request of the party secretary to the President of the Chamber.<br>For European elections:<br>(1) A fund of 15 billion lire is allocated among all parties that won at least 1 seat on the European Parliament during the June 1979 election.<br>(2) 20% of the sum is distributed to all parties. The rest (80%) is divided proportionally according to electoral results.<br>(3) The sums are paid upon the request of party secretaries to the President of the Chamber. |
| | Law No. 659<br>18 Nov. 1981 | (1) Henceforth 20% (not 15%) of the total fund is distributed to all national parties and 80% (not 85%) is |

divided proportionally (still to all parties and according to election result).

(2) Sums are paid by the President of the Chamber upon the request of the parties' legal representatives.

For regional elections:

(1) Financial aid is provided for any party participating in regional elections. Within a global fund of 20 billion lire, a sum is allotted to any single regional election in proportion to regional population.

(2) The sums are paid by the President of the Chamber upon request of the party legal representative.

(3) In order to integrate the 1980 law, and in relation to the election in regions with a special status held before the enactment of the above mentioned law, parties are entitled to receive (all together) a global contribution of 5 billion lire. The sum for any single region is fixed on the basis of the number of voters.

For European elections:

(1) Financial aid is provided for any party winning at least 1 seat on the European Parliament. The global fund is fixed at 15 billion lire.

(2) The sums are paid by the President of the Chamber upon the request of the parties' legal representatives.

Law No. 413  
8 Aug. 1985

The state subvention for national elections is fixed at 30 (not 15) billion lire.

For regional elections: the state subvention is fixed at 40 (not 20) billion lire.

For European elections: the global fund is fixed at 30 (not 15) billion lire. An additional contribution of 5 billion lire is allotted as partial reimbursement for the June 1984 European elections.

*Source*: Adapted from L. Bardi and L. Morlino (eds.) 'Italy', in R. Katz and P. Mair (eds.) *Party Organizations: A Data Handbook* (London: Sage 1992) pp.458–618.

## Problems and Perverse Effects

But how has the law functioned in practice? There are several clear weaknesses. Although in theory party budgets became public and were standardised by the 1974 law, in practice the law proved quite ineffective in ensuring that the parties revealed their total revenues, either at the centre or the periphery.

- First, there was in fact no clear standardisation of spending categories. This meant that each party could interpret the requirements of the law in a different way: each party itemised different types of spending, for example, under different categories making it virtually impossible to make cross-party comparisons. Nor was there any effective way of verifying the income received or its source. The flagrant abuse of the system was revealed by massive underreporting of 'other income' (i.e.

contributions from private sources) by the larger parties. Thus, the Christian Democrats – the largest Italian party until its collapse in the early 1990s – regularly reported lower revenue from non-official sources throughout the 1980s than some of the smallest, such as the tiny Radical Party – a party which has always refused to accept state subsidies for party operations as opposed to campaign funding. In 1984, the Radicals declared the highest amount of income of any party under the heading 'external contributions from agencies, associations or private individuals' – 855 million lire – compared with the DC's 110 million lire. In fact, during the first year in which the 1974 law became effective, only three parties – the Social Democrats, the neo-fascist Italian Social Movement and the Liberals – declared any income under this category at all, and the sums reported by other parties after that date steadily diminished.[14] Other sources of revenue – for example, interest on financial investments and banking deposits – were also suspiciously small in the reports of most of the parties. Nor were the costs of electoral campaigns borne by candidates – nor the contributions and personal payments gathered to fund them – reported in party balance sheets and, therefore, cannot be quantified.

• Second, given the unverifiable content of the party's balance sheets, it was very difficult to impose the sanctions made available by the law. Although it is difficult to comment on this issue with any certainty, there were actually fewer corruption prosecutions against politicians in the period after the law was introduced (1976–79) than in the period immediately preceding it (1963–76).[15] This is unlikely to have been because of any change in the behaviour of politicians. In any case, anecdotal evidence suggests that parties could easily evade accusations of impropriety, regardless of the new procedures introduced by law 195. Zolo describes how a governing party evaded prosecution when forced to admit that it had received 1 billion lire from a fraudulent banker: it simply said that the party had borrowed the money and then paid it back.[16] This problem reflects the more general difficulty of imposing sanctions in a system based on collusion between multiple actors and the absence over a very long period of any alternation in power

• Third, as Auci argues, there was no guarantee that the provincial or regional federations of the parties revealed full details concerning revenue or expenditure or reported these to the centre.[17] And even if they were reported, there was no way of ensuring that the sums were consolidated into the central parties' budgets. Indeed, the Christian Democrats – riven by factionalism and highly decentralised – reveal a very low degree of transfers of funds between their central and branch organisations, reflecting the fact that the official party structure conveys little of the reality of the organisation. This reality was one in which the party's local organisations – and their diffused structure of relations with associated interest groups and agencies – were largely autonomous financially from the centre. This was true also, to a greater or lesser degree, of the other parities of the governing coalitions in this period – the Socialists, Social Democrats, Liberals and Republicans. In the late 1970s it was estimated that the inclusion of income and expenditure on the part of local branches would have doubled the sums presented in official accounts[18] – and much of this revenue would have come from illicit sources. By contrast, large transfers from the central apparatus of the PCI to its federal branches reflected the high degree of centralisation of that party. Thus, while in the case of the DC, for example, public funding served to enrich the central organs of the party, the party factions – where the real power of the party lay – and local branches continued to finance themselves in time-honoured fashion. Indeed, it was because of the structure of Italian parties that one of the major academic critics of the 1974 law – Gianfranco Pasquino – opposed the introduction of a state system of party finance.[19]

- And fourth, by establishing strict and cumbersome regulations and procedure, the law made *legal* contributions very difficult as well. As pointed out above, in the absence of effective sanctions against members of parliament, this may have encouraged the proliferation of illegal financing. For example, given their dependence on funding from public companies – which had been made illegal by the law – parties were unable to switch to other such ready sources of finance and so continued to pursue those practices that had produced the law on party finance in the first place. The funding limits established by the law may also have detracted from its 'moral enhancement' effect since it established a fund – whose size could only be changed by law – to be divided among all parties represented in parliament. There were very few and infrequent increases in the size of this fund (from a theoretical maximum of 60 billion lire in 1974 to one of about 183 billion lire in 1985),[20] which in years of high inflation, such as those following the implementation of the law, caused sizeable decreases in parties' officially recorded real incomes and expenditures. The decrease is especially noticeable for the DC, whose other income sources, especially membership fees, did not make up for the deficit.

However, it is unlikely that by amending this aspect of the law its failure to deal with the proliferation of political corruption could have been rectified. Higher sums would still have been spent on party organisations rather than on the *functioning* of parties. Moreover, it is unlikely that recourse to 'kick-backs' and other sources of illicit funding would have been scaled back, given the motives which lay behind the quest for even greater sums of money. The scale of the funds accumulated in this fashion are incredible. The exact quantity of *tangenti* is of course impossible to estimate accurately, but a study carried out by Cazzola in the late-1980s obtained reasonably precise figures on the sums involved in 101 corruption cases between 1945 and 1987. According to the data – which only represent the 'tip of the iceberg' – between 1979 and 1987, Italian parties received on average at least 60 billion lire per year (in 1986 lire) in illegal funding, equal to about 75 per cent of the total public fund for the subvention of parliamentary parties.[21]

## The Causes of Corruption

What drove this quest for higher and higher amounts of illicit funding? As Cazzola points out, there are numerous schools of thought on this topic, and each may contribute part of the answer.[22] These range from the specific to the more general and include the increasing costs of politics; administrative decentralisation and the growth of bureaucracy; the absence of alternation in power and the colonisation of the state apparatus by a hegemonic Christian Democratic Party; new forms of political professionalisation, including the emergence of party agents dedicated to the accumulation of resources which, in parties with a weak ideology, can become an end in itself; and the degeneration of political morality so that the 'governing of the public sphere becomes a means rather than an end, while public power becomes an end rather than a means'.[23] All of these are, in fact, very closely connected.

We can briefly consider the relative weight of these arguments and relate them to the issue of party finance. Firstly, as in other democracies, the cost of politics – especially in running party organisations and campaigns – has increased enormously. This is, therefore, a factor that can be more easily separated analytically from the others. Political costs were always high in Italy, in part because of the length of political campaigns and the importance, until recent years, of competition within party lists for preference votes – a practice that not only increased the ferocity and expense of campaigns but also encouraged personalised and often corrupt forms of campaigning and party organisation.[24] The 'media revolution' has clearly exacerbated this problem by allowing previously-prohibited private broadcasts and pushing up information, propaganda and campaign costs. At the same time, the 'office revolution', caused by the spread of new technologies (personal computers, photocopying and fax machines), required large investments to provide party headquarters and party owned newspapers with new equipment. Finally, although officially Italian parties are very sparsely staffed and salaries are very low, salary expenditures reveal real increases in the major parties' official budgets. More generous party funding may have allowed such costs to be covered legally, but comparative research also shows that public funding tends in itself to encourage a 'bureaucratisation' of parties, to lessen dependence on membership and membership dues and promote a centralisation of party power.[25] These factors may have been as important in increasing costs as the effects of the 'media revolution'. The latter raises an additional issue, however, which will be explored briefly below: maintaining fair competition among parties in an era when access to media has become vital and *equal* access increasingly difficult to ensure.

The other factors need to be considered together against the backdrop of changes in party organisation and inter-party relations during the 1970s and 1980s. First of all, let us accept as a premise that well before the 1974 law, the established practice was to fund parties and party factions with *tangenti* from public sector and private sector organisations: while the public sector was already highly politicised because of the well-established practice of *lottizzazione* (the sharing out of political spoils) and the private sector had long been involved in clientelistic relations with leading politicians. The controllers of the spoils system – and past masters at colonising the various parts of Italy's extensive public apparatus – were the Christian Democrats whose hegemony in the system (which lay at the root of the problem of alternation in power in Italy) was complete until the 1960s. From that point on, they simply parcelled out areas of influence to their coalition partners – first, the Republicans, Liberals and Social Democrats and later on the Socialists. This was the origin of the *stato dei partiti*, a public administration that was progressively 'balkanised' by clientelistic relations between parties and bureaucracy.[26] But in the 1970s, two important changes occurred. First, the expansion of the welfare state and the accompanying increase in public spending provided many more opportunities for the extension of party – and party faction – influence at central and local levels of government. The second important development was the accession to the leadership of the PSI in 1976 of Bettino Craxi whose modernisation and transformation of that party in the late-1970s made it the vanguard of a new and growing component of the political class – a 'modernising', but self-interested, bourgeoisie.

### Systemic Corruption and the Party System

The influence of the PSI began to increase in the late 1970s when the PCI moved back firmly into opposition after the failure of the *compromesso storico*. Under the rather authoritarian style of the Craxi leadership, this party not only began to attract well-to-do younger voters (indeed, it became *the* party of the so-called *rampanti* – Italy's 'yuppies'), but it also began to attract and promote a new type of politician – the professional, careerist party bureaucrat whose ascent in the party mirrored a parallel decline in the number of dedicated party militants. To use Pasquino's term, the party quickly became 'presidentialised' by Craxi, subordinated to a caste of 'political gamblers and entrepreneurs' and entrenched in *partitocrazia* (a party-dominated system).[27] The source of the PSI's power was not so much its vote (which increased from around 9 to 14 per cent of the vote between 1976 and 1987) but rather the pivotal role this increase allowed it to play at a time when the DC's vote was declining. This meant that Craxi could exert 'coalition blackmail' power over the DC, establishing a relationship with that party that would be based less on political compromise (one effect of the Craxi leadership was to shift the party firmly away from its left-wing origins) than on the distribution of spoils. The distribution of some of the key spoils of state to the Socialists began in the late 1970s. In 1979, ENI (Italy's national hydro-carbons agency) became a Socialist fiefdom and subsequently a battleground for influence between the party's left and right-wing factions, as well as a source of *tangenti* for numerous parties (see below). After Craxi became Prime Minister in 1983, this relationship became the basis for coalition formation, for the rationale that had kept the DC-led coalitions in power from the 1950s to the 1970s – the Communist threat – was becoming less and less credible. Subsequently, the rationale for government became the occupation of the positions of power itself, and from the end of the 1980s, this objective was pursued with determination by Craxi in close alliance with the centre-right factions of the DC – led by Arnaldo Forlani and Giuliano Andreotti (*creating the so-called CAF axis*) – against both the Communist (by now increasingly 'post-Communist') opposition and the DC left led by Ciriaco De Mita.[28] The power and role of Craxi's Socialists in these circumstances was less that of a force for 'modernisation' – as the party's rhetoric always insisted – than what Sapelli has described as a specific form of southern European *caciquismo* – a party-leader based clientelism, linking an 'amoral' élite with the "clients of the clientelistic welfare state" and the other actors of a widespread illegality'.[29]

The role of party finance in these circumstances became highly problematic. As pointed out above, some secular trends – such as the 'media revolution' – had exacerbated the already costly nature of party organisation and political campaigning in Italy. But from the early 1980s, another development made the struggle to obtain vast funds of money via illicit channels even more ferocious – the decline in the ideological content of Italian politics. In the past, contributions from abroad (from the USA to the DC and from the Soviet Union to the Communists) had allowed these parties to finance expensive party apparatuses. In the case of the DC and its satellite parties in government, these funds were augmented and increasingly replaced by contributions from business, also motivated by the fear of Italian Communism. But as this threat diminished, business had less reason to contribute. Indeed, following the revelations of the 'oil scandal' of the early-to-mid 1970s, many businesses abandoned the national associations that had acted as intermediaries in the business-party financial nexus. At the same time, as pointed out by Napoleone Colajanni, the increasingly bland – if not vacuous – nature of party programmes dissuaded contributions of a less venal nature as well.[30] In these circumstances, parties – and above all the party factions and their barons – became engaged in a struggle for survival. For as revealed in the testimonies of those involved in illicit party financing in the 1980s, money had become the key not just to success in electoral competition but to positions of power within the party bureaucracies themselves. It was this moral and organisational degradation of the parties that led to an expansion of the *tangenti* system in the 1980s and, eventually, to the collapse of the traditional party system.

### 'Tangenti' and the Degeneration of the Parties

A brief description of the *tangenti* system at work in this period illustrates the degeneracy of the parties and their leadership and the 'vicious circles of corruption'[31] in which they had become involved. Three cases reveal the type of relations that were common between leading politicians and both public and private-sector companies in the 1980s.[32]

• As mentioned above, ENI had become a Socialist fiefdom from the late 1970s onwards. But what is surprising about its role in the *tangenti* system of party finance is that it was involved in subsidising all parties, not just the PSI with which it clearly had the closest links. As investigations revealed by 1993, the ENI 'affair' was a complex one, involving multiple deals and covert kickback arrangements that were linked to other public companies such as ENEL, the state electricity authority. In March 1993, the Socialist senator, Franco Reviglio, was forced to resign from the finance portfolio in the government of Giulio Amato after being accused of receiving illicit funds while ENI chairman between 1983 and 1989. In the same month, his Craxi-appointed successor at ENI, Gabriele Cagliari, admitted paying 4 billion lire to a representative of the PSI to secure a contract on a power station being built by ENEL. In one of the more tragic episodes of the *Tangentopoli* investigations, Cagliari committed suicide after 133 days in prison, but not before revealing to the magistrates that he knew of at least 50 billion lire in illegal funding through ENI and its subsidiaries to the Socialists and Christian

Democrats. Former ENI finance director, Florio Fiorini, revealed that 1.2 billion lire per annum had been channelled from the company to both parties and the Liberals and Social Democrats during the 1970s and 40 million lire a month to the DC and PSI in the 1980s. This was facilitated by the role of Valerio Bitetto who confessed to being placed on the board of ENEL by Bettino Craxi for the explicit purpose of procuring bribes. The ENEL connection also hastened the fall of Franco Nobili, the chairman of the giant state holding company, IRI, who was arrested in May that year on charges of arranging a 600-million lire payment to the PSI arising from an ENEL contract.[33]

- The second case also reveals the complex web of relations between the parties and public companies, but introduces a private sector component as well. These linkages emerged from an exposure of the machinations behind the 'Montedison/Enimont' affair in which the state over-compensated the private-sector Montedison (part of the large Ferruzzi group controlled by the colourful industrialist Raul Gardini) after the collapse of its joint venture with ENI in Enimont. In July 1993, testimony from Giuseppe Garofano, a former Montedison chairman, and from two other former Ferruzzi executives, revealed that kickbacks worth a massive 130 billion lire were handed over to leading politicians at the time of the Enimont breakup in return for the purchase at an inflated price of Montedison's 40 per cent stake in Enimont. Craxi was alleged to have received 75 billion lire and Arnaldo Forlani – the second figure in the CAF axis and then DC secretary – allegedly received 35 billion lire. The rest was said to have been divided among numerous figures including Craxi's second-in-command in the Socialist Party, Claudio Martelli. Raul Gardini was later to join Gabriele Cagliari among the growing list of 'illustrious corpses' whose suicides were linked to the *Tangentopoli* investigations.

- A third case illustrates the role of the parties in taking *tangenti* in the process of awarding public contracts. All companies which obtained contracts for the third line of the Milan Metro Underground system were required to pay bribes equivalent to four per cent of the contract's overall value; according to the prosecutors the DC's and the PCI/PDS' shares were equal to one per cent, whereas the PSI's was two per cent. This revealed the transversal nature of party collusion in corrupt practices (see below). In some cases at the local level the practice involved a 'consortium' of more than one party. For example a representative of one of the parties (usually DC or PSI) would collect bribes and then distribute agreed upon 'shares' among the consortium parties. These, according to the prosecutors in one of the investigations concerning

Bettino Craxi, included the former Communists (the PDS), and sometimes the Social Democrats and the Republicans. At the national level, those entrepreneurs who were interested in obtaining advantages through corruption would normally directly deal with individual parties' administrative secretaries. As discussed below, the role of such figures had become central to the organisation of Italian parties by the 1980s.

*The Logic of Corruption*

The logic behind such complex webs of corruption – and its destructive effects on traditional forms of party organisation – has been revealed in the testimony of leading figures such as the Socialist, Mario Chiesa – the first major figure to be indicted on corruption charges at the outset of the *Tangentopoli* investigations[34] – and in the penetrating work of Della Porta and Vannucci.[35] The generalisation of corrupt practices throughout the political system created a 'market place' for hidden transactions in which the powers and functions of certain types of politician, bureaucrat and party professional took on a greater value than those of others. First it strengthened the role of so-called 'resource seekers' in the parties and public administration, and one of the key roles of party bosses became that of placing such figures (as in the case of Valerio Bitetto at ENEL) in positions where they could accumulate *tangenti*. In the political 'market place', political careers became based increasingly on the capacity to control certain essential goods – mainly illicit funds – which were vital for the survival of the 'hidden' structure of the party. Much of this money – as has been revealed by the investigations – has ended up in personal Swiss bank accounts; but much was also invested in political careerism, as illustrated by the confessions of Mario Chiesa.

This money was used for multiple purposes, including the 'purchase' of faithful party members, conquering positions on electoral lists, buying the patronage of a party boss and acquiring political placements in the management of state-owned companies and government agencies. The building up of a faithful clientelistic base could be an expensive business, for it involved creating a 'court' of faithful followers – the stakes of which were increased by competition between factions. Securing patronage was also costly, for it frequently involved delivering 'packets of votes' to politicians in return, for example, for management positions in public authorities. The distribution of power in the party itself became linked to the capacity of local leaders to provide economic contributions to party leaders. Switching from one faction to another – if that faction was in the ascendant, for example – might require a substantial financial contribution to the faction bosses. The prevalence of such practices led to the rise of illicit professionalism at the expense of traditional party functions and the emergence of an organised, invisible structure both within particular parties and transversally between them. Della Porta and Vannucci discuss four different types of career that became prestigious and pre-eminent in the Italian parties in the 1980s: bosses of public-sector agencies and companies appointed by political parties (e.g. Gabriele Cagliari at ENI); 'party cashiers' (who co-ordinated party funding); *portaborse* (responsible for organising illicit activities in the public administration); and 'card-carrying bureaucrats' (senior administrators faithful to party or faction bosses).[36]

The ascent of these figures went hand in hand with the degradation of party sections and the exclusion of party militants of the traditional variety from influence. The most extreme example of this phenomenon was the PSI. Mario Chiesa reveals in his testimonies a party which became fragmented into competing factions with hard core 'falanges' of faithful supporters. In the process, the party sections became dedicated to the recruitment of *falsi tesserati* (false members) and *truppe cammellate* ('camel-borne troops') who could be mobilised by particular party bosses in the bitter struggle for internal supremacy.[37] Apart from the degeneration of party organisation that accompanied these developments, corruption and amoral politics were fostered by the impact of these practices on the public administration and local politics via a process of 'illicit socialisation'.[38] At the same time, relations between the parties were transformed. Behind the surface political struggles between the parties lay an increasingly important transversal structure of invisible collusion. The real conflicts, henceforth, were within the parties themselves and between competitors for resources in the political market place. This, in turn, had an important impact on costs, for these practices triggered an inflationary dynamic in the *mercato occulto* (hidden market): the higher the cost of political activity (including not just election campaigns but the struggle for internal party power), the more incentives there were to raise funds from *tangenti*; and the more possible it was to raise funds from this expansion of illicit sources, the more funds could be spent on electoral and factional competition.[39] In the process, of course, the notion of the 'public interest' was destroyed by the effective 'privatisation' of the public sphere.[40]

The scale of the funds involved in these hidden transactions is impossible to ascertain accurately; but clearly the estimates made by Cazzola, referred to above, in 1988, represented just the 'tip of the iceberg': his own revised estimates, which are substantiated by revelations that major private and public companies have been funnelling enormous sums (up to 800 billion lire each year from one single company) into party coffers, place the total amount obtained illegally by Italian political parties at 3,400 billion lire per annum.[41] This represents at least ten times the total official income of all Italian political parties (about 280 billion lire in 1989) including those, such as the Radicals, the Greens and the neo-fascist MSI, which were not part of the *tangenti* system.

In 1986, one commentator on the issue of party financing remarked with some prescience that he doubted that any parliamentary commission could reform the parties: only something similar to an Italian 'Watergate', he wrote, could restore a degree of principle and morality to the political system that these parties had destroyed.[42] The Italian Watergate began on 17 February 1992 with the arrest of Mario Chiesa, the director of the Pio Albergo Trivulzio, the Milanese old people's home and the first Socialist to be caught in the act of collecting kickbacks. The subsequent investigations which led to all levels of the political system provoked the collapse of the traditional party system and the drying up of the flow of *tangenti* to the major political parties. As a result, these parties quickly became bankrupt, the PSI being the worst off (see Table 2).[43]

*The 1993 Referendum and Law on Party Finance*

The popular revolt against the traditional parties, expressed in their collapse in membership and at the polls, created the opportunity for a major reform of the electoral system and, at the same time, of the system of party financing. In the 19 April 1993 referendum on party finance (one of 10 on institutional reform), 90.3 per cent declared themselves in favour of abolishing public financing for parties, both for campaigns and organisations. As in the 1991 referendum on the single-preference vote, the vote reflected not so much a response to the literal meaning of the question at hand but instead the desire for more general political change. When the referendum was held the old party system was already divided, fragmented and decapitated.[44] Also by the time of the referendum, the parties were being run by new (or sometimes not-so-new) faces and many of these supported reforms that their predecessors would have opposed only several years earlier. In fact, all parties supported the abolition of public finance by the time of the referenda. Given the hostility of public opinion, they could not have done otherwise.

As it turned out, the direction taken by the subsequent new law on party financing was quite different from the proposals for reform that had been advanced in the 1980s. For instance, Gianfranco Pasquino who, in the mid-1970s had been opposed to the direct public funding of parties, had changed his mind by the mid-1980s, becoming convinced that a different form of party financing could indeed be a powerful incentive for the reform of the Italian parties, producing greater and more open competition between

TABLE 2

THE FINANCIAL BALANCE SHEETS OF MAJOR ITALIAN PARTIES, 1991–94

| | Income | Expenditure | Annual Deficit | Accumulated Debt |
|---|---|---|---|---|
| *DC/PPI* | | | | |
| 1991 | 77,713,299,445 | 76,856,797,809 | 856,501,636 | −12,361,064,050 |
| 1992 | 107,334,589,538 | 107,325,911,575 | 8,677,963 | −12,352,386,087 |
| 1993 | 23,437,893,107 | 42,695,276,238 | −19,257,383,131 | −31,609,769,218 |
| 1994 | 17,037,677,081 | 31,278,374,998 | −14,240,697,917 | −45,850,467,135 |
| | | | | |
| *PDS* | | | | |
| 1991 | 103,213,606,672 | 108,840,933,419 | −5,627,326,747 | −43,451,614,804 |
| 1992 | 49,815,322,828 | 50,383,026,259 | −567,703,431 | −44,019,318,235 |
| 1993 | 31,528,208,101 | 31,872,581,145 | −344,373,044 | −44,363,691,279 |
| 1994 | 58,149,147,600 | 55,016,886,156 | 3,132,281,444 | −41,231,409,835 |
| | | | | |
| *Rifondazione Comunista* | | | | |
| 1991 | 2,542,774,424 | 2,550,422,549 | −7,648,125 | −7,648,125 |
| 1992 | 7,284,206,346 | 8,518,556,830 | −1,234,350,484 | −1,234,350,484 |
| 1993 | 11,366,176,679 | 11,236,146,089 | 130,030,590 | −1,104,319,894 |
| 1994 | 14,429,503,510 | 10,254,526,830 | 4,174,976,680 | 3,070,656,786 |
| | | | | |
| *Forza Italia* | | | | |
| 1994 | 38,578,310,020 | 35,793,589,780 | 2,784,720,240 | 2,784,720,240 |
| | | | | |
| *PSI* | | | | |
| 1991 | 60,472,860,418 | 61,202,845,150 | −729,984,732 | −26,599,325,426 |
| 1992 | 49,864,149,866 | 71,134,286,225 | −21,270,136,359 | −47,869,461,785 |
| 1993 | 13,003,459,631 | 17,517,850,384 | −4,514,390,753 | −52,383,852,538 |
| | | | | |
| *PRI* | | | | |
| 1991 | 7,474,857,200 | 6,428,781,656 | 1,046,075,544 | −3,287,729,420 |
| 1992 | 11,829,583,353 | 12,213,332,229 | −383,748,876 | −3,671,478,296 |
| 1993 | 6,327,233,240 | 4,831,765,913 | 1,495,467,327 | −2,176,010,969 |
| 1994 | 3,227,607,838 | 2,634,506,942 | 643,100,896 | −1,532,910,073 |
| | | | | |
| *PSDI* | | | | |
| 1991 | 8,781,955,713 | 8,282,485,259 | 499,470,454 | −9,398,151,078 |
| 1992 | 9,020,427,741 | 10,872,465,984 | −1,852,038,243 | −11,250,189,321 |
| | | | | |
| *Federazione dei Verdi* | | | | |
| 1991 | 3,859,162,275 | 4,199,996,261 | −340,833,986 | 132,040,616 |
| 1992 | 5,337,064,972 | 5,236,323,644 | 100,741,328 | 232,781,944 |
| 1993 | 3,995,323,560 | 3,107,324,694 | 947,998,866 | 1,120,780,810 |
| | | | | |
| *PLI* | | | | |
| 1991 | 4,943,232,180 | 5,693,821,720 | −750,589,540 | −9,413,631,089 |
| 1992 | 4,660,754,173 | 7,845,005,569 | −3,184,251,396 | −12,597,882,485 |
| | | | | |
| *Lega Nord* | | | | |
| 1991 | 2,190,875,425 | 2,446,622,815 | −255,747,390 | 194,207,330 |
| 1992 | 12,564,616,843 | 10,373,661,781 | 2,190,955,062 | 2,385,162,392 |
| 1993 | 22,970,666,098 | 19,430,743,829 | 3,539,922,269 | 5,925,084,661 |
| 1994 | 24,993,768,568 | 22,904,338,602 | 2,089,429,966 | 8,014,514,627 |

TABLE 2 cont

|         | Income         | Expenditure    | Annual Deficit  | Accumulated Debt |
|---------|----------------|----------------|-----------------|------------------|
| *MSI/AN* |                |                |                 |                  |
| 1991    | 7,107,129,667  | 10,217,444,886 | -3,110,315,219  | -4,306,491,173   |
| 1992    | 9,656,503,952  | 10,233,358,795 | -576,854,843    | -4,883,346,016   |
| 1993    | 11,720,894,589 | 9,739,438,756  | 1,981,455,833   | -2,901,890,183   |
| 1994    | 25,168,635,312 | 11,577,694,965 | 13,590,940,347  | 10,689,050,174   |

*Source*: P. Ignazi and R.S. Katz (eds.) *Politica in Italia: I fatti dell'anno e le interpretazioni*
        (Bologna: Il Mulino 1995) p.290 and M. Caciagli and D.I. Kertzer (eds.) *Politica in
        Italia: I fatti dell'anno e le interpretazioni* (Bologna:Il Mulino 1996) p.307.

them and a more extensive participation by citizens.[45] This was set out in
1985 where he recommended, parallel to proposals by the Socialist MP,
Valdo Spini, a transfer of party funds and assets to a foundation which would
become the 'legal subject' responsible for all financial activities including
private donations which would be public and registered. Public finance
would be targeted not at the structure (i.e. the bureaucracy) of the parties
but at their functioning. He also recommended an effective regulation of
electoral campaigns (including advertising) and limits on time and spending
in the mass communications. Budgets would be audited by specialised
companies, while parties would be fined in relation to scale of the offence
up to banning a party from state finance for one year and restricting
candidates from presenting themselves for public office.[46] Ciaurro suggested replacing cash grants wholly or partly with the provision to parties
of certain free services and in-kind donations, accompanied by a drastic
reduction in certain types of expenses – particularly electoral expenses.[47]

Many of these propositions were in fact advanced by the traditional
parties in the debate that preceded the April 1993 referendum, with the
former Communists, the Socialists and Christian Democrats emphasising
in particular the utility and desirability of political foundations to take
responsibility for party finances.[48] However, the massive vote against state
funding of parties, the collapse of the traditional parties in local elections
and the accompanying haemorrhage of membership created a completely
new context for new legislation on the matter. As a result, the new law (law
no. 515, 10 December 1993 – 'Disciplina delle camapagne elettorali per
l'elezione alla Camera dei deputati e al Senato della Repubblica') departed
completely from the 20-year tradition of party finance in Italy and introduced a system based primarily on the *reimbursement* of campaign spending
to *candidates*, rather than *subventions* (excluded by the referendum) to
*parties*. It also innovated in a number of other ways, and embraced in one
piece of legislation not just party funding but access to the media (including
for the first time the private sector), controls on the use of opinion polls

close to the election – an absolute novelty in Italy – limits on funding and spending and a new regulatory structure for monitoring the behaviour of parties, alongside a series of severe sanctions for contravening the new rules (see Table 3 for details).[49] In short, the main thrust of the legislation is to make candidates and lists of candidates the subjects of funding – via reimbursement rather than subsidy – and to cut all funding to party organisations as such.[50]

TABLE 3

PARTY FINANCE REGULATIONS, LAW NO. 515, 10 DECEMBER 1993

| | |
|---|---|
| Campaign Finance | Campaign subsidies are replaced by campaign reimbursements. New rules on media access, on limits on campaign spending and campaign contributions are introduced: |

(1) The media is required to guarantee equal access to candidates, lists and groups of candidates;
(2) Polls cannot be published 15 days or less before the elections date;
(3) Election spending per candidate is restricted to 80 million lire plus 100 lire per citizen in a single seat constituency and L10 per citizen in a multi-seat constituency;
(4) Election funding can only be obtained via an electoral agent who is responsible for registering them;
(5) Campaign contributions in excess of 10 million lire must be named; no single contribution should exceed 20 million lire;
(6) The total sum for the reimbursement of electoral spending for the 1994 election was fixed at 1,600 lire for the number of citizens in Italy at the most recent census, redistributed regionally according to the size of the population of each region;
(7) The quota is distributed to candidates in proportion to their votes gained. Campaign spending for Senate elections is reimbursed in the case of groups of candidates which have one of more elected or get at least 5 per cent of the vote; those not attached to lists are reimbursed if elected or get at least 15 per cent of the vote. For the lower house, spending is reimbursed to parties or groups with more than 4 per cent of votes or with at least one elected candidate and 3 per cent of the vote;
(8) Campaign spending is limited for every party, movement, list or group of candidates to a sum obtained by multiplying the number of inhabitants for constituencies in the lower house or colleges for the Senate in which they campaign by 200 lire;
(9) Candidates and lists of candidates are entitled to special discounts on postal spending connected with the campaign and to special IVA (VAT) rates on typographic material.
For European elections:
(1) The global fund is fixed at the sum obtained from multiplying the number of inhabitants of Italy at the last general census by 800 lire;
(2) This sum is distributed among parties and political movements according to the percentage of the vote they obtain at the national level.

| | |
|---|---|
| Regulatory System | (1) Representatives of parties, movements, lists and groups of candidates must present accounts on spending and sources of funds to the presidents of the upper and lower chambers to be sent to the National Audit Office where the documents will be examined by three magistrates with a special staff who will report within six months; |

(2) In each region a collegio di garanzia elettorale is established composed of magistrates and specialists in law and administration, with access to specialised staff from regional appeal courts; elected members of the national and European parliament and communal, provincial and regional councillors are excluded;

(3) The purpose of the collegio regionale di garanzia elettorale is to scrutinise campaign spending and contributions as set out in art. 7 of the law.

Sanctions    (1) For breaking the law on campaign publicity, fines of between 50 million and 200 million lire can be made. This can be doubled or tripled if the offence takes place, respectively, between the 21st and 11th day preceding the election and in the last 11 days before the election; and for offences taking place during the campaign, the government can suspend the licence of the radio or television service concerned:

(2) In the case of a violation of campaign spending limits, the collegio di garanzia elettorale can fine the offending party a sum not less that the total excess or not more than three times this amount;

(3) The offending party can be made ineligible for the elections or for the post to which they are elected:

(4) If the required details of spending and contributions are not deposited with the Collegio regionale di garanzia, the offending party will be fined between 50 million and 200 million lire. Persistent refusal to provide details will lead to the removal of the party from elected office;

(5) If spending limits are exceeded by a sum which is double or more the limit, then the candidate will lose office.

*Source*: Ministro di Grazia e Giustizia, 'Legge 10 dicembre, n. 515, "Disciplina dell campagne elettorali per l'elezione alla Camera dei Deputati e al Senato della Repubblica"', *Gazetta Ufficiale della Repubblica Italiana*, Supplemento Ordinario, n. 292, 14 Dec. 1993.

---

## A Preliminary Assessment

It is much too early to know how well this new law will function, and it is also hard to say how far the 'revolution' in Italian politics has gone in removing the practices of *partitocrazia* that fuelled the financial corruption of the past. It is possible, however, to make some preliminary assessments by way of conclusion. First of all, the new regulatory institutions – which include not just the national Court of Accounts (National Audit Office) but also regionally-based monitoring 'colleges' (*collegi regionale di garanzia elettorale*) – have been assiduous in monitoring party funding and expenditure and the Court of Accounts imposed a series of sanctions against most political parties just eight months after the March 1994 general elections. While equitable access to the media seems by and large to have been achieved during the 1994 election campaign (even if the two media oligopolies – the RAI and Fininvest – were frequently impartial in their portrayal of the parties and their leaders) – there were clear contraventions of the new regulations with regard to campaign spending limits and the declaration of sources of income. In both of these areas, the Court of Accounts has imposed fines which, in certain cases, are extremely heavy. The fact that this has occurred at all marks a major departure from past practice. Thus, two parties – *Forza Italia* and the Christian Democratic Centre (CCD) and one electoral alliance – the *Polo della Libertà* (Forza Italia plus Alleanza Nazionale and the small remnants of the old DC) – stand accused of exceeding spending limits by 6,867 million lire, 1,134 million lire and 1,928 million lire respectively. They have been levied identical fines as a penalty. Eight parties are being fined for not revealing the sources of their funds: the PDS (100 million lire), *Rifondazione Comunista* (100 million lire), the *Polo delle Libertà* (64 million lire), *La Rete* (42 million lire), *Alleanza Nazionale* (33 million lire), the Progressive Alliance (the PDS plus the smaller parties of the left) (30 million lire), *Lega Nord* (11 million lire), and the Popular Party (PPI) (10 million lire). At the same time, discounts on advertising given by Publitali, (the advertising arm of Berlusconi's media empire, Fininvest) are also being considered a covert form of party financing by the Court of Accounts, and Publitalia has been forced to revise its approach to political party advertising.[51] This is clearly a sign that the parties will find it hard to abandon their traditional practices, even if many of them are presenting themselves as untainted by the traditional political class.

On the more general issue of *partitocrazia* and corruption, it is clear that this has not yet disappeared. Under the Berlusconi government, which endured for only eight months, the practice of political placements continued and new corruption allegations are being made daily by the magistracy against politicians, businessmen and even fellow judges and magistrates. Many of these relate to crimes allegedly committed in the early 1990s, but many also concern illicit affairs that have taken place in, or continued to run into, the mid-1990s. In September 1996, there began a new phase of investigations (immediately nick-named '*Tangentopoli 2*') following revelations that public-sector managers had been diverting large sums of public money for private purposes. More generally, the consequences of the referendum, the limits imposed by the new law and the more general crisis of Italy's political parties caused by their loss of legitimacy and haemorrhage of membership, means that the issue of party funding will not go away. The bankruptcy of the major parties is a severe problem, as shown by the recent experience of the PDS. The former Communists hit the limits of extended credit in 1994 and have had to go cap in hand to their members and MPs for contributions to a national collection campaign. They have also had to sell most of their real estate, simply to secure new loans to help pay off their massive accumulated debt which, by the end of 1995 amounted to 350 billion lire. The financial – and organisational – collapse of these parties, especially at a time of major electoral turbulence and the emergence of new political forces, such as Berlusconi's *Forza Italia* – Europe's first, fully-fledged media party, led by a telegenic media magnate and staffed from his media organisations – presents as much a threat to the functioning of democracy as the systemic corruption of the past.

## NOTES

Martin Rhodes would like to thank Luciano Bardi for his help and advice in the preparation of this article.

1. H.E. Alexander and R. Shiratori, 'Introduction', in idem and R. Shiratori (eds.) *Comparative Political Finance Among the Democracies* (Boulder, CO: Westview Press 1994) p.2.
2. See D. Zolo, 'Una legge per i partiti', *MicroMega* 2 (1986) pp.34–49.
3. D. Della Porta, *Lo scambio occulto: Casi di corruzione politica in Italia* (Bologna: Il Mulino 1992).
4. For an exploration of the contrasts between the 'political opportunity structures' of corruption in different parts of Western Europe, see Y. Mény and M. Rhodes, 'Illicit Governance: Corruption, Scandal and Fraud' in M. Rhodes, P. Heywood and V. Wright (eds.) *Developments in West European Politics* (London: Macmillan 1997) pp.95–113. On Southern Europe, see G. Sapelli, *Southern Europe since 1945: Tradition and Modernity in Portugal, Spain, Italy, Greece and Turkey* (London and NY: Longman 1995) p.195ff.
5. G.F. Ciaurro, 'Public Financing of Parties in Italy', in H. E. Alexander and J. Federman (eds.) *Comparative Political Finance in the 1980s* (Cambridge UP 1989) pp.153–71.
6. F. Cazzola, *Della Corruzione: Fisiologia e patologia di un sistema politico* (Bologna: Il Mulino 1988).
7. See G. Pasquino, 'Contro il finanziamento pubblico di questi partiti', *Il Mulino* 23 (1974) pp. 233–55, repr. as Ch.2 of idem, *Degenerazione dei partiti e reforme istituzionale* (Roma–Bari: Laterza Editori 1982) pp.73–108.
8. See A.M. Chiesi, 'I meccanismi di allocazione nello scambio corrotto', *Stato e Mercato* 43 (1995) pp.145–7.
9. Ibid. p.147.
10. See G. Sapelli, *Cleptocrazia: 'il meccanismo unico' della corruzione tra economia e politica* (Milan: Feltrinell 1994).
11. The investigations into the P2 Masonic Lodge revealed a vast network linking many politicians from the Socialists to the DC right in a nexus of clientelism, economic corruption, financial power and covert politics, as illustrated by the close links between P2 and the biggest banking scandal of the post-war period – the collapse of the Banco Ambrosiano and the assassination of its chairman, Roberto Calvi. For one of the best accounts of the P2 affair, see M. Teodori, *P2: la controstoria* (Rome: SugarCo Edizioni 1986).
12. Chiesi (note 8) p.153.
13. See Ciaurro (note 5) and C. Landfried, *Parteifinanzen und politische Macht: Eine vergleichende Studie zur Bundesrepublik Deutschland, zu Italien und den USA* (Baden-Baden: Nomos 1994).
14. Ciaurro (note 5) p.162.
15. See Cazzola (note 6) p.119, Table 4.
16. Zolo (note 2) p.39.
17. E. Auci, 'Verità e problemi dei bilanci dei partiti', *Il Mulino* 253 (1978) pp.65–73.
18. See Ciaurro (note 5).
19. See Pasquino (note 7).
20. The law provides for four different funds: (a) to the parliamentary party (basically this is *the* party subvention); (b) national election campaign fund; (c) sub-national election campaign fund; (d) European election campaign fund. Only the first two were applicable

between 1974 and 1979. The theoretical maximums refer to election years. From 1980 they refer to years in which the unlikely coincidence of three elections should occur.
21. Cazzola (note 6) pp.138–9.
22. Ibid. pp.142–63.
23. Ibid. p.156.
24. See G. Pasquino, *Restituire lo scettro al principe: proposte di riforma istituzionale* (Roma–Bari: Editore Laterza 1985).
25. See Landfried (note 13).
26. Sapelli, *Cleptocrazia* (note 10) p.108.
27. G. Pasquino, 'Modernity and Reform: the PSI between Political Entrepreneurs and Gamblers', *West European Politics*, 9 (1986) pp.118–41.
28. M. Rhodes, 'The 'Long Wave' Subsides: the PSI and the Demise of Craxismo', in S. Hellman and G. Pasquino (eds.) *Italian Politics: A Review, Volume 8* (London and NY: Pinter 1993).
29. Sapelli, *Cleptocrazia* (note 10) p.123.
30. N. Calojanni, *Mani Pulite? Giustizia e politica in Italia* (Milano: Arnaldo Mondadori Editore 1996) p.16.
31. D. Della Porta and A. Vannucci, *Corruzione politica e amministrazione pubblica* (Bologna: Il Mulino 1994).
32. These are analysed in their wider political context in M. Rhodes, 'Reinventare la sinistra: le origini dell'Alleanza progressista', in C. Mershon and G. Pasquino (eds.) *Politica in Italia: I fatti dell'anno e le interpretazione* (Bologna: Il Mulino 1994), pp.91–118.
33. Ibid. pp.97 and 114.
34. See M. Andreoli, *Andavamo in Piazza Duomo: Nella testimonianza di Mario Chiesa* (Milano: Sperling & Kupfer 1993).
35. See D. Della Porta, *Lo scambio occulto: Casi di corruzione politica in Italia* (Bologna: Il Mulino 1992) idem, 'I circoli viziosi della corruzione in Italia', in idem and Y. Mény (eds.) *Corruzione e democrazia: Sette paesi a confronto* (Napoli: Liguori Editore 1995) pp.49–66 and Della Porta and Vannucci, *Corruzione politica e amministrazione pubblica*.
36. Ibid. p.429ff.
37. See Andreoli (note 34).
38. Della Porta and Vannucci (note 35).
39. Ibid. p.483.
40. See M. Magatti, 'La modernizzazione fallita della società italiana: Tra fiducia personale e fiducia istituzionale', *Quaderni di Sociologia* 38–39/8 (1994–95) pp.33–53.
41. See interview with F. Cazzola in *La Repubblica*, 20 Feb. 1993, p.7.
42. Zolo (note 2).
43. In spring 1993, PSI indebtedness was estimated by resigning party Secretary Benvenuto at 160 billion lire. Other official sources placed the total debt at about 130 billion lire, while unofficial estimates placed it at 300 billion lire. Its historical, *Via del Corso*, headquarters in Rome were put up for sale, as were most PSI real estate possessions. By May 1993, when the leadership of the collapsing party was passed on to Ottaviano Del Turco, the day-to-day functioning of the party ground to a halt when due to unpaid bills the party's phones and electricity were cut off. For a party that had received vast sums in bribes and kickbacks, this was an extraordinary state of affairs. It was paralleled in the Social Democrats where the resignation of its secretary, Carlo Vizzini, in March 1993 was provoked in part by the party's bankruptcy. Vizzini – who soon became caught up himself in the burgeoning investigations – had discovered that the rent on the party's headquarters had not been paid for years and that, with debts amounting to 20 billion lire, public finance had been going straight to the Banco di Napoli, the party's principal creditor. See Rhodes, 'Reinventare la sinistra' (note 32).
44. P. Corbetta and A. Parisi, 'Ancora un 18 aprile: Il referendum sulle legge eletorale per il Senato', in C. Mershon and G. Pasquino (eds.) *Politica in Italia: I fatti dell'anno e le interpretazione* (Bologna: Il Mulino 1994) pp.141–60.
45. G. Pasquino, 'Con i partiti, oltre i partiti', *Il Mulino* 258 (1978) pp.548–65.
46. Pasquino, *Restituire lo scettro al principe* (note 24).

47. Ciaurro (note 5).
48. A. Somma, 'Circolazione di modelli superati: Il legislatore italiano e il sistema tedesco di finanziamento della politica', *Politica del Diritto* 24/4 (1993) pp.623–46.
49. For full details see Ministro di Grazia e Giustizia, 'Legge 10 dicembre, n. 515, "Disciplina dell campagne elettorali per l'elezione alla Camera dei Deputati e al Senato della Repubblica"', *Gazetta Ufficiale della Repubblica Italiana*, Supplemento Ordinario, n.292, 14 Dec. 1993.
50. For a full analysis of the law, see C. Fusaro, 'Media, sondaggi e spese elettorali: la nuova disciplina', in S. Bartolini and R. D'Alimonte (eds.) *Maggioritario ma non troppo* (Bologna: Il Mulino 1995) pp.109–46.
51. *La Repubblica*, 14 Dec. 1995.

# Party Organisations and Alliances in Italy in the 1990s: A Revolution of Sorts

## JAMES L. NEWELL and MARTIN BULL

*This study analyses the changes which have taken place in Italian political parties and the alliances they have formulated in the 1990s, changes which are visible at three levels: the disappearance of old parties and their replacement with new organisations; organisational innovation in many of the new parties, and a new pattern of alliances – which is increasingly shaped by bipolarity. The changes are analysed in three periods, each of which culminates in a landmark national election: 1987–92, 1992–94 and 1994–96. The conclusion assesses the significance and likely permanence of the new constellation of parties and alliances.*

Of the various changes in the Italian polity in the 1990s, the most dramatic, visible and complex have been those affecting the political parties and the alliances they have formulated. Three levels of change have been witnessed: (1) the long-standing traditional parties have disappeared and been replaced by a myriad of parties, some new, some 'recycled', many of which have been short-lived. (2) these new parties (or in some cases, 'party-movements'), generally speaking, differ from the traditional parties, in being 'lighter' in structure and more open to loose forms of membership and to federation with other parties. (3) the alliances which both old and new parties have formulated have broken with the pattern established in the first 50 years of the Republic, and are shaped increasingly by bipolarity.[1] Since the Italian polity has long been dubbed a *partitocrazia* ('partyocracy') – because of the dominance of parties over all aspects of state and society – the importance of these changes should not be underestimated. They are essential to an understanding of the broad dynamic of political change in Italy in the 1990s and to an analysis of the party system as a whole.[2] We analyse these changes by outlining the configuration of parties in the first 50 years of the Republic and then document and explain the basic trajectories taken by the main organisations and alliances from the late 1980s in three periods, each of which culminates in a landmark national election: 1987–92, 1992–94 and 1994–96. The conclusion assesses the significance and likely permanence of the new constellation of parties and alliances.

1945–1987: HEGEMONIC DC AND ANTI-SYSTEM PCI

From 1945 to 1992, Italian politics were dominated by the Christian Democrats (DC) who were able to remain in power continuously as a result of the so-called *conventio ad excludendum*: an unspoken agreement between the DC and its governing allies permanently to exclude from office the second-largest party, the Italian Communist Party (PCI), because of its perceived anti-system nature. Though it enjoyed an absolute majority of seats in the legislature only once during this period (from 1948 to 1953), the DC, as the largest party and mainstay of every possible coalition, was able to sustain itself in office permanently on the basis of a shifting pattern of alliances with four much smaller parties – the Socialists (PSI), the Social Democrats (PSDI), the Republicans (PRI) and the Liberals (PLI) – whose combined average vote share over the period did not reach two thirds that of the Christian Democrats (Table 1).

TABLE 1

MEAN SHARE OF THE VALID VOTE RECEIVED BY ITALIAN PARTIES AT GENERAL ELECTIONS 1946–92

| Party | DC | PCI | PSI | PSDI | PRI | PLI | MSI | Others |
|---|---|---|---|---|---|---|---|---|
| Mean vote share | 38.2 | 26.1 | 13.2 | 4.5 | 3.0 | 3.8 | 5.5 | 8.6 |

*Key*: DC (Christian Democrats), PCI (Communists), PSI (Socialists), PSDI (Social Democrats), PRI (Republicans), PLI (Liberals), MSI (Italian Social Movement = neo-fascist party).

*Note*: Percentages do not add up to 100 since the means for each party have been calculated over those elections where they stood as independent organisations (e.g. the PSDI did not exist in 1946 and ran joint lists with the PSI in 1968, so their mean is calculated over ten rather than 12 elections).

The *conventio ad excludendum* had three consequences which would undermine electoral support for the governing parties in the long term. First, governments were highly unstable (since parties which knew that they would remain in office indefinitely could afford to quarrel). Second, governments were ineffective (because the effective absence of electoral constraints removed the need for parties to compete on policies). Third, governing-party rivalry gave rise to a politicisation of the state apparatus as the governing parties engaged in a 'sharing out' (*lotizzazione*) of ministerial and administrative posts according to the bargaining power of each. This allowed the parties to maintain and develop clientelistic ties with their electoral constituencies, a practice which frequently degenerated into out-and-out corruption. As a consequence, the Italian polity was characterised by a profound alienation of the citizenry from the political system and from the early 1970s surveys carried out by the Eurobarometer consistently found Italians to be far less satisfied with 'the way democracy works' in their country than the citizens of any other country in the European Union.

The governing parties, and especially the Christian Democrats, were for long protected from the adverse electoral consequences of such voter dissatisfaction by the strength of Catholicism, anti-Communism and the existence of two territorially-based subcultures – the 'white' and the 'red' – which also served to underpin support for the two main parties. From the mid-1970s, however, this started to change as the electorate began increasingly to be made up of those cohorts whose outlooks had been most affected by the dramatic social changes of the 1950s and 1960s: growing secularisation, higher levels of geographical and social mobility, an expansion of education and of the mass media of communications, a decline in the hold of the subcultures – all consequent upon rapid rates of economic growth. Voter dissatisfaction was now reflected in changed electoral behaviour and it could be seen in terms of: first, declining turnout – between 1976 and 1979, turnout fell from 93.4 per cent to 90.6 per cent and it has declined at every election since then to reach 82.7 per cent in 1996;[3] second, growing fragmentation – between 1968 and 1987 the number of parties in the Chamber of Deputies rose from nine to 14 and in 1992 to 16, while the proportion of the electorate voting for the three largest parties (DC, PCI and PSI) declined at every election but one between 1976 and 1992 and went down from three-quarters in the former year to under a half in 1992;[4] and third, increasing aggregate volatility – as measured by Pedersen's index, it rose from an average of 5.8 between the election pairs of 1953/58 and 1972/76 to an average of 9.1 between 1976/79 and 1987/92.

In short, whatever weight should be given to changing proclivities on the part of voters (as opposed to changes in the nature of the political supply) in explaining the altered party configurations of the early 1990s, it was a process that was not new but that had been going on for a decade and a half. Against this backdrop, the period after 1987 witnessed an acceleration in the pace of party-system change which was a precursor to the rapid collapse of the long-standing party configurations after 1992.

## 1987–92: THE TRADITIONAL PARTIES SHAKEN

The acceleration of change in the traditional parties came about as the result of two developments: the end of the 'communist question' and the emergence of new 'party-movements'. The collapse of the Berlin Wall in the autumn of 1989 led Achille Occhetto, the PCI leader, to propose a transformation of the PCI into a non-communist party with a new name, the Democratic Party of the Left (PDS).[5] The significance of this was that it entailed a final renunciation of the desire to achieve any change, however mild, of a structural or irreversible kind, and a removal of any ambiguity surrounding the 'anti-system' orientation of the main party of the left. However, the proposal unleashed an unprecedented degree of internal conflict and provoked a major party split leading to the formation of *Rifondazione Comunista* (RC – Communist Refoundation) which would not accept the change.

Yet, although the instigators of the RC breakaway came from the pro-Soviet wing of the PCI, the party was, in fact, composed of a far more heterogeneous band of forces, this as a result of the decision of *Democrazia Proletaria* (DP – Proletarian Democracy), a vestige of the 1960s and 1970s leftist surge, to dissolve and merge with the new party. This brought in individuals whose concerns were wide ranging (and which included libertarians, ecologists and feminists) but who nonetheless shared the view that the PDS would devote itself more to institutional manoeuvring than to aggressive social struggles.[6] In effect, the collapse of communism (and the sudden irrelevance of differing interpretations of the nature of the Soviet Union, which had once been the source of implacable hostility between DP and parts of the PCI) brought *rapprochement* on the left; and this, and its status as a small opposition party, meant that RC found that its eclecticism was not damaging to it. Hence, the first consequence of the PCI's transformation was to leave Italy with two significantly sized left-of-centre parties in place of the previous one.

A second consequence of the end of the 'communist question' was to create significant difficulties for the DC because the claim that the main party of opposition was an 'anti-system' party could hardly any longer be sustained, and this, in turn, undermined the effectiveness of the DC's perennial appeal that it was the main bulwark against communism. Since by far the larger of the PCI's two heirs was manifestly *no longer* a communist party, the DC's capacity to prevent a significant proportion of its voters now choosing 'exit' as their response to a long-standing disgust with its lack of policy achievements and its corruption, was definitively destroyed. As one anonymous voter put it following local elections in the autumn of 1992, 'There's no more fear of communism, so now we can vote as we like.'[7] This directly enhanced the fortunes of two hitherto insignificant 'movement-parties': the Lega Nord (Northern League) whose vote at the 1992 election rose from 0.5 to 8.7 per cent, and La Rete (the Network), which won 1.9 per cent of the vote in 1992 despite fielding candidates in only two-thirds of the constituencies.[8]

Taking advantage of the 'tax backlash' that had developed as the costs of the welfare state became harder to sustain through the recession, the Lega Nord argued that a corrupt, party-dominated bureaucracy in far-away

Rome sought to appropriate the resources of the North in order to maintain its own power in the underdeveloped South. Therefore, it argued that a set of federalist arrangements were needed as these – by limiting the functions of the state to external defence, internal security, the administration of justice and the provision of only the most indispensable of public goods – would remove from the central authorities all those functions which allowed it to tax the North without giving anything in return. In this way the Lega Nord managed to use the taxation issue to focus discontent on a single and (as it saw it) inescapable conclusion: the need for regional autonomy. Apparently wasteful public expenditure on the southern regions, combined with the fact that the larger proportion of the total tax take needed to finance it of necessity came from the richer North, allowed Bossi and other leaders of the Lega Nord to argue that the tax and spending activities of the *partitocrazia* were regionally biased against the North.

If the Lega Nord was a reaction against some of the effects of corruption in politics, the Rete was a reaction against the influence of organised crime in politics. Emerging from within Christian Democracy itself, its leaders regarded it, not as a party, but as a 'movement for democracy' whose principal purpose was to expose, and to campaign against, the influence of organised crime in public life. Reflecting an eclectic mixture of Catholic, leftist and libertarian values, its programme called for an end to parliamentary immunity, a reduction in the number of parliamentarians and greater powers for the judiciary in the fight against the Mafia (Sicily), 'Ndrangheta (Calabria) and Camorra (Naples).[9]

The general election of 1992 was the first compelling confirmation that the Northern League, and to a lesser extent the Rete, were forces to be reckoned with. Increasing its share of the northern vote from 2.6 to 17.3 per cent, the Lega scored its most striking successes in traditional DC strongholds[10] while the Rete averaged 2.3 per cent of the vote in those constituencies in which it fielded candidates. In Sicily, where it was especially strong, it seemed (as might have been expected of an organisation more closely identified with the left than the right) to win votes mainly at the expense of the PDS. Indeed, dubbed by the Italian media as an 'earthquake', the election produced the most significant change in the configuration of parties since the war. The traditional parties of government and the opposition parties of the left suffered a combined net loss of votes that amounted to 10.8 per cent of the total, while the new parties of protest saw their combined share of the vote rise by 9.0 per cent (see Table 2). The DC and the PDS experienced striking falls, while the PSI notably failed to make any gains from the collapse of the ex-communist vote. The share of the vote of the three largest parties (DC, PDS, PSI) tumbled from 75.2 per cent in 1987 to 59.4 per cent. Finally, the four parties of government (the

DC, PSDI, PLI and PSI) lost the overall majority of votes (though not of seats) that they had enjoyed in 1987, something that was interpreted by many as a vote of no-confidence in the outgoing coalition.[11]

TABLE 2

THE CHAMBER OF DEPUTIES ELECTIONS OF 1987 AND 1992

|  | 1987 | | | 1992 | | Diff. 1987–92 | |
|  | Votes | Seats | | Votes | Seats | Votes (gains/losses) | Seats (gains/losses) |
|  | % | | | % | | % | |
| DC | 34.3 | 232 | | 29.7 | 206 | –4.6 | –26 |
| PSI | 14.3 | 94 | | 13.6 | 92 | –0.7 | –2 |
| PRI | 3.7 | 21 | | 4.4 | 27 | 0.7 | 6 |
| PSDI | 3.0 | 17 | | 2.7 | 16 | –0.3 | –1 |
| PLI | 2.1 | 11 | | 2.8 | 17 | 0.7 | 6 |
| MSI | 5.9 | 35 | | 5.4 | 34 | –0.5 | –1 |
| PCI | 26.6 | 177 | PDS | 16.1 | 107 | –10.5 | –70 |
| DP | 1.7 | 8 | RC | 5.6 | 35 | 3.9 | 27 |
| Greens | 2.5 | 13 | | 2.8 | 16 | 0.3 | 3 |
| Pannella | 2.6 | 13 | | 1.2 | 7 | –1.4 | –6 |
| Rete | – | – | | 1.9 | 12 | 1.9 | 12 |
| LN | 0.5 | 1 | | 8.7 | 55 | 8.2 | 5 |
| Others | 2.8 | 8 | | 5.1 | 6 | 2.3 | –2 |
| Total | 100 | 630 | | 100 | 630 | | |

*Key*: DC (Christian Democrats), PSI (Socialists), PRI (Republicans), PSDI (Social Democrats), PLI (Liberals) = the traditional governing parties. MSI (Italian Social Movement) = neo-fascist party. PCI (Communists), DP (Proletarian Democracy), PDS (Democratic Party of the Left), RC (Communist Refoundation) = opposition parties of the left. Greens, Pannella (formerly, the Radical Party), Rete (the 'Network'), LN (Northern League) = new parties of protest.

In the absence of any politically viable alternative, however, the election's immediate aftermath saw the temporary resurrection of the outgoing four-party coalition, this time under the Socialist, Giuliano Amato, as Prime Minister. Yet, the fear of many (and the hope of some) that this marked a reassertion of the control of the traditional governing class over public life was not borne out by events. On the contrary: in the period up to the next election in March 1994, members of this class were all but swept away and the party system itself underwent a complete collapse.

1992–94: COLLAPSE OF THE OLD, BIRTH OF THE NEW

Two factors above all accounted for the collapse of the old parties: the continuation of an anti-corruption drive initiated by prosecuting magistrates in Milan in February 1992; and a referendum on the electoral system held in April 1993. This led to a significant turnover in political parties and the formation of new alliances.

## The Anti-Corruption Drive

In one sense, the fact that the anti-corruption drive developed when it did was a matter of chance, in so far as corruption scandals were not new; and while its essence was the exposure of a series of 'mutually beneficial linkages'[12] involving extensive illegal payments to the political parties in exchange for public works contracts, it was the decision of the first defendant, Mario Chiesa, to confess in early 1992, which set the investigations (known as *Mani Pulite* – 'clean hands') in motion by implicating subsequent defendants, whose confessions in their turn implicated still others. Consequently, the scandals, dubbed *Tangentopoli* ('Bribe City'), rapidly spread from Milan to other cities.

At a deeper level, however, it was not a chance affair because it depended on the actions of judicial investigators who, unusually among constitutional democracies, carry out much investigative work that elsewhere is carried out by the police, and who can initiate penal proceedings not only at outside request but also at their own discretion. Prior to February 1992, there had been a number of celebrated cases of judges using their authority to pursue the powerful in corruption cases, but now that resolution of the communist question had subverted whatever ideological justifications there had once been for being lenient towards the more dubious clientele practices of the governing class, so the judges, it seems, supported by public opinion in the aftermath of the election, had become even keener to use their powers as the champions of a campaign to moralise public life. Likewise, it has been argued that the end of communism made entrepreneurs more willing to co-operate in judicial investigations than they might otherwise have been; for, faced with the increasing costs of corruption,[13] the end of communism led big business to conclude, for the first time in 45 years, that it 'could foster a major crisis of the political system without risking its own survival'.[14]

The significance of *Tangentopoli* was that it thoroughly undermined the traditional governing parties, not only through its effect on public opinion, but also more directly by subverting the parties' financial and organisational resources. Major sources of funding were eliminated at a stroke (the PSDI, for instance, effectively went bankrupt at the end of March 1993). The membership base of several parties was weakened not only through the resignations of disenchanted members who were honestly motivated, but also by the destruction of the incentives which had influenced others to join. The acceptance of bribes for public works contracts had become a central element of the politics of clientelism and of the 'partitocratic system' as a whole.[15] To the extent, therefore, that a party lacked a membership with a sufficient degree of the *ideological* commitment necessary for maintaining its effectiveness on the ground, its very existence as a free-standing organisation was inherently fragile, and once the flow of resources from above dried up, it was vulnerable to complete collapse. Finally, *Tangentopoli* created tensions and splits at leadership level between those who had been directly compromised by the investigations and were thus on the defensive, and those who, though uninvolved, still had to bear the political costs of the crisis. In this way, divisions opened up between 'conservatives' and 'reformers', such divisions leading to eleventh-hour attempts at renewal and to acrimonious splits.

The immediate electoral consequences of *Tangentopoli* can be seen from Table 3 which shows the results of the regional, provincial and communal elections which took place between the general elections of 1992 and 1994. The figures are not, of course, comparable because of the differing electorates in each case, but they do serve to document the sheer scale of the electoral disaster provoked for the governing parties by *Tangentopoli*. By the time of the series of elections which took place on 6 June 1993, all of the traditional governing parties had begun to experience breakaways on the part of local federations which felt that the only way to save themselves was to field, in defiance of their national leaderships, their own lists of candidates under different names, or joint lists with other parties. Hence the very low, and non-existent, figures for governing-party candidates in columns 4, 5 and 6 reflect not only voter disenchantment, but also the fact that the disintegration of these parties as organisations had already become irreversible.

*Electoral Reform*

If the traditional parties were being cut down by the anti-corruption drive, they were being placed under a different sort of pressure by the referendum movement. The movement consisted of a variety of cross-party organi-sations (spearheaded by the dissident Christian Democrat, Mario Segni) which sought to adopt the tactic first experimented with by the Radicals in the late 1970s of seeking to impose political change on an unwilling establishment by means of strategic use of the referendum device. Since 1970, Italian law has allowed referenda to be held when requested by half a million citizens. Although referendums can only be used to strike down existing laws, or parts of laws, and not to make new ones, it was soon realised that they could be used in this way *de facto* – either because of the particular clauses chosen for repeal, or because the repeal of a given clause would create legal anomalies which would then put pressure on legislators to carry through change of the kind desired.

The referendum movement in the 1990s sought to undermine the

TABLE 3

NATIONAL, REGIONAL, PROVINCIAL AND COMUNAL ELECTIONS
APRIL 1992–NOVEMBER 1993

(Votes %)

|          | (1)  | (2)  | (3)  | (4)  | (5)  | (6)  | (7)  | (8)  |
|----------|------|------|------|------|------|------|------|------|
| DC       | 29.7 | 14.0 | 24.3 | 22.3 | 18.7 | 12.1 | 14.3 | 10.7 |
| PSI      | 13.6 | 7.2  | 9.9  | 4.7  | 2.5  | 0.6  | 0.6  | 1.2  |
| PRI      | 4.4  | 1.5  | 3.6  | 1.7  | 0.7  | 0.2  | 0.5  | 0.2  |
| PSDI     | 2.7  | 0.8  | 4.9  | 1.6  | 0.8  | 0.4  | 0.9  | 0.9  |
| PLI      | 2.8  | 1.2  | 2.9  | 1.3  | 0.2  | –    | –    | 0.1  |
| MSI      | 5.4  | 3.2  | 7.2  | 8.3  | 4.0  | 5.3  | 7.4  | 12.0 |
| PDS      | 16.1 | 17.8 | 11.4 | 9.9  | 7.7  | 19.8 | 4.6  | 12.1 |
| RC       | 5.6  | 6.7  | 6.3  | 5.5  | 5.1  | 8.0  | 1.3  | 5.3  |
| Greens   | 2.8  | 2.4  | 1.6  | 5.4  | 1.0  | 3.4  | 3.4  | 3.5  |
| Pannella | 1.2  | –    | 0.8  | –    | –    | –    | –    | 0.9  |
| Rete     | 1.9  | 2.7  | 4.0  | 1.8  | 2.0  | 1.8  | 5.2  | 3.1  |
| LN       | 8.7  | 33.9 | 13.7 | 26.7 | 11.7 | 30.5 | 9.6  | 6.2  |
| Others   | 5.1  | 8.6  | 9.4  | 10.8 | 45.6 | 17.9 | 52.2 | 43.8 |
| Total    | 100  | 100  | 100  | 100  | 100  | 100  | 100  | 100  |

Key
(1) General Election, 5 and 6 April 1992
(2) Provincial elections, Mantova, 28 Sept. 1992
(3) Comunal elections, 55 comunes, 14 Dec. 1992
(4) Regional elections, Friuli Venezia Giulia, 6 June 1993
(5) Partial comunal elections (1,192 comunes), 6 June 1993
(6) Provincial elections (Gorizia, Ravenna, Viterbo, Mantova, Pavia, Trieste, Varese, Genova, La Spezia), 6 June 1993
(7) Regional elections, Trentino Alto Adige, 21 Nov. 1993
(8) Partial comunal elections (424 comunes), 21 Nov. 1993

established political class by using the referendum to promote institutional reform. The outstanding success of the referendum (held on 9 June 1991) which reduced the number of preference votes which could be expressed in elections from four to one, confirmed the presence of a groundswell of opinion for change. Encouraged by this, referendum campaigners were able to gather the number of signatures required to request several further referenda, eight of which were eventually held on 18 April 1993, and most of which aimed to strike a blow at the heart of the *partitocrazia*. Of these, the most important was that which sought to abolish the so-called 65 per cent clause in elections for the upper house, since the effect of doing this would be to introduce the single-member, simple plurality system for three-quarters of the Senate seats.[16] As anticipated, the positive outcome of this referendum placed parliament under immediate pressure to amend the law governing elections to the Chamber of Deputies (because the two houses have co-equal legislative powers). As introduced in August 1993 the new electoral law replaced the old party-list system of proportional representation with a hybrid system whereby three quarters of the members of both houses are elected by the single-member, simple plurality method, the remaining quarter of the seats being distributed proportionally.[17]

The impact of this reform should not be understated, not just because it led to a suspension of party government.[18] Electoral systems influence the characteristics of party systems not only *directly* – by determining the manner in which votes are translated into seats – but also *in*directly by creating a structure of opportunities and constraints for parties in the pre-election period. Hence, while the party system was subject to the *de*composing effects of *Tangentopoli*, it was subject to the *re*composing effects of the new electoral system which placed intense pressure on the parties to find allies before the 1994 elections. Consequently, a twofold process can be traced in the period between 1992 and 1994: a fragmentation of party organisations and a regrouping of these organisations into new types of alliance.

### New Party Organisations

The traditional ruling parties proved unable to weather the anti-corruption storm. In the autumn of 1992, the DC appointed a new secretary, Mino Martinazzoli, who, it was hoped, would engineer a reform of the party that was sufficiently thoroughgoing to save it from the electoral oblivion towards which it seemed to be headed. But Martinazzoli at once found himself at the mercy of the party's powerful factions which were unwilling or unable to make the sacrifices that effective adaptation would have entailed. By the beginning of 1994, the party had split into four groups: Segni's Pact for National Renewal; the left-leaning Social Christians (CS) under Ermanno Gorrieri; the Centre Christian Democrats (CCD), a more conservative grouping under Clemente Mastella and Pierferdinando Casini; and the largest component, the Italian Popular Party (PPI) under Martinazzoli himself.

The PSI underwent a similar experience. In the aftermath of 1992, Craxi's leadership was weakened not only by the result itself but by his reaction to the anti-corruption investigations, which was one of extreme defensiveness and hostility. Not only did this attitude fly in the face of overwhelming popular support for the judges, but it was particularly damaging to a party dominated by Craxi's personalised and autocratic leadership, where the image of the *party* was virtually indistinguishable from that of its *leader*. Craxi's position was made untenable when he himself fell under the suspicion of the *Tangentopoli* investigating magistrates at the beginning of 1993; but given the sheer strength of the personal ties he had built within the party, he and his followers were effectively able to prevent his successor, Giorgio Benvenuto, from establishing sufficient control over the party to be able to achieve any real reform at all. The party broke up into three groups: Giorgio Benvenuto's *Rinascita Socialista* (Socialist Renewal – RS), Del Turco's PSI (i.e. with the same name as the old party but a new symbol), and finally, the *craxiani* (Craxi supporters) which set up the Democratic Socialist Federation (FDS). The first two groupings eventually surfaced in the Progressive Alliance while the third entered the right-wing Freedom Alliance.[19]

With the meltdown of the two main parties, combined with similar problems besetting the smaller parties, new umbrella-type organisations emerged which were designed to catch the fallout from the implosion of the older formations and which appeared to herald the end of the 'party apparatus'. The most important of these were the Democratic Alliance (AD), the National Alliance (AN), and *Forza Italia*, (FI, literally 'Come on Italy'). The AD was launched in the spring of 1993 and was designed to bring together all the progressive forces of the centre-left, while refusing entry to parties as 'apparatuses' in their existing form. The AN, on the other hand, was formed (in January 1994) with the decisive backing of the Italian Social Movement (MSI) which sought, thereby, to overcome its pariah status as a party which traced its inspiration to the pre-war fascist experience. In fact, as Piero Ignazi points out, the birth of AN can be placed in a long line of attempts by the MSI to overcome its historic isolation by giving life to organisations with broader support bases than its own. Therefore, AN was correctly viewed as little more than a cosmetic exercise behind which stood the MSI with its neo-fascist ideology and classic mass-party format remaining fundamentally unchanged.[20]

Finally, FI, a completely new formation, offered a further contrast in as much as it presented a 'party model' that was totally original: the *partito azienda*, or 'business party'. Formed by the media magnate Silvio Berlusconi as a means of bringing together the forces of the right, it deliberately eschewed – in an endeavour to project itself as a modern organisation in which voters could have confidence as a force for political renewal – the mass-party format; for it was the mass parties, with their bureaucracies and large memberships in need of servicing which had occupied and pillaged the resources of the state, and according to the analyses of Berlusconi's advisers, in a world of declining ideologies and growing disaggregation, they were destined to disappear.[21] Hence FI was less a political party in any hitherto commonly-understood sense than a large and sophisticated marketing organisation designed to promote, above all else, the image and policies of its leader. Run along business-management lines similar to the entrepreneur's multinational company Fininvest; staffed by members of his publicity agency, Publitalia; and marketed using sophisticated opinion research techniques and the media magnate's three television channels, it became the largest political organisation in Italy and the linchpin of the alliance of the right.

*New Party Alliances*

The events and negotiations which gave rise to the electoral alliances which fought the 1994 elections were complex and tortuous. On the right, Berlusconi began organising in the spring of 1993: 'His followers claim that he saw immediately that the electoral system, set up by the April 1993 referendum, would split Italy into right-wing and left-wing coalitions; that there was scant place for centrist parties and that the left began with an advantage, because the only well-organised force to survive the [*Tangentopoli*] investigation was the PDS.'[22] However this may be, the decisive event in bringing together the forces of the right were the mayoral elections held on 21 November and 5 December 1993. As a result of a change in the law governing communal and provincial elections introduced in March 1993, the mayors of provinces and communes of over 15,000 inhabitants were now to be elected directly by means of the double ballot system with the first two candidates entering a second round in the absence of an absolute majority for any one candidate at the first round. The left swept to power in several major cities, and, largely owing to the collapse of the DC, the MSI emerged as the dominant party in the south entering, among others, two high-profile run-offs in Naples and Rome. Meanwhile, the Lega Nord did less well than hoped, failing to capture two of the cities (Venice and Genoa) it had targeted.

The elections, therefore, had three effects: first, they raised the spectre of a victory of the left; second, they suggested that the MSI would have to be part of any coalition strong enough to defeat the left; third, they revealed that the Lega needed an ally. However, an alliance between AN and the Lega was never likely as an axis on which to build a right-wing alliance. The Lega stood for the North, economic dynamism, self-sufficiency and federalism (when it was not demanding secession). AN, on the other hand, stood for the South, economic assistance, welfare handouts and centralisation. Furthermore, the other forces available for coalition on the right – the CCD and the surviving Liberals in the *Unione di Centro* (UdC) – were too small to act as the basis for a winning coalition. On the other hand, Berlusconi could act as a link between AN and the Lega, by virtue of the fact that if these latter were split on two fundamental issues vital to their own identities – the unity and integrity of the nation state, and levels of state intervention – he could agree with AN on the first issue and with the Lega on the second. Berlusconi, then, was essential if an alliance of the right was to be tenable, and he was thus able to conclude stand-down arrangements with AN in the South (where the alliance became known as the 'Alliance for Good Government') and with the Lega in the North (where the alliance became known as the 'Freedom Alliance', and AN fielded its own candidates). The CCD and the UdC joined the alliance because their small size and the electoral system meant that they were likely to be obliterated if they failed to find a large ally.

In the centre, Mario Segni, having resigned from the DC in March 1993 and helped to found AD in May, then left the latter organisation because of the PDS's unwillingness to enter the umbrella movement on his terms, or to renounce a possible alliance with RC. He launched his own Pact for National Renewal in November 1993, and then tried to engage the Lega and the PPI in a three-way alliance in January 1994. This failed largely because of the hostility of the members of the latter two organisations to each other. Martinazzoli (as the leader of an organisation containing a variety of conflicting centre-left and centre-right tendencies) located his party clearly in the centre, rejecting alliances both with Occhetto and Berlusconi. His options having effectively run out, Segni had little alternative at this point but to ally his Pact for National Renewal with the PPI in what became known as the 'Pact for Italy' (PI) which opposed both coalitions to left and right.

Finally, on the left, it was clear that the PDS was the essential pivot around which any alliance had to be built, and its own objective represented an attempt to avoid the choice between a genuinely left-wing alliance (which would exclude forces deemed to be too centrist, as RC wanted) or an alliance of the centre-left (which would exclude RC, as AD wanted). Essentially, the PDS was faced with a dilemma which it tried to escape by embracing the widest alliance possible: on the one hand, it did not want to lose votes to its left by excluding RC, on the other hand its leaders were aware that if it wanted to win more centrally placed voters it would have to include groups such as AD and the CS. In the end, therefore, what became the 'Progressive Alliance' was an unwieldy and conflict-ridden coalition consisting of eight partners: the PDS, PSI, RS, AD, RC, CS, the Rete, and the Greens (see Figure 1).[23]

## The Victory of the Right

The nature of the victory of the Freedom Alliance in the March 1994 elections (see Table 4) had four consequences vital to the further shifts in the party landscape that would take place in the months following the elections.[24] First, by bringing about a dramatic growth in support for AN, the elections confirmed that the legitimacy which the alliance with Berlusconi had conferred on this organisation had been successful in allowing it to emerge from the political ghetto to which it had hitherto been confined. Second, the elections confirmed that the Lega's alliance with

FIGURE 1

EVOLUTION OF THE MAIN PARTY ORGANISATIONS
AND ALLIANCES 1991–96

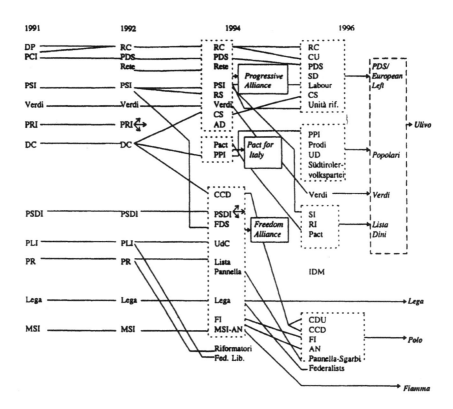

*Key*: DP = Proletarian Democracy; PCI = Italian Communist Party; PSI = Italian Socialist
Party; Verdi = Greens; PRI = Italian Republican Party; DC = Christian Democrats;
PSDI = Italian Social Democratic Party; PLI = Italian Liberal Party; PR = Radical
Party; Lega = Northern League; MSI = Italian Social Movement; RC = Communist
Refoundation; PDS = Democratic Party of the Left; Rete = Network; CS = Social
Christians; AD = Democratic Alliance; Pact = Pact for National Renewal; PPI = Italian
Popular Party; CCD = Centre Christian Democrats; FDS = Democratic Socialist
Federation; UdC = Union of the Centre; Lista Pannella = Pannella List; FI = Forza
Italia!; AN = National Alliance; Riformatori = Reformists; Fed. Lib. = Liberal
Federation; CU = United Communists; SD = Social Democrats; Unità rif. = Reformist
unity; UD = Democratic Union; Südtirolervolkspartei = South Tyrolese People's Party;
SI = Italian Socialists; RI = Italian Renewal; IDM = Italian Democratic Movement;
CDU = Christian Democratic Union; Fiamma = Tricoloured Flame.

Berlusconi was very much a double-edged sword. On the one hand, the Lega had needed Berlusconi because of the overlap in the nature of the two parties' electoral appeals and core support; on the other hand, this same similarity meant that an alliance might threaten the Lega's separate identity leading to just that slippage of votes to FI which the alliance had been designed to avoid. In the event, although the Lega more or less held its position in aggregate, exit polls revealed that at the individual level there had indeed been a considerable movement of support from the Lega to FI. This, and the fact that so many of the newly-elected Lega deputies (whose number rose from 55 to 117) so obviously owed their seats to FI votes (given the electoral system), meant that conflict between the two parties in the election's aftermath was hardly surprising. Third, the election results confirmed that the attempt to field candidates lying in between powerful opponents to the left and to the right was, in a single-member, simple plurality context likely to be an unproductive exercise. Of the 46 seats won by the Pact for Italy, only four came to it via the plurality formula, confirming the tendency for voters' effective choices to be reduced, constituency by constituency, to two front runners, one of the left and one of the right.[25] Fourth, however, in bringing about, against expectations, a further increase in the number of parties represented in Parliament, the elections confirmed that the process of forming electoral alliances had led to what one writer called the 'proportionalisation of the plurality system' allowing the party system to continue in a state of extreme flux.[26]

1994–96: TRIPOLARITY OR BIPOLARITY?

In becoming Prime Minister of a new centre-right government, Berlusconi had apparently achieved three things. First, he had – through FI – broken the traditional organisational mould of Italian parties, showing that a new type of party could be created in a short space of time with considerable electoral potential. Second, he had – through the Freedom Alliance and the Alliance for Good Government – activated the latent strength of the political right-of-centre, showing its electoral and governing potential when unified. Third, in doing so, he had apparently resolved Italy's short-term crisis and long-term problem of the absence of alternation in government. His success, however, was short-lived. Indeed, it could be argued that his achievements were questionable from the outset. The success of the new type of party could only really be tested by a period of opposition, and not by success in one election; the political right-of-centre could hardly be viewed as unified when it consisted of two alliances, not one (and in no region had the electorate been able to vote for or against the entire coalition which subsequently made up the government); and whether or not

TABLE 4

THE CHAMBER OF DEPUTIES ELECTIONS OF 1994 (630 SEATS)

| Parties & alliances | List votes | | Proportional seats | | Plurality seats | | Total seats | |
|---|---|---|---|---|---|---|---|---|
| | N (millions) | % | N | % | N | % | N | % |
| PDS | 7.86 | 20.4 | 37 | 23.9 | 72 | 15.2 | 109 | 17.3 |
| RC | 2.33 | 6.0 | 12 | 7.7 | 27 | 5.7 | 39 | 6.2 |
| Greens | 1.04 | 2.7 | 0 | 0.0 | 11 | 2.3 | 11 | 1.7 |
| PSI | 0.84 | 2.2 | 0 | 0.0 | 14 | 2.9 | 14 | 2.2 |
| Network | 0.72 | 1.9 | 0 | 0.0 | 6 | 1.3 | 6 | 1.0 |
| AD | 0.45 | 1.2 | 0 | 0.0 | 18 | 3.8 | 18 | 2.9 |
| CS | | | | | 5 | 1.1 | 5 | 0.8 |
| RS | | | | | 1 | 0.2 | 1 | 0.2 |
| Ind. left | | | | | 10 | 2.1 | 10 | 1.6 |
| Total Progressive Alliance | 13.24 | 34.3 | 49 | 31.6 | 164 | 34.5 | 213 | 33.8 |
| PPI | 4.27 | 11.1 | 29 | 18.7 | 4 | 0.8 | 33 | 5.2 |
| Patto Segni | 1.79 | 4.7 | 13 | 8.4 | 0 | 0.0 | 13 | 2.1 |
| Total Pact for Italy | 6.06 | 15.7 | 42 | 27.1 | 4 | 0.8 | 46 | 7.3 |
| FI | 8.12 | 21.0 | | | | | | |
| FI | | | 25 | 16.1 | 74 | 15.6 | 99 | 15.7 |
| CCD1 | | | 7 | 4.5 | 22 | 4.6 | 29 | 4.6 |
| UdC | | | | | 4 | 0.8 | 4 | 0.6 |
| Pld | | | | | 2 | 0.4 | 2 | 0.3 |
| Riformatori | | | | | 6 | 1.3 | 6 | 1.0 |
| AN | 5.20 | 13.5 | 22 | 14.2 | 87 | 18.3 | 109 | 17.3 |
| Lega Nord | 3.24 | 8.4 | 10 | 6.5 | 107 | 22.5 | 117 | 18.6 |
| Lp | 1.36 | 3.5 | 0 | 0.0 | 0 | 0.0 | 0 | 0.0 |
| Total Freedom Alliance | 17.92 | 46.4 | 64 | 41.3 | 302[2] | 63.6 | 366 | 58.1 |
| SVP | 0.23 | 0.6 | 0 | 0.0 | 3 | 0.6 | 3 | 0.5 |
| Lista Valled'Aosta | | | | | 1 | 0.2 | 1 | 0.2 |
| Lega d'Azione Meridionale | 0.06 | 0.2 | 0 | 0.0 | 1 | 0.2 | 1 | 0.2 |
| Social-democrazia | 0.18 | 0.5 | 0 | 0.0 | 0 | 0.0 | 0 | 0.0 |
| Lega Alpina Lumbarda | 0.14 | 0.4 | 0 | 0.0 | 0 | 0.0 | 0 | 0.0 |
| Verdi-Verdi | 0.03 | 0.1 | 0 | 0.0 | 0 | 0.0 | 0 | 0.0 |
| Other Leghe | 0.13 | 0.3 | 0 | 0.0 | 0 | 0.0 | 0 | 0.0 |
| Autonomist lists | 0.03 | 0.1 | 0 | 0.0 | 0 | 0.0 | 0 | 0.0 |
| Other lists | 0.57 | 1.5 | 0 | 0.0 | 0 | 0.0 | 0 | 0.0 |
| Total others | 1.37 | 3.6 | 0 | 0.0 | 5 | 1.1 | 5 | 0.8 |
| Total | 38.59 | 100.0 | 155 | 100.0 | 475 | 100.0 | 630 | 100.0 |

*Source*: Stefano Bartolini and Roberto D'Alimonte, 'La competizione maggioritaria: le origini elettorali del parlamento diviso', *Rivista Italiana di Scienza Politica*, XXIV, No. 3, Dec. 1994, Table 2.

*Abbreviations*: PDS: Partito Democratico della Sinistra (Democratic Party of the Left); RC: Rifondazione Comunista (Communist Refoundation); PSI: Italian Socialist Party; AD: Alleanza Democratica (Democratic Alliance); CS: Cristiano Sociali (Social Christians); RS: Rinascita Socialista (Socialist Revival); PPI: Partito Popolare Italiano (Italian Popular Party); FI: Forza Italia; CCD: Centro Cristiano Democratico (Christian Democratic Centre); UdC: Unione di Centro (Centre Union); Pld: Polo Liberal-Democratico (Liberal Democratic Alliance); AN: Alleanza Nazionale (National Alliance); Lp: Lista Pannella (the Pannella List); SVP: Südtiroler Volkspartei (South Tyrol People's Party)

*Notes*:
1. The list votes won by CCD (which presented a separate list only in Molise) have been included under 'Other lists'; the seven proportional seats obtained have been attributed to CCD candidates on the lists presented by FI.
2. Of these seats, 164 were won by the Freedom Alliance (of which Lega Nord 107, FI 38, CCD 8, Riformatori 6, UdC 3, Pld 2); 129 by the Alliance for Good Government (of which AN 79, FI 36, CCD 13, UdC 1); 1 by FI-CCD; and 8 by AN running alone.

---

alternation in government had been achieved depended on one's interpretation of Berlusconism, and its relationship to the political space previously occupied by the DC. In short, rather than marking the beginning of a new phase in Italian politics, the Berlusconi experience proved to be another ephemeral product of Italy's ongoing political turmoil, the government bearing all the trappings of governments of the so-called 'First Republic' before the collapse of the old parties.[27] This promoted further change in the parties and alliances, and a reversal of fortunes in the 1996 elections. While the right fragmented, the centre split and the bulk of the latter successfully formed a winning alliance with the left.

## *Fragmentation of the Right*

The right's problems stemmed primarily from the deep differences between the Lega Nord, on the one hand, and FI and AN on the other, differences which came to the fore once the alliance assumed office. As already noted, the relationship between the Lega and FI had been fractious from the outset because of the latter's threat to the former's electoral base. The tensions this created were exacerbated not only by the government's failure to deliver on several of its promises (e.g. institutional reform, privatisation, jobs and the economy), but also by deep controversies surrounding Berlusconi as Prime Minister. He continually procrastinated on the critical issue of how to resolve the conflict of interests between his role as Prime Minister and that of leader of Fininvest and controller of three television channels which accounted for more than 90 per cent of commercial television audiences. Furthermore, he clashed with several important institutions, including the

Presidency, the RAI (state television network), the Bank of Italy and the magistrates. Judicial–political conflict, in particular, ensured that the Lega kept its distance from the government. The introduction of a decree law modifying the legislation on preventive custody for corruption offences was regarded with cynicism and suspicion in view of the fact that both Fininvest and Berlusconi's brother, Paolo, were under investigation by the magistrates. These suspicions appeared to be confirmed when Berlusconi himself received the notorious *avviso di garanzia* (formal notification that he was under judicial investigation). Moreover, his reaction – denouncing the action amidst accusations of a political vendetta and instigating a ministerial investigation of the Milanese magistrates – destroyed any prospect of normality in judicial-political relations while he remained Prime Minister.

The tensions between the Lega and AN stemmed from their different philosophies (noted earlier), AN's Fascist heritage (which had yet to be unambiguously repudiated), and AN's electoral success, something which, paradoxically (in view of the second factor), was put down to the legitimisation it had received through its presence in the Freedom Alliance, and which could only be reinforced the longer it remained in office. Indeed, the adept leader of AN, Gianfranco Fini, proved able to exploit both Berlusconi's difficulties (while not breaking with him) and Bossi's erratic behaviour such as to be increasingly viewed as a potential leader of a future governing coalition. It was not surprising, therefore, that the Lega was instrumental in bringing down the government after only eight months (in December 1994), and that this event spelled the end of the unity forged for the 1994 elections. Indeed, it simply confirmed what many observers had always maintained: that the FI–Lega–AN coalition had been an alliance intended to win an election, irrespective of the fact that its lack of cohesion always suggested that it would govern with difficulty.

This was not to suggest, however, that the Lega itself was united on its independent course of action. On the contrary, Bossi's decision to bring down the government and commit the party to an independent centrist course was fiercely opposed by a significant proportion of the party. Bossi's aim was to hold the balance of power in a future parliament and then demand federalism as the condition for his support of either of the coalitions. Roberto Maroni (the party's leading dissident) believed that a centrist position would leave the party isolated and marginalised, arguing that its future lay in an alliance with Berlusconi. There were also members who remained open to entering an alliance on the centre-left, depending on the latter's eventual shape. By early 1995, 50 of the 117 Lega parliamentarians had left the party over opposition to Bossi's line, most of them forming independent groupings. The issue came to a head at the party's Congress in February 1995 when Bossi, in an extravagant gesture, offered to resign over his centrist course. His resignation was rejected and the party line approved, as was a formal change of name to 'Northern League – Federal Italy'. From there on, as a mark of this independent course, and possibly also to compensate for the apparent 'centrality' of the Lega on the political spectrum, the party's platform became more radical, emphasising its secessionist aspirations.

For AN, the Berlusconi government (even though short-lived) constituted a significant step on the road to gaining full legitimacy. AN had originally been created as an umbrella grouping to attract new members of the right and present the MSI with a softer image (hence the official name, AN-MSI). In fact, as argued above, it was little more than a name change. After the fall of the government, Fini argued that it was time to 'put out the flame' (the MSI's symbol), formally replacing it with AN. The MSI hard-liners, however, were vehemently opposed to this idea, and, when the party congress of January 1995 approved Fini's line, they left the party to form a new neo-Fascist party, the *Fiamma Tricolore* (Tricoloured Flame) led by Pino Rauti, which stood alone to the right of the Freedom Alliance.

Besides the addition to the alliance of the small and maverick Pannella–Sgarbi list, the other gain for the right was the Christian Democratic Union (CDU) which formed a federation with the CCD (which had been part of the Freedom Alliance in 1994) for the 1996 elections (see Figure 1). The CDU was the product of a significant split in the PPI, marking the collapse of the old centre which, in 1994, had refused to recognise the bipolar logic of the new electoral system.

## The Old Centre Crumbles

As already noted, the results of the 1994 elections seemed to confirm that the centre was a redundant place in the party system. Yet, divisions over whether to opt for the left or the right made a split in the centre inevitable. Segni was still convinced that there was sufficient political space for a centre party, and attempted, in vain, to relaunch his Pact in late 1994. The PPI was ready to abandon the centre but was divided over whether, in doing so, to join the left or the right. Party leader Rocco Buttiglione believed that the PPI's future lay in an alliance on the centre-right. Indeed, he argued that there was no alternative since any coalition on the left meant allying with an ex-Communist party which was big enough to dominate the PPI. He had, with the Lega, engineered the downfall of the Berlusconi government, expecting FI, once in opposition, to collapse, leaving a centre-right-oriented PPI to inherit the floating votes. He also felt that this move would reinforce the centrist weight of the alliance, thus constraining AN either to democratise further or become isolated.

The left of the party, however, was fiercely opposed to any alliance with

AN, whose fascist roots remained all too apparent, and they were reluctant to renounce links forged with the PDS at the local and regional levels, even though recognising the dilemmas of entering a national alliance with a larger party to the left of the PPI. Their solution was to persuade a progressive ex-Christian Democrat, Romano Prodi, to launch a new centre-left coalition, the Olive Tree (*Ulivo*) within which the PDS and centre parties could form an alliance. The birth of the Ulivo in early 1995 made a split in the PPI inevitable. Buttiglione broke away and formed the Christian Democratic Union (CDU) which, as already noted, formed a federation with the CCD in the Freedom Alliance. Gerardo Bianco, meanwhile, led the PPI into the Ulivo, followed, somewhat reluctantly, by Segni and the PI (see Figure 1).

### The Ulivo: Alliance for Government

The electoral defeat of 1994 (combined with similarly poor results in the June 1994 European elections) was shattering for the Progressives. The leaders of the PDS, PSI and AD all resigned and the alliance began to shed its component parts and formed a single, four-party, grouping (called the Progressive Federation) in the Parliament, made up of the PDS, CS, the Greens and the Rete. The main problem for the left was the PDS which, paradoxically, was both a source of strength and weakness.

The 1994 elections confirmed that the PDS was more important than ever to the left, representing something like 80 per cent of all left-of-centre voting support in the country, and was (with AN) one of only two parties remaining organisationally intact from the 'First Republic'. Yet, at the same time, the party was insufficiently large by itself to act as an alternative to the centre-right. This meant allying with others and it was at this point that the PDS became the main stumbling block. This was not just because of disagreement inside the party about how far to the centre and to the left such an alliance should stretch, but because of the fear of other partners of being dominated by the PDS. The PDS's organisational inertia, it was argued by many, lay at the heart of what was viewed as the failure of both the transformation of the PCI and, subsequently, the Progressive Alliance. The transformation of the PCI, it was argued, rather than leading to an innovative experiment in party organisation which was genuinely open to new members, had resulted in the PDS being effectively captured by the old apparatchiks. The PDS had then refused to consider alternative organisational experiments such as AD, thus ensuring their failure; and the Progressive Alliance, besides being organisationally deficient, had included, on the PDS's insistence, RC – the very party which had been formed out of opposition to the transformation of the PCI in the first place, and whose inclusion was viewed as a major cause of the defeat.[28]

Many called on the PDS to resolve this dilemma by formally dissolving itself such that a genuine new organisation could be formed in the absence of the suffocating effect of its party structures. Yet, for all their rhetoric about the PDS becoming a new and different type of party, this was something neither Occhetto or Massimo D'Alema (who became the new leader in the summer of 1994), were willing to countenance. Nevertheless, on becoming leader, D'Alema was ready to build on the experience and lessons of the Progressive Alliance, and this change of attitude was to prove to be significant.

D'Alema argued that the principal cause of the Progressives' defeat was the failure to extend the alliance to the centre. The Progressives had based their appeal on the assumption that voters of the centre would change their allegiance, something which they proved unwilling to do. He argued that the PDS should continue to renovate its identity with a view to becoming increasingly free of the influence of RC, and available to form a permanent federation with other parties of the left and centre (something he dubbed a 'liberal revolution'). This federation would be led by a single leader, who could be chosen by a primary election and should probably come from a party other than the PDS. He was ready, he said, to put the PDS's resources at the disposal of such a 'coalition of democrats' and even to change the name and symbol of the party – though not to dissolve its organisation and membership.

Irrespective of the PDS's willingness to evolve, the outlook for this strategy looked bleak in the summer of 1994. Three factors, however, hastened the realisation of a variant of D'Alema's 'coalition of democrats': the Olive Tree alliance, which successfully brought together the more progressive elements of the centre and the left in one coalition. The first factor was the fall of the Berlusconi government and its replacement with a government of technocrats. D'Alema's decision, in the autumn of 1994, to bury any spirit of the Westminster model of opposition (which Occhetto had espoused in the immediate aftermath of the defeat) by refusing to recognise the legitimacy of the Berlusconi government, hastened its downfall. At the same time, since no alternative coalition could be found, it ensured another suspension of party government, and Berlusconi's Treasury Minister, Lamberto Dini, formed (like Ciampi in 1993) a government of technocrats. The nature of the majority which, over time, came to support this government was significant. The Dini government was subjected to seven votes of no confidence in all of which both FI and AN, anxious for immediate elections, voted against the government. Dini came to depend on the PDS, the PPI and the Lega Nord, and was even once dependent for its survival on the abstention of RC. This experience of centre and left working together was important for the development of the Ulivo, and proved to be crucial when, in early 1996, Dini decided to form his own political force and, against his natural instincts, to locate it in the Ulivo in recognition of the parties which had kept him in office during the previous year.

The second factor was the role of Prodi and the nature of the Ulivo. Prodi's reputation (as former President of the state holding group IRI) was one of honesty, efficiency and popularity with businessmen and the markets. He appeared to be the epitome of reasonableness and modesty and refused to use the election campaign techniques typical of Berlusconi. More importantly, in launching the Ulivo, he was not asking any of the parties to sacrifice anything in organisational terms beyond supporting him, as leader of the alliance and candidate for Prime Minister, and a moderate programme whose main characteristic was continuity with Dini. The Ulivo's objective was simply to forge an alliance between the more progressive elements of the centre and left. In this it succeeded. The third factor which encouraged the formation of the Ulivo was the results of the regional elections of April 1995 which showed promising gains for the centre-left and the likely potential of its vote at the national level.[29]

This is not say, however, that the formation of the Ulivo was unproblematic. On the contrary, it provoked opposition from within the PDS (many of whose members objected to Prodi's leadership and the diluting of the PDS's left-wing identity through the alliance), and reservations on the part of several centre parties. It was the product of a long and tortuous process of negotiations and tactical manoeuvrings between a myriad of parties and movements on the centre and left, the outcome of which was never certain and which was finalised only shortly before the April 1996 elections.

The Ulivo, in its final shape, was made up of four component parts, three of which contained within them several separate elements (see Figure 1). The largest component was the PDS-European left, whose size is evident from the fact that it provided approximately half of the Ulivo's candidates in the 1996 elections. It consisted of the PDS and the so-called 'shrubs' (*cespugli*), six tiny parties which were close to the PDS but unwilling to be completely absorbed by it: the *laburisti* (Labour, led by Valdo Spini), the United Communists (the product of a split in RC, and led by Sergio Garavini), CS (led by Piero Carniti), the Social Democrats (led by Schietroma), *Unità riformista* (Reformist Unity) and (although some would question its position as a 'shrub') the anti-Mafia, Rete (Network).

The second component was based around the PPI and was known as the *Popolari*. In addition to the PPI (led by Bianco), there was the Prodi Group, the Democratic Union (*Unione Democratica*, led by Antonio Maccanico), and the *Südtiroler Volkspartei* (South Tyrolese People's Party). The UD, moreover, was an alliance in itself, bringing together members of the old PLI, PSI and PRI, including well-known names such as Valerio Zanone, Giorgio Benvenuto and Giorgio La Malfa.

The third component was the Dini List (*Lista Dini*), which was made up of a small group based around Lamberto Dini (*Movimento Rinnovamento Italiano*, Italian Renewal), the Italian Socialists (*Socialisti Italiani* (SI), official heirs of the PSI, and led by Enrico Boselli), the *Pattisti* (led by Mario Segni), and the Italian Democratic Movement (led by Sergio Berlinguer). The final component consisted of the Greens.

RC was not included in the coalition, but stand-down arrangements were reached for the 1996 elections which gave RC a clear run at 27 seats in the Chamber and 17 in the Senate in return for not putting up candidates against Ulivo candidates in other constituencies, something which prevented the left's vote being split in key areas. A formal inclusion of RC in the Ulivo was not wanted by any of the latter's constituent parts: for the PDS leadership, RC's inclusion in the Progressive Alliance had been a primary factor in the Alliance's defeat in 1994; for the centre parties, RC's adherence to Marxism ruled it out, and they would not enter the Ulivo if RC were to be included. RC, for its part, regarded the Ulivo as too centrist a construction, and disagreed with key parts of its programme (e.g. privatisation, European Monetary Union and the refusal to reinstate the wage-indexation system). There was no attempt, therefore, to paper over the differences, as had happened in 1994, and the agreement with RC was frankly acknowledged as being almost wholly motivated by electoral expediency.

### The Victory of the Ulivo

The nature of the success of the Ulivo in the 1996 elections suggests that its *raison d'être* (that of bringing together the centre and left, rather than attempting to win over voters to a new organisational formation) was correctly identified by people like Prodi and D'Alema. The Ulivo's victory owed more to tactical ingenuity than to a major realignment of the electorate. This is not to suggest that there were no shifts in the distribution of the vote. But three factors suggest substantial stability. First, the centre-right declined only marginally, despite the defection of the Lega, which became the new 'centre', thus preserving the tripolar nature of the competition. In fact, if the Lega is included, the centre-right actually increased (from 46.4 per cent to 52.2 per cent of the Chamber list vote). Second, aggregate volatility (24.3), as measured by Pedersen's index, was lower than in the 1992/94 pair of elections (37.3), and by far the greater part of this (19) could be attributed to splits and mergers, the appearance and disappearance of party formations. Finally, the level of fragmentation of the vote barely changed, with the three largest parties (PDS, FI and AN) taking 57.4 per cent of the vote as compared to 55 per cent in 1994.[30] In short, the fact that the Ulivo received 9 per cent more of the vote and a much higher proportion of seats than the Progressive Alliance in 1994, was more the result of a widening of the alliance towards the centre and clever tactical exploitation of the electoral system (particularly with regard to RC) than it was a realignment of voters. The Ulivo contrasted strongly with the tactical disarray of the Freedom Alliance where the loss of the Lega and the split in AN cost it dearly in seats (see Table 5).

TABLE 5

CHAMBER OF DEPUTIES ELECTIONS 1996

|  | List votes | | Proportional seats | | Single-member seats | | Total seats | |
|---|---|---|---|---|---|---|---|---|
|  | N | % | N | % | N | % | N | % |
| PDS | 7,897,044 | 21.1 | 26 | 17 | 146 | 31 | 172 | 27 |
| Popolari | 2,555,082 | 6.8 | 4 | 3 | 63 | 13 | 67 | 11 |
| Dini | 1,627,191 | 4.3 | 8 | 5 | 16 | 3 | 24 | 4 |
| Greens | 937,684 | 2.5 | 0 | 0 | 21 | 4 | 21 | 3 |
| Total Ulivo | 13,017,001 | 34.7 | 38 | 24 | 246 | 51 | 284 | 45 |
| RC | 3,215,960 | 8.6 | 20 | 13 | 15 | 3 | 35 | 6 |
| Lega | 3,777,786 | 10.1 | 20 | 13 | 39 | 8 | 59 | 9 |
| FI | 7,715,342 | 20.6 | 37 | 24 | 86 | 18 | 123 | 19 |
| AN | 5,875,391 | 15.7 | 28 | 18 | 65 | 14 | 93 | 15 |
| CCD-CDU | 2,190,019 | 5.8 | 12 | 8 | 18 | 4 | 30 | 5 |
| Total Polo | 15,780,752 | 42.1 | 77 | 50 | 169 | 36 | 246 | 39 |
| Pannella | 701,033 | 1.9 | 0 | 0 | 0 | 0 | 0 | 0 |
| Fiamma Tricolore | 338,721 | 0.9 | 0 | 0 | 0 | 0 | 0 | 0 |
| Others | 663,712 | 1.7 | 0 | 0 | 5 | 2 | 5 | 1 |
| Total | 37,494,965 | 100.0 | 155 | 100 | 475 | 100 | 630 | 100 |

*Key*: PDS = Democratic Party of the Left; Popolari = Italian Popular Party (PPI) and allies; Dini = Dini List; Ulivo = Olive-Tree Alliance; RC = Communist Refoundation; Lega = Northern League; FI = Forza Italia; AN = National Alliance; CCD = Centre Christian Democrats; CDU = Christian Democratic Union; Polo = Freedom Alliance; Pannella = Pannella–Sgarbi List; Fiamma Tricolore = Tricoloured Flame.

Nevertheless, it should also be noted that in the single-member district ballot for the Chamber, the centre-left won approximately half a million more votes than its combined list-vote totals for each of the parties making up the alliance, while the Freedom Alliance won one-and-a-half million votes less than the combined list-vote totals. This shows that, despite the stability in voting behaviour, the centre-left nevertheless had a capacity to mobilise support beyond the ranks of its target electorate. This can probably be explained by a tendency of voters to perceive the centre-left as something more than simply the sum of its parts, something which, in turn, would have been assisted by two factors: first, the voting context created by the single-member ballot which, unlike the proportional ballot, was in effect inviting voters to make a straight choice between alternative governing coalitions (so that it was quite possible, therefore, that some whose preferred party belonged to a coalition other than the centre-left, nevertheless preferred the latter as a potential governing coalition); second, by the skill of Prodi in portraying himself as a leader who at once stood above the centre-left's parties while also being the essential element of their cohesion. This suggests that the Ulivo may have been more organisationally innovative than at first appeared to be the case.

## CONCLUSION: ORGANISATIONS AND ALLIANCES IN FLUX

The significant changes which have occurred in the configuration of parties and alliances in the 1990s have marked a sharp break with the configuration which characterised the first 50 years of the Republic. The changes are unlikely to stop, however, as long as political turmoil continues. First, it is not clear if, and for how long, the new party organisations will last, because they remain substantially untested by time. Indeed, it is even unclear as to whether the revival of old parties can be definitively ruled out. The idea of a revived DC is not just casual rumour: it is based on a deeply held belief of some that there is the need and the space for one united party to represent political Catholicism. Second, even though the early 1990s seemed to herald the end of the era of the 'party apparatus', it remains unclear as to whether genuinely new forms of organisation will last. FI is the most successful innovative party structure to have appeared in Italy in 50 years, but its existence continues to be fragile, dependent, as it is, on the resources and personality of one man. Of note, is the fact that the two organisations remaining substantially intact from the 'First Republic' (the PDS and AN) have not made any major changes to their basic structures. Third, the alliance structure of the (changing) parties is still fluid. Under pressure from the new electoral system, there has been a gradual transition towards bipolarity, but it is one which remains incomplete. In a first phase (which culminated with the 1994 elections), the centre remained small, but intact, leaving left and right coalitions to include the extremes to try to ensure victory. In a second phase (culminating in the 1996 elections), the left and centre merged, and the extreme left was formally excluded from the alliance. Meanwhile, the centre-right fragmented, creating a new centre (the Lega), while the extreme right split, giving AN more legitimacy with the Fiamma Tricolore excluded from the alliance.

This state of flux in the number and type of organisations raises the question of the prospects for party development under the Ulivo government; for, just as with the Berlusconi government, it cannot be assumed that the victory of the Ulivo will bring an end to the evolution of party organisation and alliances. If the 'normalisation' of their country's politics means anything to ordinary Italians, it means the achievement of two moderate centre-left and centre-right coalitions which can alternate in government, and it is too early to say that this has been achieved. Moreover, the more ambitious see 'normalisation' as constituting the formation of two moderate parties which, even in the presence of one or two smaller formations in the centre, can alternate in government. What is the likelihood of this occurring?

The question is complex because any moves in this direction by one particular set of parties has repercussions and implications for others. Yet, aside from the question of whether or not FI will survive in the long-term (something which will have a determining impact on the development of the centre-right), the key issue in this legislature will be what happens to the centre-left. Indeed, the Ulivo's victory, rather than resolving anything, has simply made more urgent the issue of whether the PDS should be organisationally superseded and, if so, how and by what. This is an issue which will go beyond the question of the Ulivo government, even though (like the Berlusconi government) its performance in office will have an influence on developments.

There are, broadly speaking, two scenarios. The first is the construction of a centre-left 'Democratic Party' on the back of the victory of the Ulivo, thus bringing together the centre and left under one organisation. This idea was formally launched shortly after the election by the President of the Prodi Group, Giancarlo Bressa. The idea is that it would begin as a federation within which individual membership would be acceptable, and would evolve from there (the French UDF is cited as an example to follow). The idea has sympathy with Prodi and those around Walter Veltroni in the PDS.[31] The second scenario is the creation of a party in the European social democratic mould which aims at uniting the socialist and ex-Communist traditions in one party. This is the vision of the PDS leader, Massimo D'Alema, who, in June 1996, opened a debate on the *Cosa 2* ('Second Thing', recalling the term – *La Cosa* – used in 1990 to refer to the PDS before it had been given a name). D'Alema argues that creating a single party of the centre and left is not possible because of the resistance to such a project from various centrist components. Moreover, such an operation would leave Italy largely as it had been before the dramatic changes of the

1990s: without a reformist non-Communist party of the left. The Italian anomaly, in short, would continue. His view is that a genuine new democratic Socialist party should unite the various 'shrubs' and the PDS, and might, in the process, attract RC members, if not the party as a whole (something currently rejected by RC's leadership).[32] Much, therefore, will depend on the PDS's next Congress. Critical also to these developments will be the centrist components of the Ulivo. It is no secret, for example, that Lamberto Dini's instincts are against being in an alliance with ex-communists, and that he harbours ambitions to recreate a *grande centro* ('large centre') which could compete against the PDS. Yet, whether that aspiration would persist if the PDS were to dissolve and be replaced by a party with no link to the communist past remains an open question.

In short, party organisations and alliances in Italy are still in a state of considerable flux, and it is difficult to predict which alliances and parties will be shaping party government in the millennium. Yet, beneath this immense complexity, there has been an important change which may last. Even though the centre persisted in the 1994 elections and was recreated (in the form of the Lega) in the 1996 elections, the basic dynamic between the organisations and alliances is one of bipolarity, something which is markedly different from the situation existing until 1992 when the DC still occupied the centre. And though the pattern of party *organisations and alliances* seems likely to undergo further significant change, in terms of the *interactions* between them, the most likely scenario is that, in the absence of additional 'exogenous shocks' (such as further electoral reform) an underlying bipolar mechanism will persist.

## NOTES

1. As one might expect, changes in the party superstructure have been accompanied by changes in the patterns of political recruitment, which amount to the effective removal and regeneration of an entire political class, and which have themselves had an impact on the features of the party system. Though important, this is not an issue dealt with here. It is explored by E. Recchi, 'Fishing from the Same Schools: Parliamentary Recruitment and Consociationalism in the First and Second Italian Republics', *West European Politics* 19/2 (April 1996) pp.340–59; and Luca Verzichelli, 'I nuovi parlamentari', in P. Ignazi and R. S. Katz (eds) *Politica in Italia. I fatti dell'anno e le interpretazioni. Edizione 95* (Bologna: Il Mulino 1995) pp.139–60.
2. On which see R. D'Alimonte and S.Bartolini, '"Electoral Transition"' and Party System Change in Italy' (this volume).
3. If one adds to these figures those who cast either blank or spoiled ballot papers, then one ends up with a rising trend in support for the so-called 'non-vote party' that by 1996 had reached 23.2 per cent – larger than the support given to any other party.
4. The period from the mid-1970s witnessed the emergence and growth of 'new-politics' parties such as the Radicals, Greens and Proletarian Democracy (whose combined share of votes and seats rose from 2.6 and 10, to 6.8 per cent and 34 respectively between 1976 and 1987).

5.  See M.J. Bull, 'Whatever Happened to Italian Communism? Explaining the Dissolution of the Largest Communist Party in the West', *West European Politics* 14/4 (Oct. 1991) pp.96–120.
6.  J.M. Foot, '"The Left Opposition" and the Crisis: Rifondazione Comunista and La Rete', in S. Gundle and S. Parker (eds.) *The New Italian Republic: From the Fall of the Berlin Wall to Berlusconi* (London: Routledge 1996) p.174.
7.  V. Testa, 'Il piacere di bastonare Roma', *La Repubblica*, 1 Oct. 1992.
8.  Foot, 'The "Left Opposition" and the Crisis' (note 6) p.181.
9.  Ibid. p.180.
10. J.L. Newell, 'The Scottish National Party and the Italian Lega Nord: A lesson for their rivals?', *European Journal of Political Research* 26/2 (1994) pp.616–47.
11. See M.J. Bull and J.L. Newell, 'Italian Politics and the 1992 Elections: From "Stable Instability" to Instability and Change', *Parliamentary Affairs* 46/2 (1993) pp.203–27.
12. S. Waters, "Tangentopoli' and the Emergence of a New Political Order in Italy', *West European Politics* 17/1 (Jan. 1994) p.170.
13. D. Della Porta, 'La capitale immorale: le tangenti di Milano', in S. Hellman and G. Pasquino (eds.), *Politica in Italia: I fatti dell'anno e le interpretazioni* (Bologna: Il Mulino 1993) pp.219–40.
14. M. Calise, 'Remaking the Italian Party System: How Lijphart Got It Wrong by Saying it Right', *West European Politics* 16/4 (Oct. 1993) p.556.
15. For instance, if it had become an established practice that appointments to many of Italy's numerous public agencies would be made on a party basis, and if an appointee then used their position to collect bribes, the money so gathered could then be used to control packets of votes in the party's internal organs. This meant that the motives for joining a party were often largely self-regarding, which in turn meant that the rank-and-file tended to be highly passive.
16. M.J. Bull and J.L. Newell, 'The Italian Referenda of April 1993: Real Change at Last?', *West European Politics* 16/4 (Oct. 1993) pp.607–15.
17. Until the referendum, the electoral law for the Senate provided that any candidate who won more than 65 per cent of the votes in 237 single-member seats was automatically elected with any remaining seats being distributed proportionally. Abolishing the '65 per cent' clause means that these seats are distributed according to the plurality formula with votes then being aggregated at regional level in order to affect the proportional distribution of the region's share of the remaining 78 seats. For the Chamber, the voter has two votes – one for the plurality-distributed seats, the other for the proportionally distributed seats (the so-called 'List Vote'). For detailed accounts of the system's operation see R.S. Katz, 'Electoral Reform and the Transformation of Party Politics in Italy', *Party Politics* 2/1 (1996) pp.31–53; M.J. Bull and J.L. Newell, 'Electoral Reform in Italy: When Consequences Fail to Meet Expectations', *Representation* (Winter 1996) forthcoming ; R. D'Alimonte and A. Chiaramonte, 'Il nuovo sistema elettorale italiano: quali opportunità?', *Rivista Italiana di Scienza Politica* 22 (1993) pp.513–47; and A. Agosta, 'Maggioritario e proporzionale', in I. Diamanti and R. Mannheimer (eds.), *Milano a Roma. Guida all'Italia elettorale del 1994* (Rome: Donzelli Editore 1994) pp.15–27.
18. The Prime Minister, Giuliano Amato, resigned after the result was known, announcing the 'death of a regime' and making way for a transitional government (headed by ex-Governor of the Bank of Italy, Carlo Azeglio Ciampi) which governed Italy from April 1993 until the elections a year later. Amato's resignation marked the final end of governing coalitions dominated by the DC.
19. On the PSI meltdown see M. Rhodes, 'Reinventing the Left: The Origins of Italy's Progressive Alliance', in C. Mershon and G. Pasquino (eds.) *Italian Politics: A Review Volume 9* (London: Pinter 1994) pp.113–34.
20. P. Ignazi, 'Alleanza Nazionale', in Diamanti and Mannheimer, *Milano a Roma* (note 17) pp.43–52.
21. P. McCarthy, 'Forza Italia: nascita e sviluppo di un partito virtuale', in Ignazi and Katz, *Politica in Italia* (note 1) pp.49–72.
22. P. McCarthy, 'Forza Italia: The New Politics and Old Values of a Changing Italy', in S.

Gundle and Parker, *New Italian Republic* (note 6) p.137.

23. On the formation of the Progressive Alliance see M. Rhodes, 'Reinventing the Left' and M. J. Bull, 'The Reconstitution of the Political Left in Italy: Demise, Renewal, Realignment and ... Defeat', in R. Gillespie (ed.) *Mediterranean Politics:Volume 2* (London: Pinter 1996).

24. On the election results see M.J. Bull and J.L. Newell, 'Italy Changes Course? The 1994 Elections and the Victory of the Right', *Parliamentary Affairs* 48/1 (Jan. 1995) pp.72–99; and S. Bartolini and R. D'Alimonte, 'Plurality Competition and Party Realignment in Italy: the 1994 Parliamentary Elections', *European Journal of Political Research* 29/1 (Jan. 1996) pp. 515–59.

25. On the general collapse of the centre pole see L. Morlino, 'Crisis of Parties and Change of Party System in Italy', *Party Politics* 2/1 (1996) pp.5–30.

26. A. Di Virgilio, 'Dai partiti ai poli: la politica delle alleanze', *Rivista Italiana di Scienza Politica* 24/3 (Dec. 1994) pp.493–547.

27. See P. Ignazi and R.S. Katz, 'Introduzione. Ascesa e caduta del governo Berlusconi', in idem, *Politica in Italia* (note 1) pp.27–48.

28. See M.J. Bull, 'Il fallimento dell'Alleanza progressista' in ibid. pp.97–120 and M. Rhodes, 'The Italian Left between Crisis and Renewal', in R. Leonardi and R.Y. Nanetti (eds.) *Italy: Politics and Policy*, Vol.1 (Aldershot: Dartmouth 1996) pp.108–33.

29. On the results of the regional elections see, R. D'Alimonte, 'La transizione italiana: il voto regionale del 23 aprile', *Rivista Italiana di Scienza Politica* 25/3 (1995) pp.515–59.

30. See J.L. Newell and M.J. Bull, 'The April 1996 Italian General Election: the Left on Top or on Tap?', *Parliamentary Affairs* 49/4 (Autumn 1996) pp.616–47.

31. See, for example, the interview with Veltroni, 'Veltroni: non può voltarsi indietro la sinistra del 2000', *La Repubblica*, 30 June 1996. Veltroni is careful not to commit himself to the idea of the *Ulivo* actually becoming a party, but the general drift of his ideas is clear.

32. See the interview with D'Alema, 'D'Alema: una rosa al posto di falce e martello', *La Repubblica*, 29 June 1996.

# 'Electoral Transition' and Party System Change in Italy

## ROBERTO D'ALIMONTE and STEFANO BARTOLINI

*This account assesses the relevance of the principal party and electoral changes of the 1990s for the functioning of the Italian party system. Focusing on the interactive structures of the party system, it evaluates change in four dimensions: the number of units constituting the system; interaction between those units; the distribution of their electorates; and the prevalent dynamics of competition. This analysis demonstrates how much the Italian party system has changed in the 1990s and how exactly it differs from the system which characterised the first 50 years of the Republic.*

THE NATURE OF THE ITALIAN CRISIS

The Italian Republic of the late 1980s and early 1990s experienced a crisis of parties, political class, institutions and the state. That crisis has been further accentuated by the complex political events of 1992, 1994 and 1996. This powerful combination has produced four fundamental changes with respect to the past: (1) a new vitality in the field of electoral reform, entailing significant changes to all electoral laws apart from those regulating European elections; (2) a high turnover of political and parliamentary élites with a distancing of many (but not all) sectors from the influence of the parties and pre-1994 governments; (3) a reorganisation of the old centre parties, substituted by new formations or presented under new names, winning minimal shares of the vote and split into different groups; (4) a radical realignment of electoral coalitions and of the experimental governmental coalitions of 1994 to 1996 – the most innovative element of which was the entry into government of the two parties which historically had been excluded from power, namely the Democratic Party of the Left (PDS) – the former Italian Communist Party (PCI) – and the National Alliance (AN), the former Italian Social Movement (MSI).

'Second Republic', 'regime change' or 'new politics' are expressions used by many commentators but for the moment they exaggerate the nature and extent of these changes. So far, Italy has not witnessed any constitutional revisions and its parliamentary system has retained its principal characteristics. Any changes to date have been restricted to political parties and the electoral arena. To what extent these political and electoral changes can modify the functioning of institutions or even produce tangible reforms remains to be seen, and is almost impossible to predict. Indeed, we might say that so far, the 'new' Italian political system is still embryonic and recent developments must be seen as intermediate and unstable. Nothing stands in the way of a more sweeping institutional change in the future which would justify the term 'regime change'[1] (presidentialism, 'chancellorism') or which would involve a change in the form of the state (some version of federalism). However, it seems clear that the pressures for change coming from sources *external* to existing political forces (such as movements proposing institutional reform, political and judicial scandals, and public opinion) are losing their impetus, if they have not already expired. This implies that any future phases of electoral/institutional/state reform will result from pacts and negotiations between the current political actors who have regained control of the political agenda.

In short, changes in Italian politics between 1992 and 1996 have occurred in the electoral mechanisms and the party landscape, and such changes should be analysed in terms of a shift in the party system. It is for this reason that the title of this contribution contains the unusual term 'electoral transition', emphasising that the process of change has been restricted to party and electoral development and that the process is far from over. In fact, the numerous and often complex new electoral rules have provided a strong basis for electoral mobility and party realignment well beyond that which has occurred to date. It should be remembered that Italians currently vote according to many different electoral systems,[2] five of which have recently undergone major reforms. Nevertheless, the new system, with new incentives, deriving from an accentuation of the majoritarian element, towards alternation and bipolar coalitions, has met with resistance from some party actors and parts of the electorate. The result has been tension between institutional incentives, on the one hand, and electoral and party behaviour on the other: thus the state of the party system is one of unstable transition. This is our main hypothesis.

A knowledge of the principal party and electoral changes in the 1990s is essential to understanding the current state of this transition, and these changes are outlined in the article by James Newell and Martin Bull in this volume.[3] Here we will focus on the systemic relevance of these changes, in other words, on their significance with regard to the traditional functioning of the Italian party system.

DIMENSIONS OF CHANGE IN THE PARTY SYSTEM

We do not intend to analyse the results of the March 1994 elections in great detail, since they have already been the subject of an in-depth study, or of the April 1996 elections, on which we still await book-length studies.[4] The results of these elections are presented in Tables 1 and 2. Our interest lies in looking at the *type* of party system that emerged from the electoral earthquake of 1994–96. How much did the Italian party system change? How does it differ from its predecessor?

TABLE 1

1994 GENERAL RESULTS OF THE CHAMBER OF DEPUTIES BY ELECTORAL CARTELS AND PARTIES

| Parties | propor-tional | single-member | total seats | total seats % | Electoral cartels | total seats | total seats % |
|---|---|---|---|---|---|---|---|
| RC | 12 | 27 | 39 | 6.2 | | | |
| PDS | 37 | 72 | 109 | 17.3 | | | |
| Verdi | 0 | 11 | 11 | 1.7 | | | |
| PSI | 0 | 14 | 14 | 2.2 | | | |
| Rete | 0 | 6 | 6 | 1.0 | Progressisti | 213 | 33.8 |
| AD | 0 | 18 | 18 | 2.9 | | | |
| CS | 0 | 5 | 5 | 0.8 | | | |
| RS | 0 | 1 | 1 | 0.2 | | | |
| Ind. Sin. | 0 | 10 | 10 | 0.6 | | | |
| PPI | 29 | 4 | 33 | 5.2 | Patto per l'Italia | 46 | 7.3 |
| Patto Segni | 13 | 0 | 13 | 2.1 | | | |
| Lega Nord | 10 | 107 | 117 | 18.6 | | | |
| Forza Italia | 25 | 74 | 99 | 15.7 | | | |
| CCD (1) | 7 | 22 | 29 | 4.6 | | | |
| UDC | 0 | 4 | 4 | 0.6 | Polo delle Libertà + | 366 | 58.1 |
| PLD | 0 | 2 | 2 | 0.3 | Polo Buon Governo | | |
| Riformatori | 0 | 6 | 6 | 1.0 | | | |
| AN | 22 | 87 | 109 | 17.3 | | | |
| LP | 0 | 0 | 0 | 0.0 | | | |
| Others | 0 | 5 | 5 | 0.8 | Others | 5 | 0.8 |
| Total | 155 | 475 | 630 | 100.0 | Total | 630 | 100.0 |

(1) The 7 proportional seats have been attributed to CCD candidates present in the Forza Italia list.

The answer depends on the starting point for the comparison and on the aspects of change we choose to consider. A glance at the results of the past four elections – in particular the proportional results of 1994 and 1996 (summarised in Table 3 below) – reveal that the 1992 elections represented a turning point for the classic post-war model, and that the elections of 1987 were, therefore, the last to fit this model.[5] In 1987 the pattern of actors still resembled that of the early elections of 1948–53. There were no consistently strong autonomist movements in the North, and an opposition to the

TABLE 2

1996 GENERAL RESULTS OF THE CHAMBER OF DEPUTIES BY ELECTORAL
CARTELS AND PARTIES

| Parties | propor-tional | single-member | total seats | total seats % | Electoral cartels | total seats | total seats % |
|---|---|---|---|---|---|---|---|
| RC | 20 | 15 | 35 | 5.6 | | | |
| PDS | 26 | 141 | 167 | 26.5 | | | |
| Verdi | 0 | 16 | 16 | 2.5 | | | |
| Popolari-Prodi | 4 | 66 | 70 | 11.1 | Ulivo + RC | 319 | 50.6 |
| Lista Dini | 8 | 18 | 26 | 4.1 | | | |
| La Rete | 0 | 5 | 5 | 0.8 | | | |
| Independent Ulivo. | 0 | 10 | 10 | 0.6 | | | |
| Lega Nord | 20 | 39 | 59 | 9.4 | Lega Nord | 59 | 9.4 |
| Forza Italia | 37 | 86 | 123 | 19.5 | | | |
| CCD-CDU | 12 | 17 | 29 | 4.6 | Polo delle Libertà | 246 | 39.0 |
| AN | 28 | 66 | 94 | 14.9 | | | |
| Others | 0 | 5 | 5 | 0.8 | Others | 5 | 0.8 |
| Total | 155 | 475 | 630 | 100.0 | Total | 630 | 100.0 |

PCI/PDS had still not appeared and been consolidated on the left. Furthermore, the dominance of the Christian Democrats (DC) showed no signs of waning. All these things occurred in 1992 and were strengthened further in 1994, via a phase of local elections which, although unimportant in the analysis of a national party system, gave some idea of the changes taking place. Thus, an analysis of the change of the party system must start from the events of 1987, and consider the 1992 elections as a transitional phase.

As for the dimensions of change, we need to look at those important from a systemic perspective, that is those which affect the *nature* of a party system. A party system can be characterised by the competitive interaction which exists between its parties. In the 1960s, Giovanni Sartori used the term 'polarised pluralism' to describe the Italian party system, and then expanded its use to denote a more general *type* of party system in his typology.[6] Such a type of party system has a high number of parties spread across a broad ideological left–right space which the parties themselves try to extend. This type is also characterised by a high level of ideological polarisation and party fragmentation; a multipolar distribution of party preferences; the occupation of the centre ground and of the median voter by a strong party; centripetal coalition forces based upon the pivotal role of the centre party; the exclusion of the extreme wings, which are too ideologically distant and/or are perceived as democratically untrustworthy; and centrifugal forces in electoral competition, where the multipolar distribution of political preferences and the occupation of the centre render centripetal convergence unrewarding as a strategy. In contrast to 'polarised pluralism', the party system type known as 'moderate pluralism' has quite different characteristics in terms of the number of parties, the ideological distance between them and the prevailing bipolar logic.

TABLE 3

PERCENTAGE OF LIST VOTES, 1987–1996

| | 1987 | 1992 | 1994 | Diff. 1992–1994 | 1996 | Diff. 1994–1996 |
|---|---|---|---|---|---|---|
| Dem. Proletaria | 1.7 | – | – | – | – | – |
| Rif. Comunista | – | 5.6 | 6.0 | +0.4 | 8.6 | +2.6 |
| PCI/PDS | 26.6 | 16.1 | 20.4 | +4.3 | 21.1 | +0.7 |
| Rete | – | 1.9 | 1.9 | 0 | – | –1.9 |
| L. Verde/Fed. Verdi/Verdi | 2.5 | 2.8 | 2.7 | –0.1 | 2.5 | –0.2 |
| AD | – | – | 1.2 | +1.2 | – | –1.2 |
| PSI | 14.3 | 13.6 | 2.2 | –11.4 | – | –2.2 |
| PRI | 3.7 | 4.4 | – | –4.4 | – | – |
| PSDI | 3.0 | 2.7 | – | –2.7 | – | – |
| PLI | 2.1 | 2.9 | – | –2.9 | – | – |
| DC/PPI | 34.3 | 29.7 | 11.1 | –18.6 | 6.8 | –4.3 |
| Patto Segni | – | – | 4.7 | +4.7 | – | –4.7 |
| Lista Dini | – | – | – | – | 4.3 | +4.3 |
| Lega Lomb./Nord | 0.5 | 8.6 | 8.4 | –0.2 | 10.1 | +1.7 |
| P. Radic./L. Pannella | 2.6 | 1.2 | 3.5 | +2.3 | 1.9 | –1.6 |
| CCD–CDU | – | – | – | – | 5.8 | +5.8 |
| Forza Italia | – | – | 21.0 | +21.0 | 20.6 | –0.4 |
| MSI–DN/AN | 5.9 | 5.4 | 13.5 | +8.1 | 15.7 | +2.2 |
| Other minor lists | 2.8 | 5.1 | 3.4 | –1.7 | 2.6 | –0.8 |

One way of assessing change in the Italian party system would be to ask whether the system is moving away from polarised pluralism towards moderate pluralism.[7] In other words, does the system now have the smaller number of parties, bipolar party preferences, coalition alternatives and centripetal competition that characterise this type? The problem is that the degree of change in Italian politics from 1992 to 1996 is such that studying them in purely typological terms – transition from one type to another – is too limited. The typological approach is ideal for analysing relatively stable periods, but less satisfactory for dynamic processes. For example, there is no doubt that, at the end of the 1970s, Italian politics experienced ideological depolarisation and a more centripetal dynamic in party competition. Nevertheless, there is still the problem of measuring the extent of this change, and assessing what aspects of the past persist in the behaviour of élites and voters. Forcing these trends to fit a model more suited to the dynamics of stable systems would only produce misleading assessments of the current situation. Therefore, while remaining true to the basic dimensions that party system theory has provided, it seems more useful to separate these and analyse them individually, rather than to combine them in a type which can only approximate the present state of the Italian system. In what follows, we will analyse the four aspects which seem crucial to our understanding of the current state and potential development of competitive interaction between parties. Such interaction essentially depends on: (1) how many units constitute the system, (2) how these units organise and coalesce, (3) how their electorates are distributed in the political space, and how 'compatible' and 'combinable' they are, and (4) the prevalent dynamics of competition.

A NEW MORPHOLOGY?

Let us begin with the morphology of the new party system. Such a morphology can be defined by the number of formations in the party system arena and by their relative strengths. The number indicates the *format* of the party system; the distribution of the electoral forces indicates the concentration of the relative resources within this format.

*The Proportional Format*

How many units are there in the new party system? Taking the 1987, 1992, 1994 and 1996 elections we can compare the number of lists which obtained at least 0.5 per cent of the vote, the number of lists that obtained seats and the number of parliamentary groups formed in the Lower Chamber and in the Senate. This comparison provides a picture both of stability and a surprising increase in the fragmentation of the actors (see Table 4). In the 1987 elections, 14 parties or lists obtained more than 0.5 percent of the vote. In 1992, the number rose to 16 but in 1994 returned to 14. In 1996, it dropped to 11. In the light of a persistent and significant fragmentation of actors in the proportional arena, we would expect the introduction of the majoritarian system to have a noticeable effect at the parliamentary level. But this is not borne out by the facts. Nineteen parties won representation under the majoritarian system in 1994 and 13 in 1996 – more or less at the same level, in fact, as in the proportional results of 1989 and 1992. Looking at this figure, we might doubt whether there had been a radical change at all in the electoral system between 1987/92 and 1994/96.

TABLE 4

NUMBER OF PARTY ACTORS

|  | 1987 | 1992 | 1994 | 1996 |
|---|---|---|---|---|
| Lists with more than 0.5 per cent of the vote | 14 | 16 | 14 | 11 |
| Number of lists obtaining seats | 14 | 16 | 20 | 13 |
|  |  |  | of which: | of which: |
|  |  |  | in proportional 7 | in proportional 8 |
|  |  |  | in majoritarian 19 | in majoritarian 13 |
| Number of parliamentary groups*: |  |  |  |  |
| Lower Chamber | | 12 | 13 | 8 | 9 |
| Senate | | 9 | 10 | 10 | 11 |

* At the beginning of the legislature

If we compare the number of lists which obtained seats under the proportional and majoritarian systems, we notice that the difference is substantial: only seven under proportionality but 19 under the majoritarian system in 1994; and then eight and 13 respectively in 1996. Proportionality has been far more selective than the majoritarian system, reducing fragmentation in a much clearer way. This is due to the four per cent threshold in the Lower Chamber. The national threshold is a real obstacle and reduces the number of parties which can receive seats, while the majoritarian threshold, which seems much higher, is only a potential hindrance which can be avoided via agreements, exchanges, divisions and similar manoeuvres. If it is to reduce fragmentation, the majoritarian system must demand far more precise conditions for political aggregation. This is not true of a proportional system with a threshold. Reaching agreements between lists is far more complex than sharing constituencies. The threshold eliminates weak actors, but the majoritarian constituency, under certain conditions, offers them a means of defence. Constructed in this way, the new electoral system is able to offer everybody the maximum possibility of such protection. In 1994, a medium-strength party, such as the *pattisti* (adherents of the pact led by Mario Segni), even though isolated in terms of alliances, could defend itself in the proportional arena. An electorally weak list, such as the Centre Christian Democrats (CCD), could defend itself in the majoritarian sector with a divisive alliance. The situation had not changed substantially by 1996. The actors heavily penalised by the new system were the weak parties which were, in addition, unable to make alliances in the majoritarian sector. There was a very poor potential selection, and, in fact, almost nobody attempted to bargain. It is not surprising, then, that the new electoral system reflects much the same party format as before, being no less fragmented than its predecessors. The 1996 figures indicate only a small reduction in fragmentation, with the disappearance of parties with small lists.

## The Concentration of Electoral Forces in the Proportional System

The second dimension to the morphological change of the party system concerns the profile of electoral distribution among the various groups. The number of party units can stay more or less the same, but the distribution of strength among them may give the system a different configuration. From 1987 to 1994, such a tendency is clearly definable. If we look closely at the percentage of votes obtained by the first four parties (see Table 3), we can see that it dropped from 81.1 per cent to 60 per cent, and then rose to 66 and then 67.5 per cent. Taking into account the distribution of votes among the main parties, we can see that the system seems to have moved from a standard 'imperfect bipartism' configuration, with two large parties a long way ahead of the medium and small groups (1987 and 1992), to a configuration of equitable distribution, characterised by four or five medium-sized parties with little difference between them in strength.[8] The ratio between the first and the fourth party was from 1:6 in 1987, but 1:2 in 1996. The results from 1994 and 1996 tell us that beyond the first four parties, there are none bigger than those of 1987–92. In short, the distribution has levelled out: the strongest parties have a smaller share of the vote than before, while that of the smaller ones has increased.

To summarise, as far as fragmentation is concerned, the party system has not notably changed: the trends existing before electoral reform are ongoing and, indeed, have been slightly accentuated. Evidently, it is always possible that, without the new electoral system, fragmentation would still be great. Overall, however, it would seem fair to conclude that the new electoral laws have not halted, let alone reversed, existing party system dynamics.[9]

## The Majoritarian System and the Distribution of Parliamentary Strength

The train of argument used so far is open to one fundamental objection. Why analyse the format and distribution of actors within the party system by referring to the proportional part of the vote? After all, the novelty of the situation is to be found in the majoritarian system and its effects: and arguably we should study the morphology of party system change at the parliamentary level because it is precisely there that the impact of the majoritarian logic on the grouping of actors is revealed. We could reply to this objection by simply stating that the format of a party system is determined by the number of parties alone,[10] and that the parties, independently of their coalitions and alliances, maintain a specific identity, as can be seen from the complex parliamentary activity of 1994 to 1996.

Nevertheless, this criticism should not be underestimated and it is worth considering its implications. Certain parties have obtained only proportional seats, and others have not presented lists, relying instead on majoritarian seats. Thus, the party system as a proportional/majoritarian mix *at the parliamentary level* is different from that which emerges from the distribution of proportional electoral strength. How different is it? At this point we encounter the problem of finding a reference-point. The above argument implies that parties and lists are no longer the 'effective' unit within the system, and that something else has replaced them, consequently diminishing their relevance. This 'something else' needs to be analysed if we are to characterise the system. What other units should we consider? In fact, only three other units could replace the parties as a reference-point: parliamentary parties, parliamentary groups, or parliamentary alliances (or 'poles') under the majoritarian system.

Let us look at the first possibility – the *parliamentary parties.* Comparing Tables 1, 2 and 3, the distribution of strength between the electoral parties (the proportional system percentage) and the parliamentary parties (percentage of seats) is effectively the same. If we look at the *parliamentary groups* (see Table 4) the party system format appears. The 20 and 13 parties/lists which obtained seats in the Lower Chamber in 1994 and 1996 respectively formed eight and nine parliamentary groups, half of which were medium-sized, and half of which were small. The number still remains high, varying little from those resulting from the proportional elections of 1987 to 1992. The reduction is noticeable in the Lower Chamber – where the number of groups grew between 1994 and 1996 – but there is no change in the Senate. It does not appear, then, that parties and parliamentary groups constitute a different system to those that result from the proportional vote.

The situation is more complex if we look at the aggregation around electoral poles. After both the 1994 and 1996 elections, the system appears to be configured around three poles: left, right and a centre formerly arranged around the ex-DC in 1994, and which passed to the Lega Nord (LN – Northern League) in 1996. Can the new morphology of the party system be found among this data? Are we looking at a pattern of three groups which, during this transitional phase, have not yet consolidated their party organisation but which is the major reference-point for future developments?

In our opinion, it is too early to speak in such terms. The three poles of 1994 did not last, and those of 1996, although more solid in appearance, still possess many internal contradictions. In 1994, the main question was how to describe the centre-right electoral pole – or rather, how to quantify it. The 58.1 per cent of deputies in the chamber who constituted the centre-right were not a unified pole, but a collection of various electoral poles (see

Table 2). One pole with 30.3 per cent of the deputies was clearly definable as an alliance between *Forza Italia* (FI), its allies and the southern AN (known as the *Polo del buon governo*, Alliance for Good Government). For the sake of detail, if the aggregative principle to be employed is that of electoral alliances, then we must keep distinct those deputies from FI and AN who were elected in situations where the two parties were competing against each other. In the North, AN obtained 11 seats – 10 proportional and 1 majoritarian – where it opposed Forza Italia's *Polo delle Libertà* the Freedom Alliance with the Lega Nord). In the South, AN won 10 parliamentary seats against FI, and FI won four proportional seats and a single majoritarian one in areas where it opposed AN. Beginning with the electoral coalitions of 1994, then, we can identify at least three poles on the centre-right: FI–Lega, FI–AN and AN on its own in the North. FI and AN belong to different poles in different arenas. The ambiguity and confusion that this situation could potentially cause was reinforced after the elections and it is no coincidence that internal conflicts within the centre-right undermined the Berlusconi government from the outset. We can conclude that the three centre-right poles on which Berlusconi based his 1994 parliamentary majority cannot be considered as fundamental units of the party system, bearing in mind their collapse just six months after the election. In 1996, the 39 per cent of deputies who reconstituted the right pole seemed more homogeneous. This time, the alliance (known as the *Polo delle Libertà* – Freedom Alliance) was unique and covered the whole country, and secondly, the political homogeneity of the three groups within it was much higher.

The composition of the left pole also changed substantially between 1994 and 1996. The Progressive Alliance of 1994 transformed itself into a layered grouping: the PDS and the Italian Popular Party (PPI) formed the nucleus, around which were attached agreements with Communist Refoundation (RC) on the left, and Dini's Italian Renewal party in the centre. The centre-left alliance of 1996 was thus more composite than the Progressive Alliance of 1994, unlike the centre-right transformation. Taking into account the uncertainty surrounding RC's capacity to support the Prodi government, and the flirtation by Dini and the centrists with the right-wing pole, this alliance may prove to be less than solid. In any case, bearing in mind its five distinct components (RC, PDS, Greens, PPI, Dini), one cannot consider it a unitary actor in the new party system, even if its internal differences are less acute than those in Berlusconi's 1994 centre-right coalition.

We can state categorically, then, that the electoral poles of 1994 cannot be considered the final, component parts of the new party system. Undoubtedly we are witnessing the consolidation of the right pole in 1996; but at the same time the left pole is becoming more heterogeneous. In short, we might conclude that victory requires vast, diverse coalitions which, once the election has passed, can only be seen as a collection of different parties with strong elements of internal conflict.

One element of polar consolidation which has undoubtedly occurred is in the profile of government support. Berlusconi's 1994 majority and Dini's 1995 majority were formed by collections of deputies not just from different parties, but from different electoral alliances. But the Prodi government is reliant upon a coalition which, although not based on a cohesive, cross-party consensus on policy, at least covered the whole country electorally in 1996. At the same time, many other indicators show a bipolar tendency in the party system: the average number of candidates per constituency (majoritarian) dropped from five to three for the Lower Chamber (but remained constant at six for the Senate); the average winning share of the vote rose from 43.5 per cent in 1994 to 48.6 per cent in 1996 (valid for the 707 majoritarian seats in the Lower Chamber and the Senate); the average gap between first and second place dropped from 17.7 to 10.9 per cent in the Lower Chamber, and from 13.9 to 11.0 per cent in the Senate; the number of seats where the gap was reduced between first and second increased dramatically; and finally, there was a massive reduction in the majoritarian vote for third and lower candidates – from 36.4 per cent in 1994 to 16.4 per cent in 1996.[11] However, such symptoms still do not allow us to speak of bipolarism as a systemic feature. The poles are only alliances of parties, and the parties retain their identities, interests and (sometimes) individual parliamentary behaviour.

All of the above means that it is very difficult to provide a morphology of the party system in terms of the number of competitive units and their respective electoral strengths. From this point of view, it seems more profitable to refer to political parties, of which there are still at least ten in the parliament. The system resulting from the 1996 elections is perhaps less 'amorphous' and more precisely defined than that of 1994. But it is difficult to say whether in the future the parties will continue to be stronger than the electoral alliances which installed their deputies, or whether the latter will in fact impose a more formal group logic. As things stand at the moment, the parties are still the best way of defining a unit in the system, even if it is clear that the vast majority of small and medium parties owe their existence and survival to the electoral alliances and the sharing of constituencies in the majoritarian system.

Of course, it can be argued that not all the parties should be counted: there are some which have little or no effect within the system, lacking any coalition potential or effect on other coalitions, and consequently should be excluded from any morphological characterisation of the party system. According to this reasoning, numerous parties which appeared in the elections from 1994 to 1996 would not count, and the party system could therefore be considered to hinge on no more than five or six parties.[12] We do not agree with this conclusion and so have not used 'qualitative' criteria for counting: in our opinion, coalition and blackmail potential exists for the small parties and can be measured in a party constellation and under a relatively stable and consolidated coalition tradition. If party actors are electorally unstable (if there is great doubt about their long-term electoral future) and the rules of the game – the nature of the electoral system – are also uncertain, it will be difficult for these parties to fulfil their coalition and blackmail potential in the same way as others. In the Italian electoral transition there is a high level of uncertainty among the main parties as to their – and other parties' – electoral strengths under the new majoritarian rules. This has produced a kind of equal sharing of both coalition and blackmail potential, offering even the smaller groups vast scope for playing a crucial role within whatever coalition. It should be remembered that the defection of a tiny party, such as that of Marco Pannella, cost the right pole at least two regional governments in 1995, and the presentation of candidates in the party of the extreme right, *Fiamma Tricolore* (Tricoloured Flame), in 1996 cost the centre-right pole dozens of seats in the south of Italy and, in all probability, the election itself.

THE STRUCTURE OF COMPETITION

*Vote Mobility*

The second dimension of a party system is its competitive dynamics. Most commentators have stressed the fact that, in the 1994 elections, the so-called 'electoral market' was wide open, with an unprecedented availability of voters.[13] In Figure 1 we show the total volatility levels in elections from 1948 to 1996.[14] It is clear that even from 1979, the Italian electorate was starting to show signs of growing electoral volatility. From this date onwards, volatility steadily increased. In 1992 (at 11.5 per cent) it had already reached the highest level in elections since the war, excepting 1948 (23 per cent) and 1953 (14.1 per cent). In 1994, it reached 37.2 per cent – a level far higher than anything experienced during the post-war reconstruction and consolidation of the party system. At least one-third of the electorate modified its party preference between 1992 and 1994.[15] This aggregate data supports what many surveys have found, with for example a recent estimate of more than 50 per cent individual volatility.[16] In a comparative perspective, this level of volatility is exceptionally high: out of a total of 428 elections in western Europe between the turn of the century and 1989, only four manifested volatility above 35 per cent: Germany in 1919 (47.5), France in 1945

(36.4), and Greece in 1959 and 1951 (47.0, 45.1).[17] These were all elections after regime changes. Evidently, we are looking at an indicator of fundamental party system decomposition and – accepting the hypothesis that aggregate volatility can be considered as an indirect but valid indicator of individual mobility – an electorate whose mobility is amongst the highest ever recorded in Europe

FIGURE 1
TOTAL VOLATILITY (1948–96)

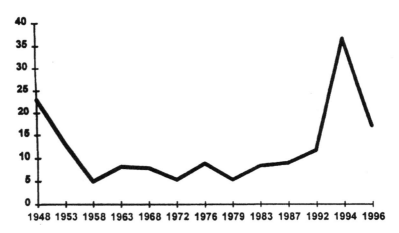

Certainly, the results of 1994 were influenced by the changing conditions of political supply – in other words the appearance of new parties – but this only partially explains why electoral dealignment preceded the birth of the new political formations. This electoral instability is not surprising if we look at the conditions under which the March 1994 elections took place. Other research has constructed a general model of the sources of aggregate electoral instability, based upon the interplay of three macro-processes. The first is the change of parties' socio-organisational roots; the second is the collection of incentives to party preference change offered by institutional change in electoral competition; the third is political supply, being the effect of differentiation between the programmes on offer by different contenders.[18] These three factors interact, and the effect of political supply in particular is heightened by the relaxation of socio-organisational links between party and electorate, and institutional incentives for mobility.

These are exactly the conditions under which the 1994 and 1995 regional elections occurred. It would be difficult to underestimate the effect of

*Tangentopoli*; the same applies to Berlusconi's own efforts. Thus, political supply and its positive/negative assessment dominated the scene during these elections. Nevertheless, we should not forget that this occurred in an election where time had already weakened the historical links of ideology and organisation between parties and voters, and maximised institutional incentives for mobility[19] to a level previously only seen between 1958 and 1962 in France. We are thinking especially of: the numerous referendums called for by voters freed from party choice and influence, local election reforms which imposed unusual party alliances and transfers of votes to second party choices, the abolition of the preferential vote,[20] and, not least, the national electoral reform with its implicit incentives for tactical voting. Faced with the weakened social links of parties and institutional incentives for electoral betrayal of traditional loyalties, it is not surprising that political supply became the decisive factor for most voters. For them, the supply provided something new; for the experts, it provided new issues and new faces. Bearing in mind the continuity of the new actors and the exhaustion of the historic confluence of new supply, institutional incentives and specific issues, it was unsurprising that in 1996, total system volatility halved, settling down at around 16 per cent.

In any case, 1994 to 1996 can be characterised as a period of high volatility in an open and competitive market. That said, it is interesting to look at the components of total volatility individually, breaking them down according to inter-bloc and intra-bloc volatility. This type of analysis is evidently not a substitute for individual movements, and is not intended to be. Rather, it aims to describe the major changes in voting in the main political camps, and to verify how much volatility is inter-bloc, and how much takes place within blocs.

In Table 5, we have tried to synthesise the information from Table 3, which is not easily comparable, according to the different political formations. The level of discontinuity in the political groupings makes it difficult to analyse the centre camp over time. The other two groups are more easily identifiable. On the right, the MSI/AN was the only formation until 1994, when the extreme right dissident, Fiamma Tricolore emerged. On the left, the PDS, RC and allied parties in the majority maintained some sort of continuity with the left of pre-1994. In the very centre we have grouped all formations which historically and programmatically have not belonged to the left or the right. We have included in this new parties such as FI and the Lega Nord.

The most noticeable result is that between 1987–92 and 1994–96, the right and the left gained at the expense of the centre. The centre lost about 12 percentage points over the decade. In other words, the appearance of FI and the Lega did not make up for the collapse of the two governing

TABLE 5

PROPORTIONAL ELECTORAL STRENGTH BY POLITICAL CAMP

|        | 1987 % votes | 1992 % votes | 1994 % votes | 1996 % votes |
|--------|------|------|------|------|
| Left   | 30.9 | 26.6 | 34.3 | 32.2 |
| Centre | 62.1 | 67.1 | 50.1 | 50.2 |
| Right  | 5.9  | 5.4  | 13.5 | 16.6 |
| Other  | 1.1  | 0.9  | 2.1  | 1.0  |

*Legend*: Left = 1987: DP, PCI, Green Lists; 1992: PDS, RC, Green Lists, Rete; 1994: PDS, RC, Greens, Rete, PSI, AD; 1996: PDS, RC, Greens. Right = 1987; 1992: MSI; 1994: AN. 1996: AN, MST

parties in the old centre, the DC and the Italian Socialist Party (PSI), or for their allies, the Italian Republican Party (PRI), the Italian Social Democratic Party (PSDI) and the Italian Liberal Party (PLI). The missing votes moved to the two extremes. Nevertheless, in spite of the gains of the left in 1994 and 1996 (after poor performances in 1987 and 1992), the novelty is the growth of the right, which tripled its vote over ten years. In terms of the politico-ideological space, the collapse of the post-war centre stimulated the creation of new political groupings and also produced a decline in consensus, to the profit of the right.

As for the historical left, there was a significant improvement between 1992 and 1994. However, the Progressives only benefited moderately from the collapse of the centre, which supplied the majority of the new votes to the new centre-right groups (especially FI and AN). In terms of inter-bloc volatility between the left and the centre, there was very little movement in 1994. These results, based on aggregate data, have recently been supported by a survey looking specifically at the mobile electorate.[21] This also confirmed the limited attraction of the left in 1994 to ex-DC, ex-PSI, ex-PSDI and ex-PRI voters.

Paradoxically, the situation remains the same for the 1996 elections, which were won by the centre-left. If we look again at the historical left, its votes can be seen to have remained almost completely stable. Similarly, the large amount of aggregate volatility concerns the interchange of votes or the internal movements in the centre (the growth of Dini's Italian Renewal and the Centre Christian Democratic-Christian Democratic Union (CCD-CDU) alliance; the decline of the PPI, and the disappearance of Segni) or between the centre and the right (the growth of AN and the success of the Fiamma Tricolore).

Overall, quite a clear picture emerges from this data. The left gained very little from the high level of electoral mobility in the centre in 1994 and

1996. Few of the enormous numbers of mobile votes crossed its border from the centre. If we leave aside the improvement of the PDS in 1994 from its disastrous situation of 1992 and refer instead to 1987, the substantial stagnation of the left vote is even clearer: 30.8 per cent in 1987; 32.2 per cent in 1996. In reality, between 1992 and 1994, the electoral chaos amongst the five main parties produced a mobile electorate that either went to the right – if this is how we are defining the new formations – or reoriented themselves in the same camp within a new and less compromised group. In short, we see a picture of high volatility between the centre and the right, and a tight electoral seal surrounding the left.

These facts suggest that we should be careful in characterising the electorate as deprived of its historical identity and free to choose according to the rules of the market. These results point out substantial stability on the left as opposed to an *electoral remobilisation* on the centre-right. From this point of view, we should not be deceived either by the victory of the centre-left in the regional elections of 1995 or by its majority in 1996. Such victories are the result of wide electoral alliances – wider than the left itself – at the centre of which the left does not have a positive electoral dynamic. In the face of the defeat of the Progressive Alliance in 1994, the PDS had the option of two strategies *vis-à-vis* the centre: either attract the centre electorate, or coalesce with the parties which represent that electorate. They successfully chose the second option. But this strongly suggests that the shifting of the moderate vote to the centre was not a defection, but rather accompanied the parties of the centre when they moved into alliance with the left.

## The 'Summability' of the Votes

One of the characteristics of the new electoral system allows us to pick up on another important aspect of electoral mobility and, at the same time, to explain the competitive dynamics, and different results of the elections in 1994 and 1996. In the Lower Chamber – but not in the Senate – voters choose candidates in single-vote constituencies, and separately for the proportional quota, with two different ballot-papers. This makes it possible, in the same territorial area (the single-vote constituency) to compare electoral behaviour according to different political supply and under different electoral rules. It is not necessarily true, for example, that a voter who chooses FI under the proportional system will also vote for the *Polo* (Freedom Alliance) in the constituency.

If we assume – plausibly – that the proportional vote is a sincere vote (and thus reflects the actual distribution of electoral preferences), it is possible to quantify the value of electoral cartels, and consequently their relative competitiveness, by measuring the difference between two votes:

the votes obtained in the constituency by the candidate representing the coalition, and the votes obtained in the same constituency – but under the proportional system – by the parties which fielded that candidate. A positive difference means that the candidate has managed not only to keep the votes of his 'fielders' but has also attracted external votes. On the other hand, a negative difference indicates a difficult 'summability' of voters within the cartel. We need not emphasise the importance of this result: with a three-quarters majoritarian electoral system, a negative return in this area of competition can mean a significant loss of seats in a highly competitive election, as occurred in 1996.

Tables 6 and 7 shed light on this fundamental aspect of electoral competition. Comparison between 1994 and 1996 clearly shows the difference in effectiveness of the two coalitions, centre-left and centre-right. In 1994 (Table 4) the centre-right coalition was more competitive than the Progressive Alliance both in the north and in the south. Its candidates attracted voters beyond those who were supporting them according to their party preference. The data show that the moderate electorate transferred its vote without a problem to the heads of coalitions, even when they were from the AN. Moreover, AN candidates within the *Polo* performed better than more moderate candidates. This leads us to the conclusion that the integration of AN at the mass level had succeeded, at least in the south, in 1994. For the Progressives, the situation was completely different. With few and insignificant exceptions, the coalition candidates did not manage to safeguard the votes of the lists that they were supporting. When the candidates were from RC, the defections reached 2.8 per cent of the vote.

Given the complex nature of the competition, however, this difference in coalition effectiveness did not significantly affect the electoral result. In particular, in the North, but also in the South, the competitive advantage of Berlusconi's two alliances was such that, in every case, defections to the left did not produce a significant loss of seats. What did have an effect, however, was the nature of the Progressive Alliance, which had neither a sufficient basis of support, nor the ability even to retain it.

In 1996, the picture changed drastically, and the Polo had major difficulties. Given the diverse profile of the competing groups and the presence of many marginal constituencies, by contrast with 1994, the difference between majoritarian and proportional votes had a strong negative effect on the *Polo* and a positive one on the Olive Tree alliance (*Ulivo*), as well as on the Lega and the Fiamma Tricolore. Everybody gained between the majoritarian and proportional vote, except for the Polo which lost on average 3.7 per cent (Table 7) and, in absolute terms, about 1.4 million votes. Of these, only a part (about 500,000) defected to the Ulivo. The others went to the LN, to the Fiamma Tricolore and to other minor

TABLE 6

ELECTORAL EFFECTIVENESS OF CARTELS, 1994 LOWER CHAMBER, (% VOTES)

| Parties/ coalitions | No. candidates | % average votes to candidates (A) | % average votes to lists (B) | Difference A–B |
|---|---|---|---|---|
| *Ulivo/RC* | *454* | *41.7* | *40.1* | *+1.6* |
| RC | 27 | 42.3 | 49.5 | −7.2 |
| PDS | 182 | 32.2 | 33.7 | −1.5 |
| Verdi | 31 | 32.3 | 32.8 | −0.6 |
| AD | 49 | 31.4 | 32.6 | −1.2 |
| Rete | 39 | 27.6 | 27.6 | 0.0 |
| PSI | 38 | 30.1 | 31.6 | −1.5 |
| CS | 20 | 29.3 | 30.5 | −1.2 |
| RS | 2 | 30.9 | 30.6 | 0.3 |
| Ind. Sin. | 49 | 25.2 | 25.5 | −0.3 |
| *Polo libertà* | *235* | *40.1* | *36.7* | *+3.4* |
| FI | 61 | 37.8 | 34.1 | +3.7 |
| Lega | 148 | 41.1 | 37.7 | +3.4 |
| CCD | 15 | 34.1 | 32.0 | +2.1 |
| UDC | 3 | 49.6 | 41.8 | +7.8 |
| PLD | 2 | 49.7 | 43.1 | +6.6 |
| Riformatori | 6 | 47.8 | 43 | +4.8 |
| *Polo Buon Governo* | *187* | *37.2* | *35.2* | *+2.0* |
| FI | 63 | 35.9 | 35.6 | +0.3 |
| CCD | 21 | 38.8 | 37.7 | +1.1 |
| AN | 102 | 37.8 | 34.5 | +3.3 |
| UDC | 1 | 30.4 | 33.9 | −3.5 |

candidates. In this way, the *Polo*, which obtained 44 per cent of the proportional vote, dropped to 40.5 per cent (as against 43.4 per cent for the centre-left coalition, and 44.9 per cent for the Ulivo and RC). There is no doubt that the difference in effectiveness of the two coalitions was a reason for the success of the Ulivo/RC coalition. Regarding the latter, we can see the strong negative effect of RC. A loss of seven percentage points is an unequivocal sign of the difficulty of holding together the Ulivo mosaic when the candidates that are representing it are too ideologically diverse. It is a further confirmation of the hypothesis that, under a majoritarian regime, there is a trade-off between the ideological breadth of the coalition and its electoral effectiveness.[22]

Why are these differences so marked between 1994 and 1996? Overall, the data in Tables 6 and 7 suggest two general hypotheses. The first concerns the candidates, the second the coalitions. A candidate can lose votes for the coalition which supports him for two reasons. The first reason is linked

TABLE 7

ELECTORAL EFFECTIVENESS OF CARTELS, 1996 LOWER CHAMBER (% VOTES)

| Parties/ coalitions | No. candidates | % average votes to candidates (A) | % average votes to lists (B) | Difference A–B |
|---|---|---|---|---|
| *Progressisti* | *468* | *30.6* | *31.9* | *+1.6* |
| RC | 27 | 42.3 | 49.5 | –7.2 |
| PDS | 2152 | 44.1 | 42.2 | +2.1 |
| Verdi | 28 | 42.0 | 40.7 | –0.6 |
| Popolari | 130 | 38.9 | 36.2 | +2.7 |
| Lista Dini | 47 | 37.5 | 36.2 | +1.3 |
| Rete | 5 | 43.0 | 41.4 | +1.6 |
| PS d'az. | 1 | 43.1 | 41.5 | +1.6 |
| Ind. Ulivo | 1 | 26.8 | 21.7 | +5.1 |
| *Polo libertà* | *475* | *37.4* | *41.1* | *–3.7* |
| FI | 233 | 36.9 | 40.7 | –3.2 |
| AN | 162 | 38.9 | 42.8 | –3.9 |
| CCD/CDU | 79 | 35.7 | 39.1 | –3.4 |
| *Lega* | *228* | *19.5* | *17.9* | *+1.6* |
| *MST* | *179* | *4.3* | *1.5* | *+2.8* |

to his personal characteristics: his political past or his lack of involvement in the constituency, for example. For some electors in his camp, he may be a 'poor' candidate as compared with candidates put forward by other political groups in the constituency. An interesting aspect of this phase of electoral transition in Italy is that the majoritarian electoral system has not discouraged a significant group of voters from defecting to candidates who have no possibility of winning. Instead of voting tactically for a second choice, the voter prefers to vote sincerely even at the cost of voting for an outsider, thus favouring the opposing coalition. This phenomenon was certainly true in the case of the Fiamma Tricolore. The second reason is ideological. The coalition candidate may be too ideologically distinct and distant from that of the coalition's voters. This was the case with RC candidates in the centre-left coalition. These defections reveal the persistence of an ideological vote which makes the summability of the diverse electoral components in the coalition difficult. In these cases, the defection can also be helped by the presence of minor candidates who are ideologically closer, even though they may be uncompetitive.

The second hypothesis refers to what we might call the 'coalition' effect. According to this hypothesis, a number of voters select a coalition independently of its candidates. More precisely, they vote for the coalition, even though they do not identify with any of the component parties, because they prefer it to the others. This behaviour can result from various factors. The complex profile of the coalition is one; a second is the profile of the leader. An effective leader has the ability to function both as a linchpin in bringing together the various electoral components of his political camp, and as a magnet to attract voters from other camps. For example, this was the case for Berlusconi in 1994, but not in 1996. Contemporary electoral competition in Italy, then, is not only amongst parties, but also amongst coalitions. The impact of a coalition can vary: programmes, image and electoral campaign are all factors which can influence the result. The availability of data in reference to the proportional system allow us to test this. However, as we have already emphasised in this account, electoral coalitions are still mostly constructed on artificial grounds: they are more or less successful groups of parties, not parties in themselves or even party federations. It is still not clear today whether they will develop in this direction: on this point, the debate continues, with no hint as to its resolution. However, there is no doubt that the profile of the party system will depend on how far things proceed in this direction.

CONCLUSIONS: A COMPETITIVE PARTY SYSTEM?

Mobility and 'summability' are important aspects of electoral competition, but they do not characterise the nature of the party system *per se*. This is what we intend to do in this final section. More specifically, we want to assess whether the party system has become more competitive or not. Competitiveness at the party system level depends on the structure of competitive interactions among parties, and particularly between government parties and opposition parties. A party system is competitive if voters can choose at election time between two parties or two party coalitions, each of which has a realistic chance of gaining a majority of seats in Parliament. To this end, two conditions should be met : (1) the existence of a clear differentiation between parties in government and parties in opposition, (2) the existence of a pool of available voters located in such a position in the political spectrum to make them decisive for the success of either contender.[23]

The old party system met neither condition. The opposition was divided between an extreme right and an extreme left. The separation between government and opposition was clear at the governmental level, but very ambiguous at the parliamentary level. The available voters were few and their spatial location was within well-defined ideological blocs. Given these features, no median voter was available to act as the pivot of electoral competition and therefore as 'government maker'. The system was based on centrist coalitions which benefited from a competitive advantage created by polarisation. In short, the party system was not competitive. To what extent does the new party system meet the conditions for systemic competitiveness which we have outlined above?

The first condition defines party system competitiveness on the supply side. The condition is met if a party system is structured around two parties or two party coalitions, one of which represents the incumbent government and the second a credible governmental alternative. Does the Italian party system meet this condition today? Yes and no. To start with, even in the last elections voters did not face a clear choice between an incumbent government and a viable alternative opposition. The Dini government, which replaced that of Berlusconi, had been supported by an ambiguous centre-left parliamentary majority that, for most of the time, included the Lega, but not RC. At election time the centre-left coalition excluded the Lega and included RC. Moreover, the Lega was not a member of a unified, alternative coalition.

In the second place, the party system is neither two-party nor bipolar. We have already discussed at length the question of the format. In terms of electoral dynamics we can say that a tendency towards a bipolar pattern certainly exists, but it is far from being clearly defined. In 1994 there were three electoral coalitions competing in the single-member districts: the Progressive Alliance, the Pact for Italy, and the Freedom Alliance. In addition, the centre-right coalition – the Freedom Alliance – had a different configuration and a different name in the North (*Polo delle Libertà*) from the centre and South (*Polo del buon governo*). In 1996 there were still three coalitions. Only voters in central Italy faced a bipolar contest: the Ulivo/RC on the one hand and the *Polo* on the other. In the North, competition was tripolar with the Lega being the third competitive actor capable of winning a number of plurality seats. Not even in the South can one speak of a real bipolar contest since in many single-member districts there were Fiamma Tricolore candidates who were too weak to win any seat, but critical enough to influence decisively the contests between the candidates of the two major coalitions.

From this perspective, the picture is that of a party system in transition. Nevertheless, there are clear breaks with the old party system which cannot be neglected. The first is the disappearance of the old anti-system parties. The PCI has become the PDS and today is a crucial member of the Prodi government. The MSI has become AN and was a fully-fledged member of the Berlusconi government. Neither RC (which is not in the Prodi government, but gave its support in the confidence vote) nor the Fiamma Tricolore can be considered a threat to the democratic system. Democratic legitimacy is no longer a dimension of Italian politics. The second difference concerns the centre of the political spectrum. The DC does not exist anymore, and nor do we find in its place the PPI as we did in 1994. The split in the PPI between the *Popolari* (who sided with the Ulivo) and the CDU (which sided with the *Polo*) has 'freed' the centre from the presence of a Catholic party. This was an important element of the old polarised party system.

However, this change has not produced a truly bipolar system because the centre, evacuated by the PPI, has been re-occupied as of 1996 by the Lega. The difference between the old party system and the new, as well as between the elections of 1994 and 1996, is that today there is no longer at the national level a third party or a third coalition in the political centre. Without counting the Fiamma Tricolore, a third party exists only in the North and it has distinctive features. In fact, to characterise the Lega we need two dimensions: left-right and centre-periphery. Along the first dimension the Lega seeks to project a centrist image, whereas along the second its image has become increasingly radical. But the relative salience of these two dimensions has changed over time. In the 1994 elections, the Lega, as a member of Berlusconi's northern alliance, competed along the left-right continuum, seeking to exploit its centrist location. Since its break with the *Polo* and particularly since its decision to run alone in the 1996 elections, its leadership has increasingly emphasised the issue of federalism/independence, making the centre-periphery dimension more salient than the left–right one. Therefore, the space for electoral competition is today two-dimensional and this prevents the formation of a unified centre-right opposition. As a result, the opposition to the Prodi government is today unilateral, whereas in the old party system it was bilateral. But it is nevertheless bimodal since it is divided between the *Polo* and the Lega.

Let us now analyse the party system from the point of view of the second condition indicated above: the role of the available voters. What is the impact of these voters on the outcome of the elections? Are they critical? Do they make the difference between success and defeat? In the old party system competition was more among parties than between alternative coalitions; and the stake was not the right to form the government. In a consolidated polarised system electoral mobility between blocs is very limited. Mobility, if it exists at all, is *within* blocs and often among factions of the major incumbent party. Given these conditions, the outcome of the elections is not uncertain. The incumbent centrist parties return consistently to power. This was the Italian case.

To what extent have things changed? In spite of the different electoral outcome between 1994 and 1996, the answer is mixed in this respect as well. Many observers have emphasised the historical and political significance of the fact that, for the first time in the post-war period, there has been a rotation in power (of sorts) between the centre-left and the centre-right. But is this development the result of a massive shift of voters from one bloc to the other? On this point we have already expressed our doubts. Mobility has certainly increased, but the different outcome of the two elections is less the result of a massive spatial redistribution of electoral preferences than of a significant change of electoral alliances. In other words, competition on the demand side (voters' preferences) has changed less than competition on the supply side (what parties provide). Parties have changed, but voters less so. However, regardless of what has changed, we can say that the party system has become more competitive in comparison both with the pattern before 1992 and with that in 1994. This is clearly shown by the dramatic increase in 1996 in the number of marginal seats (249 in the Lower Chamber from 138 in 1994), namely, those seats where the difference between the winner and the second-placed candidate is less than 8 per cent of the votes. In 1994 these seats were largely concentrated in the South, which turned out to be the only competitive area, particularly in the Senate.[24] In 1996, both the North and the South have shown high levels of competitiveness, leaving the geographic centre as the only area where one alliance – the centre-left in this case – is clearly dominant.

In conclusion, a more competitive party system has emerged from Italy's 'electoral transition', but it still has an unstable structure. Its main feature is a bipolar tendency. We use the term 'tendency' rather than pattern for several reasons. The Lega is one, but it is not alone. RC is another potential problem. How long will this party continue to be a member of the centre-left coalition? The question is relevant because there are significant policy differences between RC and the other members of the Ulivo in at least two major areas, the economy and political reform. However, the major potential threat to the consolidation of a competitive party system stems from the instability in the centre of the political spectrum. This is where we find the highest levels of party fragmentation and voter mobility. The sources of this instability are numerous: the Lega, Dini's Italian Renewal party, FI and the legal problems of its leader, the manoeuvres involving the Catholic parties in both coalitions, the role of Mario Segni (the referendum leader) and that of Antonio Di Pietro (the former *Tangentopoli* investigator and prosecutor). This instability can lead to two possible outcomes which represent different types of party system. The first is the strengthening and consolidation of the two main electoral alliances which competed in the 1996 elections. In this case a stable bipolar pattern would emerge with the Lega being gradually pushed into a marginal position. The second possible outcome is the formation of a new centre party, or more likely a new centrist alliance. In this case we would see the re-emergence of a non-competitive pattern based on the critical role of a centrist actor as opposed to the critical role of centrist voters. Which of these two outcomes will prevail is too soon to say, but future decisions (if any) concerning political reform will play an important role in the evolution of the party system.

## NOTES

1. Recently, old requests for constitutional revision have been supplemented by critics who emphasise that the introduction of the majoritarian electoral system goes against many norms and the spirit of the 1948 constitution, and thus does not constitute a reform. See esp. S. Cassese, *Maggioranza a minoranza. Il problema della democrazia in Italia* (Milan: Garzanti 1995).
2. A mixed proportional/majoritarian system with some differences between the Lower Chamber and Senate; a proportional system for the European Parliament; a proportional system with majority victory for regional elections; a direct, two-ballot majoritarian system for local presidencies, mayors of local councils, and commune councils with more than 15,000 inhabitants; and a plurality system for communes under 15,000 inhabitants.
3. See James L. Newell and Martin Bull, 'Party Organisations and Alliances in the 1990s: A Revolution of Sorts' (this volume).
4. On the 1994 elections see I. Diamanti and R. Mannheimer (eds.) *Milano a Roma. Guida all'Italia elettorale del 1994* (Rome: Donzelli Editore 1994); A. di Virgilio, 'Le elezioni politiche del 27 e 28 marzo 1994. Dalla destrutturazione alla (instabile e parziale) ricomposizione', *Quaderni dell'osservatorio elettorale* 32 (1994) pp.137–210; S. Bartolini and R. D'Alimonte (eds.) *Maggioritario ma non troppo: le elezioni politiche del 1994* (Bologna: Il Mulino 1995); G. Pasquino (ed.) *L'alternanza inattesa. Le elezioni del 27 marzo 1994 e le loro conseguenze* (Catanzaro: Rubbettino 1995); S. Bartolini and R. D'Alimonte, 'Plurality Competition and Party Realignment in Italy', *European Journal of Political Research* 29 (1996) pp.102–42.
5. For an interpretation of these elections according to the model of competition prevalent from 1948, see P. Corbetta, A. Parisi and H. Schadee, *Elezioni in Italia. Struttura e tipologia delle consultazioni politiche* (Bologna: Il Mulino 1988) p.456. Taking into account the new features of the 1987 elections, they typify it as *'smobilitazione frenata'* ('dampened demobilisation') which is one of the analytical categories (the other being 'mobilisation') they use to assess elections after 1948. From 1992 onwards, it becomes impossible to use their model based on the alternation of the two types between elections, because the basic structure of competition changes significantly. To use their words, we can no longer speak of 'demobilisation *within* the model, but of demobilisation *of* the model' (p.458). See also R. Cartocci, *Elettori in Italia. Riflessioni sulle vicende elettorali degli anni '80* (Bologna: Il Mulino 1990).
6. G. Sartori, 'European Political Parties: The Case of Polarized Pluralism', in J. La Palombara and M. Weiner (eds.) *Political Parties and Political Development* (Princeton UP 1966); and G. Sartori, *Parties and Party Systems. A Framework for Analysis* (Cambridge UP 1978).
7. This is the choice of A. Pappalardo, 'Dal pluralismo polarizzato al pluralismo moderato. Il modello di Sartori e la transizione italiana', *Rivista Italiana di Scienza Politica* 26 (1996), pp.103–45.
8. On 'imperfect bipartism', see G. Galli, *Il bipartitismo imperfetto* (Bologna: Il Mulino, 1967); and idem, *Dal bipartitismo imperfetto alla possibile alternativa* (ibid. 1975).
9. On this subject, see A. Chiaramonte, 'Gli effetti distorsivi del nuovo sistema elettorale', in Bartolini and D'Alimonte, *Maggioritario ma non troppo* (note 4) pp.373–400.
10. At most we can discuss how to describe it: that is, what criteria we should adopt to count the number of important parties. On this point see Sartori, *Parties and Party Systems* (note 6) pp.121–5. It must be said that Sartori's counting rules do not work well in the fluid situation described above. For more on this, see the conclusion of this section.

11.  Note that for both chambers in the north, where the presence of the Lega produces a tripolar dynamic, such votes are more numerous.
12.  See Pappalardo, 'Dal pluralismo polarizzato al pluralismo moderato' (note 7). The difficulty of counting the number of party units is demonstrated by Pappalardo, who, before the elections, maintained that the parties which 'counted' numbered only five: AN, FI, PPI, PDS and RC. The exclusion of the Lega from the list of parties with coalition or blackmail potential is almost certainly misguided even before the 1996 elections, taking into account its pivotal role in the Berlusconi government and its fall, and in the subsequent Dini majority.
13.  I. Diamanti and R. Mannheimer 'Introduzione', in idem, *Milano a Roma* (note 4) pp.vii–xxii and G. Sani, '1992: la destrutturazione del mercato elettorale', *Rivista Italiana di Scienza Politica* 22 (1992) pp.539–65.
14.  The volatility index is calculated using the classic formula. It is worth noting that in between the data for 1992 and 1994, we have tried to reduce to a minimum the artificial volatility resulting from the change of names and from the merger and splitting of parties. In the former case, we consider a party to be new only when it has no link with the past. For example, the Pact for Italy (*Patto per l'Italia*) is considered a continuation of the DC in 1992, whereas the Segni Pact (*Patto Segni*) is considered a new party. At the same time, the various Green lists in 1992 have been compared with the single Green list in 1994. Naturally, FI is treated as a brand new party.
15.  For these aspects, linked to the mathematical significance of volatility indexes, see S. Bartolini, 'La volatilità elettorale', *Rivista Italiana di Scienza Politica* 16 (1986) pp.363–400.
16.  P. Segatti, 'Le elezioni del marzo 1994. Un caso di terremoto elettorale che conserva quanto distrugge?' (forthcoming paper).
17.  However, the Greek data should be treated with caution. No matter how much one has tried to reduce artificial volatility, the turmoil of the Greek party landscape makes comparison over time very difficult.
18.  For a detailed discussion of the model and of the three macro-process indicators, see S. Bartolini and P. Mair, *Identity, Competition and Electoral Availability. The Stabilisation of European Electorates, 1885–1985* (Cambridge, UK: Cambridge UP 1990) pp.286–308.
19.  L. Morlino 'Crisis of Parties and Change of Party System in Italy', *Party Politics* 2 (1995) pp.5–30.
20.  G. Pasquino, 'Bilancio della preferenza unica e futuro della riforma elettorale', in idem (ed.) *Votare un solo candidato. Le conseguenze politiche della preferenza unica* (Bologna: Il Mulino 1993).
21.  Segatti, 'Le elezioni del marzo 1994' (note 16) pp.6, 7 and 11.
22.  Bartolini and D'Alimonte, 'Plurality Competition and Party Realignment' (note 4) pp.102–42.
23.  For a detailed analysis of these concepts see R. D'Alimonte, 'Democrazia e competizione', *Rivista Italiana di Scienza Politica* 19 (1989) pp.301–20.
24.  Bartolini and D'Alimonte, *Maggioritario ma non troppo* (note 4).

# Politics and the Mass Media in Italy

## LUCA RICOLFI

*This examination reviews the changes which have occurred in the links between politics and the mass media in recent years in Italy. It should be stressed that such an analysis must be largely conjectural. Although empirical studies analysing media content are fairly numerous, there are very few touching upon the two areas which are essential for adequately reconstructing the events of the last decade, namely a vertical study, through panel data or comparable measures, of the evolution of public opinion,[1] or a study of the effects of the media on electoral behaviour. This analysis is divided into three sections. The first describes some of the changes which have occurred over the last few years in the links between mass media, the Italian public and the political system. The second presents the available empirical evidence on the effects of television on electoral behaviour. Finally, the third discusses various problems relating to the regulation of political communication in the mass media (the so-called par condicio – equal access regulation).*

### LINKS BETWEEN THE POLITICAL SYSTEM AND THE MEDIA

Reconstructions of the links between politics and the mass media in Italy have been frequent in the post-war period. The majority of commentators seem to agree on distinguishing between at least five periods. The first of these, extending from the immediate post-war period until the introduction of television into Italy around 1954, is characterised by the political system's domination of the media. The formation of public opinion stemmed mainly from the mass political parties – the Christian Democrats (DC), the Communists (PCI) and the Socialists (PSI) – and in the case of the intellectual élite, via the classic mechanisms of mediation by leaders of opinion. In the following 15-year period, from the birth of television to the outbreak of the student and workers' revolts, television caught up with the classic media of radio, newspapers and periodicals, and soon became the main information source for the bulk of the population. During the regional elections of 1960, the TV programme, *Tribuna Elettorale*, first appeared. This provides a good illustration of the relationship between television and politics in the 1960s: television, far from developing an autonomous role in political innovation and content, instead restricted itself to offering existing political parties a channel for communicating their respective manifestos.

The subordination of television to the political parties began to break down towards the end of the 1960s, with the concomitant onset of a difficult period of political upheaval – the student and workers' revolts, 'Red' (left-wing) and 'Black' (right-wing) terrorism, feminism, the first referendum conflicts and the crisis of the DC. Whilst remaining heavily dependent upon the party system, television used the volatility of civil society to gain some measure of independence from the political system. Giving society its own voice permitted television to contribute to the political renovation and cultural modernisation of the country.[2] This slow (and incomplete) development of independence of television from politics proceeded along two main lines: structural innovation and the diversification of supply. In the period from 1968 until the mid-1970s,[3] various experiments in political broadcasting were tried: open-house debates, popular tribunes, self-compiled propaganda, etc. At the same time, the process of pluralising televisual broadcasting, which a few years later led to the law reforming the RAI (State broadcasting corporation),[4] began with the creation of the third RAI channel, mainly contracted to the PCI, and to the birth of commercial television.

In the decade and a half which spanned the middle of the 1970s to the end of the 1980s, the situation changed once more. The end of the collective movements coincided with the emergence of an apparently renovated PSI, led by Bettino Craxi, and built on the ruins of left-wing unity, the marginalisation of the PCI, and an organic alliance of most of the small parties (except the fascist MSI) with the DC in the so-called *pentapartito* (five-party) alliance. The history of the *pentapartito* is also that of the gradual but inexorable takeover of the RAI. Having lost their vitality and their links with civil society, the Italian parties found the carving up of the broadcasting network – and of other sectors[5] – the best means of survival and self-perpetuation. Simultaneously, commercial television grew in size and power, especially in its ability to guide Italy's cultural modernisation. After an initial period of excessive proliferation, small private channels (of which there were almost one thousand at the beginning of the 1980s) yielded to the stronger entrepreneurs, and were virtually all absorbed by the beginning of the next decade. At the end of the 1980s, with the purchase of almost the entire commercial network by Silvio Berlusconi and his company Fininvest (now Mediaset, after the floating of the shares on the securities market), radio and television had developed into a duopoly, based on a division of the audience between private and public, the latter forming a kind of 'petrified pluralism' through the distribution of offices and sectors within this 'public' service. The so-called Mammì law,[6] which regulated radio and television broadcasting in Italy, served only to duplicate this situation in the legal domain.

However, even if the control of the media, both public and private, by the political system remained as solid as ever, the 1980s saw a major transformation of the relationship between the two. Through the influence of commercial television, this decade saw political parties first using advertising slots, and then politicians experimenting with new channels of communication, such as appearing on talk shows and entertainment programmes. The relationship between television and politics switched in many respects to one of mutual exchange. Whilst it is certainly true that the parties controlled television through job appointments (for the RAI) and concessions (for private channels), it is also true that the means of communication was always firmly in the hands of the operators, who consequently used politicians to glamourise their shows.

With the 1990s, this arrangement again began to change. The first evolution, very gradual and almost imperceptible, was the increasing amount of air-time given over to new political themes. The *Lega Nord* (LN – Northern League) of Umberto Bossi and the referendum movement of Mario Segni, while not actually created by the media, benefited from a boost in publicity that would have been unthinkable before television. Then, very gradually, the political system began to spiral out of control following the *'Mani Pulitie'* ('clean hands') affair, resulting in the electoral trouncing of the *pentapartito* in the elections of 6 April 1992, and the victory of the supporters of a referendum, finally held on 18 April 1993, which instigated a change in the electoral law towards a majoritarian system.

The battle between the old and fading nomenclature and the new political élites (those who were pro-referendum, members of the Lega, and ex-fascists who had previously always been excluded from the sharing-out of broadcasting) considerably broadened the role of the media which, within the space of a couple of years, found itself not only fulfilling its traditional function of agenda-setting, but also acting as the cog in the transition from old to new, from the first to the second Republic. This process culminated with the entry of Silvio Berlusconi into the fray, after the creation of *Forza Italia* (FI).

Although accepting that the role of the television channels which Berlusconi controlled directly was anything but marginal in FI's victory in the 1994 elections (as shown in sections three and four below), the key to Berlusconi's success is less his ability as a communicator (an aspect which has been over-emphasised) than his faultless timing, and the means which he used act. During a period when change was the most pressing objective, in the context of a media which was striving ever harder to create new 'spectacles', a brand new party like FI was by definition already ahead of the field. Television relies upon events, and Berlusconi's chief success was turning this political novelty into exactly that. Leaving aside the *nature* of the reaction to it by the various national channels, the birth of FI was the central event in politics for many weeks, becoming the yardstick by which other actors were measured. More fundamental even than media control was the electoral affinity with the product, and the consequent victory for Berlusconi.

After the victory of the right in the elections, and despite the growing interference of politics in television, which culminated in the appointment of the new Council for the Administration of the RAI,[7] the power of journalists over politics otherwise grew. Politics in the 1990s has an ever increasing reliance upon television, and this is not lost upon those who are working in it. As individuals they can be in the vanguard of political and economic power; but together they are propelled by a logic which is often in contradiction with their political counterparts. The realm of televisual information is acting more and more like a lobby, pursuing its own interests and ignoring the political affiliations of its members.

These changes can be illustrated by the reactions to the drawing up of the 'Gambino' law on *par condicio* – (equal access) – which aims to introduce some rules into the management of political broadcasting during elections.[8] Despite many of these regulations being inspired by the left, the editorial staff of RAI 3 – the channel closest to the *'Progressisti'* (Progressives' alliance) of the left – has been the fiercest critic of the bill, not because of its effectiveness in combating the abuse of television, but because of its negative effects on journalistic 'freedom'. Similar reasoning can be ascribed to other journalistic initiatives, such as the *'Abbonato alza la voce'* ('Subscribers, Raise your voices') campaign, the *'Telesogno'* project led by two presenters, Costanzo and Santoro,[9] and more generally the attitude of the media as a whole during the referendum on televisual information (April 1995). In all of these cases, televisual information has become a leading political issue, covering personal interests which are often opposed to the powers on which they depend.

Despite the resistance and hostility of those in broadcasting, the rules on equal access have had some sort of impact on the form of political communication. In the 1996 electoral campaign, the format of politics on television underwent a fundamental restructuring[10] and the context of competition seemed less inclined to presenting politics as a show. Furthermore, faced with the new regulations, the producers tried to synthesise them, adapting the style of political propaganda to the new equal access regime. This contributed to the cooling of competition, and to the maintenance of the broadcasting élites at the centre of political communication.

The result of these changes has been a new type of relationship between the media and politics. Midway through the 1990s, politics and journalists find themselves linked in a perverse kind of Laocoontian embrace.[11] The heat of the political and economic battles has certainly increased the reliance of journalists and their careers upon the strategies of opinion leaders. However, the centrality of television in information supply has also changed the face of politics, making it more dependent upon access to mass communication.

In this game of mirrors and exchanges between the media and the political system, the main losers are the audience. Especially during the years straddling the 11th and 12th legislatures (the three-year term from 1993 to 1995) the 'spectacularisation' of political competition opened the doors to talentless personalities with so-called 'gifts' of aggression, verbal pugnacity and domineering manners. Furthermore, the appearance of many new political groups allowed these same politicians to use the mass media ever more unscrupulously. Desperately searching to remind the voters of their existence, leaders on the left and on the right took on board a new method of survival: the continuous production and reproduction of artificial events. Slogans guaranteeing an interview; blazing declarations triggering polemic; broken alliances which were immediately patched up again; insults against adversaries which had to be countered, and which were already claimed to be responses to previous slander; and statements whose seriousness was inversely proportional to the electoral strength supporting them – these were the means by which politicians fought on television and in the newspapers, and the journalists were left to cover a political agenda which had very few *real* events to offer.

Similarly – and this should be seen as probably the most important effect of the changes since 1989 – the complex relationship between information and political alliances changed. At the point when the main interest of the media was in increasing its own freedom, the regulation policy traditionally promoted by the left finally met the interests of the broadcasting élite head on. A broadcasting network which aims to maximise its own freedom does not need to be controlled by the political right to be in tune with it. It is only natural that today, the right being the foremost supporter of market forces and deregulation in television, the latter sector should lean towards that particular political camp. The left, which for half a century has been accustomed to providing patronage for cultural movements, or at least major branches of them, does not seem to be fully aware of this major change. Winning the 1996 elections, and the probable future alignment of state television with them as a result, only makes it more difficult for the left to adapt to this change in the relationship between the political system and the media.

THE EFFECTS OF TELEVISION ON VOTING: THE 1994 ELECTIONS

The electoral campaign of 1994 was exceptional for many reasons. The 1994 elections were the first to take place under the new (partially) majoritarian electoral law, as well as being the first since *Tangentopoli* (February 1992). These two aspects are tightly interwoven in the mentality of the Italian electorate. The extraordinary success of the two referenda on electoral laws (1991 and 1993) would be inexplicable without the growing antipathy towards the political class which had dominated the scene for the past 15 years, under the guise of the *pentapartito*. The apparent concerns of the 1991 referendum on the preference vote and its 1993 successor on the majoritarian system were the electoral system, but the underlying and motivating force was to change the political class.

This context, characterised by loud demands for innovation, was stronger than ever in the spring of 1994, notably when the entrepreneur Silvio Berlusconi entered the arena at the head of FI. Newspapers, opinion polls and maps of the electoral space all attest to this. For example, some studies on perceptions of electoral space carried out a few months before the birth of FI do not arrange the parties in a uni-dimensional space (such as left-right or progressive-conservative axes) but in a bi-dimensional space.

Cross-cutting the traditional left-right axis, a second axis appeared, probably at the beginning of the 1990s, based on the juxtaposition of

FIGURE 1

DIMENSIONS OF ELECTORAL SPACE

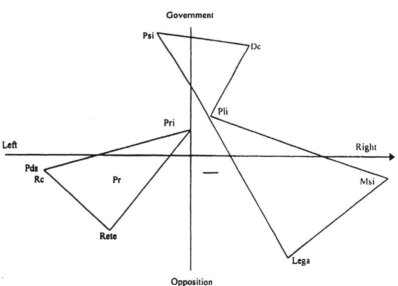

*Key*: Psi (Socialists), Dc (Christian Democrats), Pli (Liberals), Pri (Republicans), Psd (Democratic Party of the Left), Rc (Communist Refoundation), Pr (Radical Party), Msi (Neo-Fascists)

government and opposition parties, or, if one prefers, of new and old parties. Moreover, this new dichotomy became more important (or more precisely, a better description) than the old left-right axis (see Figure 1)[12].

In this situation, characterised by intense demands for change, the appearance of a new actor (Silvio Berlusconi) at the head of a new party (FI), with the technological support for the type of communication that had just become important in political competition (opinion polls, focus groups, advertising slots, political broadcasts) created a truly exceptional combination of conditions – which needs to be emphasised if we are to understand the subsequent dramatic electoral results.

In an econometric-style study of the evolution of Italian political preferences in the 1994 electoral campaign I have attempted to estimate the effects of exposure to the RAI channels (public television) and to the Fininvest channels (commercial television, controlled by Berlusconi) on voting behaviour.[13]

FIGURE 2

THE EFFECT OF TELEVISION ON THE VOTE

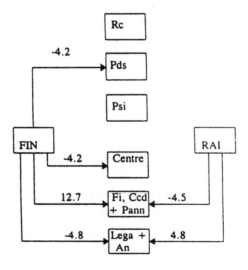

Key: FIN (Fininvest), Fi (Forza Italia), Ccd (Christian Democratic Centre), Lega (Northern League), Pann (Pannella), Rc (Communist Refoundation), Psi (Socialists), An (National Alliance), Pds (Democratic Party of the Left).

The results are impressive. The impact of the three RAI channels together is on at least five per cent of the electorate, whereas that of the three Fininvest channels is on at least 13 per cent. The total of all the movements induced by the RAI channels roughly equals zero, whilst for the Fininvest channels there is an increase of about four percentage points in favour of the centre-right, and especially at the expense of the PDS (the former communists) and of the two Catholic centre parties (the successors to the DC). To this we should add that a simulation of electoral constituencies has shown that, without the effects of television, the composition of Parliament would be very different indeed. Under the most conservative estimate, the centre parties *Partito popolare* (PPI) and the *Patto Segni* would have held the balance, and under the most likely scenario, the *Progressisti* would have won an absolute majority of seats.

These results, in agreement with both common sense and also with the most recent methodological and political science studies,[14] have caused strong reactions in Italy, especially in the broadcasting sector (worried as they are by possible negative repercussions on the level of freedom accorded to them) and amongst some mass media experts (still often adhering to the theory of limited effect). Apart from the robustness of the results, the *extent* of the effects predicted by the model is surprisingly large. Before estimating the parameters of the main behavioural equations, I expected a movement of about 3–4 per cent, whilst *a posteriori* the actual results were triple that figure. What tends to confirm the results was the emergence of two further pieces of empirical evidence congruent with the other findings, but obtained through different methods and different data.

The first piece of evidence congruent with the econometric model came from the Osservatorio di Pavia on the content of television transmissions. From these data, it is possible to see for each political party the bias in time accorded to each by the Fininvest channels and RAI channels.[15] This data can be compared with difference in vote volatility caused by the Fininvest channels and the RAI channels. Surprisingly the two series correspond almost exactly:

FIGURE 3

TIME BIAS AND VOTER MOVEMENT

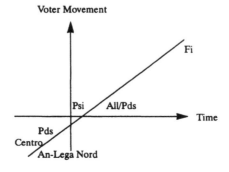

It is difficult to interpret this result in any way other than a confirmation of coverage on television – measured simply by direct coverage time – having an effect on electoral choice.

The second element of proof comes from an independent study by a young sociologist at the University of Naples.[16] The author, Angelo De Lucia, lives in the small village of San Felice a Cancello, in the province of Caserta. This locality has special characteristics because, due to the geography of the area, not all of its districts receive all television channels. RAI 3 (on the political left) and the three Fininvest channels (on the centre right) are received by different districts. San Felice a Cancello is therefore an ideal place to perform an experiment (of sorts) – and consequently a sociological rarity. Subdividing the districts according to which particular channels they receive, one can try and measure the differing effects in each. This is in substance what De Lucia did, using variance analysis to try to isolate the effects of the Fininvest channels and of RAI 3. Table 1 presents his statistically significant results.

TABLE 1

EFFECTS OF TELEVISION IN SAN FELICE A CANCELLO

|                     | Fininvest | RAI 3 |
|---------------------|-----------|-------|
| Forza Italia        | 8.9       | –     |
| Alleanza Nazionale  | –5.2      | –     |
| PDS                 | –         | 4.5   |
| Patto Segni         | 3.0       | –     |
| Others              | –4.1      | –3.6  |

Source:  A. De Lucia, 'L'influenza della televisione sul voto. Un caso esemplare: S. Felice a Cancello', *Sociologia e Ricerca Sociale* 49 (1996).

The comparability of these results with those of my study is limited by at least three factors: the different structure of political supply (in the south of Italy, the Lega does not field candidates); the weakness of the left in San Felice; and the different operationalisation of the RAI in the two studies (grouped in my study, RAI 3 is isolated from the other two channels in his). The weakness of the left, visible even in the 1992 results, particularly narrows the possible volatility of votes moving to the centre-right. This aside, De Lucia's study also demonstrates a large influence of the Fininvest channels in favour of FI (+8.9 per cent), partly at the expense of *Alleanza Nazionale* (AN) and local political groupings. Perhaps the most interesting result is the current favourable effect RAI 3 is producing *vis-à-vis* the PDS (+4.5 per cent). This reinforces one conjecture which arose from my study: it is likely that the neutrality of the three RAI channels, rather than being a by-product of the quality of their broadcasting, is a result of a talented distribution of patronage by the parties.

Even if De Lucia's results do not allow us to draw general conclusions about television influence on the vote, due to the limited sample size, they at least reinforce the results of my own study: in the 1994 elections, the extent of television's effects on the vote was of a size equal to – if not greater than – that needed to determine the outcome of the ballot (5–10 percentage points).

## A 'BRAIN-WASHED' ELECTORATE?

Should we conclude from this that the electoral result of 27 March 1994, and the victory of the forces led by Silvio Berlusconi, was due to radio-televisual 'brain-washing'? Definitely not. In reality, the depth of our study only confirmed that television almost certainly influenced the result, and that such influence was of a size sufficient to determine the outcome. But this is as much as can be claimed. It is one thing to say how much television had an effect, but quite another to say how this worked. The former describes the behavioural effects, the latter would have to explain the communicative, emotional and cognitive mechanisms through which such effects were produced.

Whilst the existence of effects from radio and television broadcasting on electoral behaviour is incontrovertible, and there is undoubtedly a serious problem of regulating the access to such a system, the analysis of such effects is open to interpretation. The influence of media on behaviour can always be read in two different ways: on one extreme, there is the theory which sees political communication as a manipulation of public opinion, while on the other, there is the opposite theory, which views communication merely as information. Evidently this does not mean that the way in which public opinion can be influenced by communication cannot be subject to empirical testing. Rather, it means that to understand what happened in the 1994 campaign we must go beyond the results of the model, and try to get inside the black box of voting behaviour.

The theory of manipulation, often promoted by the left in retrospect as a convincing (and soothing) explanation for their failure, clashes with two principal empirical problems. The first is that the two main groups on the left – the PDS and its allies – are the only ones to experience negative effects from both the Fininvest and RAI channels. Such negative effects do not appear in Figure 2 because of the lower percentage levels and significant statistical uncertainty. Table 2 presents the complete effects.

This seems to absolve the RAI from the accusation of having played to the left. But it also suggests a possible alternative perspective on voting, and one which is distinctly more worrying for left-wing leaders. The fact

TABLE 2

THE EFFECTS OF TELEVISION ON THE VOTE

| Parties | RAI | Fininvest |
|---|:---:|:---:|
| RC, Rete, Verdi, AD | (–0.6) | (–0.4) |
| PDS | (–0.7) | (–4.2) |
| PSI | (–0.4) | 1.0 |
| PPI, Patto, PRI | (1.4) | –4.2 |
| FI, CCD, Pannella | –4.5 | 12.7 |
| Lega Nord, AN | 4.8 | –4.8 |

(The figures in parentheses indicate the effects which drop below the 5% threshold of statistical significance.)

that the left on television never produces positive results in voting terms would suggest that the defeat of the left was also due to their inability to use television,[17] that is their failure to strike the correct chords in a medium largely divorced from traditional means of mobilisation (rallies, leaflet distribution, debates, etc.).

The manichean theory of a direct linkage between television and voters is also weakened by the fact that those sections of the population that turn out to be most sensitive to influence appear also to be those who 'think more', that is, who possess the greatest cognitive resources.[18] It seems that the theory of manipulation should at least provide a minimally convincing interpretation of these results. Nevertheless, the opposite approach – which absolves the media of all responsibility for the 1994 results – also encounters problems. Who would truly believe that the voters are individuals with totally free choice, blessed with complete rationality or an ability to assess relative value, which immunises them to any form of conditioning? This view not only contradicts half a century of studies on the process of decision-making, but also the surprising results presented above (Figure 3): the difference in effect of Fininvest and RAI on public opinion mirrors exactly the bias in time allocated by the two broadcasting agencies to the respective political parties.

The significant level of correspondence between the two measurements seems on the one hand to be a confirmation of the reliability of our results (otherwise, is it a near-miraculous coincidence?); while on the other it suggests that the reading of the impact coefficient should be far lighter (that is, less extreme) than those discussed until now. It may seem banal, or too close to common wisdom about politics, but our diagram (Figure 3) suggests that in general, *time is equal to approval*. Certainly, the reliability of the information, the non-sectarianism of presenters, and the balance between the different groups can also play a role, and these should surely be introduced as fundamental ethical imperatives for those working in the broadcasting sector. But, above all, visibility, time and focus – whether through advertising or report coverage – that the parties obtain for themselves are what count the most. This is the greatest lesson of advertising in the consumer sector ('As long as you get people talking about you …'); and is one of the main discoveries in international research. Television does not change opinions directly, rather it changes individual orderings by determining the salience of issues. In short, it plays a critical role in setting the agenda.[19]

If viewed from this perspective, problems such as partisan broadcasts or the freedom of voters appear in a different light. It may be that when bias or a partisan element is found in a RAI or a Fininvest broadcast, it may be due more to the planning itself than to the nature of broadcasting management. RAI and Fininvest allocated time to the different political groupings in a markedly unbalanced manner, and these differences have a significant effect on the volatility of the voters aligned with each broadcaster. The extent of the volatility caused by Fininvest is greater than that of RAI, above all because the bias in time allocated to *Forza Italia*, as opposed to the other political parties, is correspondingly larger.

This perspective considerably transforms the question of the voters' freedom of choice. The voter/viewer is not a passive subject who absorbs everything that is placed before him, but rather an information processor who reformulates the information he/she receives.[20] The crucial point is that the result of this process depends upon the quantity and content of the mix of information received. We can restate this point by saying that the voter is free by definition and that, whatever the connection between the stimuli which he receives and his behaviour, his choices are to be considered a manifestation of his true beliefs. More realistically, we might surmise that the fact that the 'menu' presented by television strongly affects our choices poses certain problems for democracy, if not to our freedom. However, before turning to this more speculative point, it is worth re-examining the effect of the media on elections under the less exceptional circumstances of 1996.

## THE EFFECTS OF TELEVISION ON VOTING: THE 1996 ELECTIONS

The lower exceptionality, or greater normality, of the 1996 elections is due to two factors. The first is a certain 'cooling' of political passions since 1994, partly due to the spontaneous reduction of tensions over the previous two years (*Tangentopoli*, rebellion against *partitocrazia*, etc.), but also because of the attempt by the Dini government (the successor to the Berlusconi government, supported by the Lega, the PPI and the PDS) to introduce elements of control and to civilise the broadcasting network. At the beginning of 1995, with the approval of the President of the Republic, the Minister for Postal and Telecommunications, Antonio Gambini, presented a bill (subsequently made into a decree) limiting the amount of advertising and opinion polls in electoral campaigns, and imposing certain regulations guaranteeing equal access to the broadcasting network and mass communication by all political groups.

The second reason for this cooling of the political climate is the absence both of a media event on the scale of Silvio Berlusconi's arrival on the political scene, and of the birth of a new party, such as FI. The entry into the political fray by prime minister Lamberto Dini with *Rinnovamento Italiano* was in no way comparable to that of its predecessor: Berlusconi created a new coalition, whereas Dini only allied himself with one of the existing alliances (Polo, Ulivo, Lega). Furthermore, Dini's entry was immediately neutralised by accusations by his adversaries of incorrect behaviour, partisan bias, lies, betrayal, all of which were immediately seized upon by the mass media and forced the Prime Minister to be constantly on the defensive.[21]

The lack of spectacle in the 1996 campaign does not mean that the public was less interested in the televisual treatment of the campaign and elections than in 1994; rather, the nature of their interest had changed. In 1994, the public's interest was suffused with emotion, caused by antipathy towards the political class, and the demonising tactics of the two adversaries. In 1996, as has been demonstrated by the Mediamonitor group in the University of Rome,[22] interest in political broadcasts took on an intensely cognitive character. The public turned to television for information-gathering and the reduction of uncertainty, rather than for the show. In spite of a reduction in the total amount of broadcasting by both RAI and Fininvest, the interest in political information remarkably increased, as revealed by the higher parity of sharing-out compared with 1994.[23]

In other words, the 1996 campaign represented a return to the old style of politics or, more exactly, an improvement in content which contrasted with the 'game of mirrors' played two years before. The use of advertising and opinion polls was drastically reduced, while the key themes of political debate returned: tax, employment, education, welfare, law and order. Moreover, in contrast to the past, the different political parties did not oppose each other by championing a single issue, but rather by promoting different programmes dealing with the same issues.[24] In the end, it was thanks to its ability to meet the public's demands that the centre-left coalition, a group with a clear disadvantage against the centre-right, managed to make up this deficit at the eleventh hour of the campaign.

The different dynamics of the two campaigns has been reconstructed using a very similar methodology to monitor television supply and public demand. Thanks to the data on political broadcasting collected by the Mediamonitor group in the University of Rome, and also to the weekly public opinion data collected by Cra-Nielson,[25] a detailed picture can be presented of the imbalance between supply and demand of political issues (Tables 3a to 3c).

TABLE 3a

THE STRUCTURE OF PUBLIC DEMAND

| Themes | 10/3 | 17/3 | 24/3 | 7/4 | 14/4 | 21/4 |
|---|---|---|---|---|---|---|
| Work and training | 46.6 | 49.0 | 50.0 | 52.1 | 53.9 | 54.9 |
| Tax and deficit | 24.8 | 22.0 | 20.8 | 19.2 | 17.4 | 15.5 |
| Welfare | 11.8 | 12.3 | 12.6 | 12.4 | 13.3 | 14.3 |
| Law & order/immigration | 2.9 | 3.6 | 3.7 | 3.8 | 3.7 | 3.5 |
| Justice/'Tangentopoli' | 2.7 | 3.3 | 3.8 | 4.0 | 3.5 | 3.3 |
| Other laws | 7.4 | 6.2 | 5.7 | 5.7 | 5.5 | 5.5 |
| Future government | 1.1 | 0.8 | 0.9 | 0.8 | 0.9 | 0.9 |
| Europe and miscellaneous | 3.0 | 2.8 | 2.5 | 2.0 | 1.8 | 2.1 |

*Source*: Cra-Nielsen.

TABLE 3b

THE STRUCTURE OF POLITICAL BROADCASTING SUPPLY FROM THE CENTRE-LEFT

| Themes | 1 | 2 | 3 | 4 | 5 | 6 |
|---|---|---|---|---|---|---|
| Work and training | 14.3 | 25.4 | 16.7 | 15.5 | 12.0 | 17.6 |
| Tax and deficit | 20.8 | 13.6 | 18.2 | 15.1 | 15.7 | 16.5 |
| Welfare | 11.0 | 20.3 | 15.3 | 11.3 | 11.6 | 12.8 |
| Law & order/immigration | 1.9 | 1.1 | 5.9 | 2.1 | 2.3 | 1.1 |
| Justice/'Tangentopoli' | 22.1 | 10.7 | 12.8 | 15.8 | 21.8 | 14.4 |
| Other laws | 16.2 | 19.2 | 16.7 | 20.6 | 25.5 | 20.2 |
| Future government | 13.0 | 9.6 | 12.8 | 16.8 | 9.3 | 13.3 |
| Europe and miscellaneous | 0.6 | 0.0 | 1.5 | 2.7 | 1.9 | 4.3 |

*Source*: Mediamonitor

TABLE 3c

THE STRUCTURE OF POLITICAL BROADCASTING SUPPLY FROM THE CENTRE-RIGHT

| Themes | 1 | 2 | 3 | 4 | 5 | 6 |
|---|---|---|---|---|---|---|
| Work and training | 8.1 | 18.8 | 17.3 | 22.9 | 26.6 | 19.3 |
| Tax and deficit | 19.4 | 18.8 | 20.4 | 12.6 | 12.2 | 12.7 |
| Welfare | 10.6 | 16.8 | 19.0 | 13.7 | 15.4 | 12.7 |
| Law & order/immigration | 3.1 | 7.4 | 0.9 | 2.3 | 3.1 | 2.0 |
| Justice/'Tangentopoli' | 16.3 | 6.9 | 5.8 | 17.1 | 11.9 | 10.2 |
| Other laws | 22.5 | 17.8 | 20.4 | 18.9 | 14.0 | 13.9 |
| Future government | 20.0 | 11.9 | 15.5 | 10.3 | 16.1 | 24.2 |
| Europe and miscellaneous | 0.0 | 1.5 | 0.9 | 2.3 | 0.7 | 4.9 |

*Source*: Mediamonitor

As can be seen, out of eight thematic areas studied, three dominate public interest over time: employment and its development, welfare, and tax and the public deficit. Contrary to what many observers believe, themes such as justice, moral questions (such as *Tangentopoli*), law and order, immigration, and broadcasting and political control are of interest mainly to the parties, whilst most voters are virtually indifferent to them. Indeed, it was due to the differing capacities of the two wings to synthesise public interests, amending their own programmes along the way, which made the difference between the centre-left and the centre-right. To measure the correlation between the content of political communication and public interest, we have constructed on a weekly basis an index of the shift between public expectations and the composition of the two camps' communications to the voters.[26] The difference between the shift on the centre-right and that of the centre-left was compared with the change in strength of the two camps (a simulation of the single vote for the Lower Chamber) collected in an electronic panel-study by Cra-Nielsen.

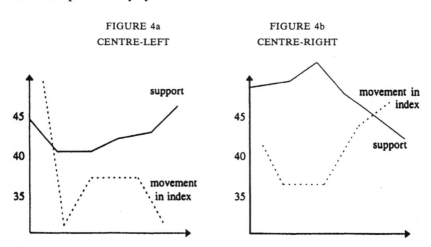

FIGURE 4a                          FIGURE 4b
CENTRE-LEFT                        CENTRE-RIGHT

The link between the shift in the composition of the parties' messages and the evolution of electoral support is quite evident. During the first three weeks, allowing for fluctuations, the movement in the index on the centre-left (Figure 4a) is greater than that of the centre-right (Figure 4b), with the centre-left suffering an electoral deficit of between about four and eight percentage points. At the beginning of the fourth week, the centre-left index begins to fall, as opposed to the centre-right's which rises. Correspondingly, the electoral handicap for the centre-left drops, eventually becoming a lead of three points. Significantly, such a change is due more to the fall of the centre-right than to the growth of the centre-left: the defecting part of the centre-right heads in the main towards the Lega and smaller parties – local movements and the *Movimento sociale–fiamma tricolore* (neo-Fascists) rather than to the centre-left.

If this analysis of the 1996 elections has a firm basis, it would be reasonable to expect that, given the greater 'nomality' of the 1996 campaign compared with that of 1994, the effects of exposure to either RAI or Fininvest channels would be smaller. At the time of writing this article, definitive and detailed estimates of the effect of television on the vote are not yet available: but some evaluations are already possible.[27] In particular, there has been an attempt to estimate the effects that exposure to RAI and Fininvest would have had just on the choice between centre-left and centre-right.[28] If we analyse these first estimates, we see the following (Table 4):

TABLE 4

EFFECTS OF TELEVISION ON 1996 ELECTIONS (INITIAL ESTIMATE)

|  | Centre-left | Centre-right |
|---|---|---|
| RAI | 2.8 | –2.8 |
| Fininvest | –3.9 | 3.9 |

Similarities with the 1994 results are quite minimal: they have in common simply that exposure to television broadcasting has some effect on voting behaviour; and the effect of Fininvest seems slightly greater than that of the RAI. The differences are far more interesting. At the moment, we can make three conjectures:

• the difference in effect between Fininvest and the RAI is much smaller than in 1994;
• the net effect of exposure to television is negligible (the effects of Fininvest and the RAI counter each other almost completely);
• and RAI broadcasting, which in 1994 only had redistributive effects within the centre-right, has ceased to be neutral.

This third conjecture is perhaps the most worrying result to emerge from the initial analyses. In spite of the RAI's position being heavily influenced after 1994 by the interests of the victors, the RAI's broadcasting during the 1996 campaign was more in harmony with the centre-left than the centre-right. This paradoxical situation can be explained by the desire of those appointed by the centre-right not to appear too supine towards their masters;[29] or, more simply, as a result of the change in majority after 1995 (the Dini government supported by the centre-left) and the traditional acquiescence of RAI journalists to the government.

The behaviour of the RAI is worrying because, in view of the history of its journalism, it is more than likely that over the next few years we will witness a pro-government stance, rather than a critical attitude towards the executive. We have become accustomed to thinking that the problem with television in Italy is the dominance of Berlusconi; and this is true to a certain extent. However, it is possible that over the next few years, the nature of this problem will change drastically. Fininvest's power is set to change after the judgement of the Constitutional Court which fixed a limit of two national channels per private owner;[30] on the other hand, there does not seem to be any move to reduce the acquiescence of the public service towards the government.

EQUAL ACCESS, BUT FOR WHOM?

In Italy, the term *par condicio* means the right of all political actors to equal access to mass communications. Until now, the regulations on equal access, contained in a series of decrees, have been applied in the 1995 regional elections, and to the 1996 legislative elections. The most severe criticisms of equal access stem from two main actors: the centre-right coalition and the broadcasting world as a whole, including many RAI 3 journalists. The regulations which govern opinion polls, advertising and, above all, the time allocated to each party are seen as an intolerable imposition on the freedom of expression, a bureaucratic and authoritarian means of regulating broadcasting.

There are many other facets to this argument, not least the idea that regulating, controlling and sanctioning on the basis of *content* is impossible, even from a technical point of view, due to the sheer size of the sector. In the west, the strength and the appeal of *laissez-faire* arguments regarding information are based on systemic considerations linked to the size and complexity of the structures which are being controlled. But, amongst the critiques of par *condicio,* there is also an underestimation of the unique position of Italy as regards broadcasting. Not only is almost the entire commercial network controlled by one individual, who also happens to lead of one of the two major political camps, but there are also two socio-historical facts of primary importance: the meagre professionalism and independence of a large number of journalists; and the long tradition of dependence of television journalists on political forces.

A more general anomaly should be added to these, one on which all discussion of links between politics, culture and means of mass communication can be based. Among western countries, Italy has the lowest average level of education and the largest cultural gap between young and old. But most importantly, it is the country in which linguistic unity has occurred most recently, and almost entirely because of television. In Italy, as opposed to other countries, high culture – learned in school, through reading and through written media – does not form a solid traditional foundation onto which television has been added, but rather something which, for about half the population, has been something of mysterious taboo area, which they would not know how, or indeed wish to, deal with. More than any other Westerners, Italians have been homogenised by television. Many have learnt to speak, to think, and even to read and write through television. Television is not simply *one* means of communication, but – for the majority of the population – the *only* means of communication, almost to the point of being an element of collective identity. This is also probably the reason why the referenda on television were won by the pro-Fininvest camp which promised to protect the integrity of radio and television broadcasting. But, above all, this is the reason why in Italy, with all its peculiarities, the problem of regulating radio and television has become an extremely delicate business. This is why it is difficult to give a balanced assessment of the equal access regulations.

The claim that journalists have the right to produce information without interference or external influence is sacrosanct. However, this claim would be more credible if its subjects could claim a long tradition of professionalism and independence, rather than their sad heritage of servitude to economic and political power. Evaluation of the equal access regulations is also difficult on purely technical grounds, and merely at the level of their effectiveness in comparison with their scope. It is true that many of them are complicated, muddled and consequently difficult to implement securely and on time. Furthermore, it is also true that the so-called *'autorità garante'* (regulating authority) has the means neither to survey the implementation process, nor to bring sanctions into force quickly enough to be effective. Nevertheless, what can be said is that, in the last two campaigns – the 1995 regional elections and the 1996 national elections – the conflict between the two camps has been decidedly more civilised than in 1994, and attention to content has been much higher. The role of a regulation is not only to prevent or punish certain behaviour, but also to discourage it, or at least to make it less likely. From this point of view, we cannot rule out the possibility that the improved electoral climate is in part a result of the equal access regulation. However debatable, intricate and difficult it may be to enforce generally, it is possible that its mere existence, backed up by observers, monitors and claims to legitimacy, may have produced in both groups and individuals a more cautious, intelligent and generally well-balanced style of communication, or simply more willingness to observe and limit oneself, if not actually to censure.

Beyond the judgements that can be made of the effectiveness of equal access regulation, there remains the fact that all debate on radio and television broadcasting in Italy revolves around the problem of competitive equality in politics. The close integration of political and media systems, and the frequent exchange of roles and functions between broadcasters and politicians, has reduced this question to little more than an internal problem of the politico-journalistic establishment. The logic of equal access regulation follows the logic of regulations which prevent unfair competition in the economic and advertising sectors. This perspective would seem to be reasonable but narrow. In the economic sphere, it is not simply reciprocal rights to market competition which are protected, but also the rights of consumers. It is not clear why the same principle does not apply to television broadcasting in general, and to the politico-electoral sphere in particular. For next to the rights of the politicians are those of the voters. There are times when there is no reason to find in favour of Party A over Party B, but rather to respect the clear right of the viewer/citizen/voter.

What is this right? Simply, it is the right to truth, the right to information that does not excessively distort the facts. This may seem like a simple nicety, or maybe even a truism, but it is not. Every day, there are thousands of violations, some of which are serious, to the right to truth which are invisible and go unpunished because the injured party (i.e. the public) is too diffuse or the organisation is not strong enough to begin legal action. Newspapers, radio and television know this all too well, and play on the fact that the right to clarification and to refutation has too high a price.

It is worth emphasising that this is first and foremost a cost–benefit mechanism, rather than an ethical shortcoming. Providing a documented, balanced service costs more time and effort than producing a montage of voices and agency clips. Producing a scandal sheet for spectacle or for effect pays better than performing a rigorous enquiry. The risk of economic or legal sanctions is almost always minimal in comparison to the rewards. Above all, it is the structure of prizes and punishments which makes for bad journalism. If the professional level of journalists in Italy is low, it is because there are no disincentives on producing shabby work. Neither laws, standard procedures nor moral sensibilities protect readers, listeners and viewers from bad broadcasting.

Amongst this lack of solid institutions answerable to the public, we can discern the weakness in the associational fabric of civic culture which has been the eternal thorn in the side of the Italian version of western democracy.[31] But on closer inspection, in this imbalance between the power of the apparatus and the rights of the individual, there is an issue of relevance to all post-industrial societies. The concentration of media ownership occurring throughout the world, together with a growing dependence of citizens on information sources, means it will become progressively more difficult to guarantee both the freedom of expression and the right to truth – or more prosaically, the pluralism of information and its accuracy. *Par condicio* (equal access ) amongst political groups is only one side of the problem. The other side is the *impar condicio* (unequal access) between the establishment which controls information (the political class, state bodies, private editors, software manufacturers, telecommunications companies, etc.) and the individual users who are always much weaker and more dependent on a system they cannot easily influence.

To resolve this problem, there have been as many *laissez-faire* and neo-conservative suggestions as there have been interventionist ones.[32] The former, whilst right to emphasise the impossibility of governing the enormous flow of information channelled by the media, seem to ignore the problems of the degradation of communication that this logic brings. The latter, whilst right to point out such dangers, do not seem to have taken on board the kernel of truth to be found in laissez-faire theory, that is, the *technical* impracticality of governing a media system via its content. The problem of integrating freedom of expression, pluralism of radio and television broadcasting, and the rights of the users to a minimum of accuracy in information does not seem to be uniquely Italian. The media landscape of the next few years will very much depend on the way in which this particular problem is confronted.

## NOTES

1. The unique exceptions being the studies on 'The reading habits of Italians' carried out by Istat every six to seven years, and opinion surveys by the RAI agency. These could potentially be valuable sources, but are underused and are almost completely unknown in sociological research.

2. This partial increase in the autonomy of information from political influence is relevant not only to television but also to the printed word. Notably in not directly political areas, such as divorce, newspapers assumed a very important role in sensitizing and educating, removing a noticeable amount of influence from the traditional party links. See C. Marletti, 'Il 'potere dei media': sulla crescente interazione fra comunicazione e politica', *Il Mulino* 4 (1983).

3. The mid-1970s is considered by most authors writing on the evolution of the media as a watershed, even if the year held to be the turning point is not always the same. In his *Dalla Tv di partito al partito della Tv* (Florence: La Nuova Italia 1995), Edoardo Novelli, for example, isolates the 1976 elections as the pivot, whereas Peppino Ortoleva, in his very original reconstruction of 'ventennio a colori' ('20 years in colour'), takes the referendum on divorce as his point of departure. See P. Ortoleva, *Un ventennio a colori. Televisione privata e società in Italia (1975–1995)* (Florence: Giunti 1995).

4. At the institutional level, the first clear indication of the new tendency was supplied by the Constitutional Court judgement no. 226, July 1974, which concerned the incompatibility between monopoly ownership of the means of mass communication and pluralised society. See *Novelli, Dalla Tv di partito al partito* (note 2) p.132.

5. As became clear after 1992, with the advent of inquiries into all aspects of society, 'sharing out' is a phenomenon occurring everywhere, and not just in information: 'At the moment when the great wave of political participation began to recede, the first manifestations

of society being highly dominated by the parties began to emerge. Still supported by mass membership, the parties set out to occupy all available spaces, a process which culminated in the 1980s' (Novelli, note 2, p.147).

6. The 'Mammì law' (from the name of its proposer, the Republican party deputy Oscar Mammì) refers to law no.223 of 1990, which for the first time regulated radio and television broadcasting, which had grown enormously during the 1980s.

7. As of the summer of 1994, the state management of television was regulated by a long series of decrees ('Urgent dispositions for the restructuring and reorganisation of the RAI'). The first of these in particular gave the Presidents of the two Chambers the power to select members of the governing council. In 1994, the two presidents (Irene Pivetti and Carlo Scogna-miglio) were both members of the centre-right (Irene Pivetti was a member of the LN until summer 1996 when she was expelled for her refusal to adopt Bossi's separatist line in place of federalism, Carlo Scognamiglio of FI).

8. The bill by Minister Gambino was never passed into law, but rather into a series of decrees, each issued at a different electoral expiry date (regional elections, single constituency by-elections, referenda, legislative elections).

9. Maurizio Costanzo and Michele Santoro are two of the most well-known presenters of current affairs programmes – the first on *Canale 5* (*Fininvest*), the second on RAI 3 (the public channel close to the PDS). In the course of 1994 and 1995, the two presenters discussed on many occasions the possibility of creating a third television group in Italy, which would be autonomous from the RAI and Fininvest. The project was named '*Telesogno*' ('Dream TV') by the mass media.

10. M. Morcellini, forthcoming in *Problemi dell'informazione*.

11. Laocoontes, a Trojan priest, was crushed to death with his two sons by two enormous serpents.

12. L. Ricolfi, 'Politica a quante dimensioni', *Il Mulino* 1 (1994) and Left, voice and God. 'Riflessioni sulla geometria del mercato Macao elettorale', *Micro & Macro Marketing* 1 (1994).

13. L. Ricolfi, 'Quanti voti ha spostato la tv', *Il Mulino* 6 (1994).

14. L. M. Bartels, 'Messages Received: The Political Impact of Media Exposure', *American Political Science Review* 2 (1993) pp.267–85.

15. F. Rositi, 'Sette televisioni nazionali quasi ventimila casi', *Problemi dell'informazione* 3 (1994).

16. A. De Lucia, 'L'influenza della televisione sul voto. Un caso esemplare: S. Felice a Cancello', *Sociologia e Ricerca Sociale* 49, 1996.

17. This incapacity can either be attributed to the limitations of the *Progressisti*'s leadership (Achille Occhetto in the 1994 elections) or, more generally, to the culture and mentality which is typical of the left in Italy. Alberto Abruzzese, *Elogio del tempo nuovo. Perché Berlusconi ha vinto* (Genova: Costa & Nolan, 1994) supports the latter explanantion.

18. Ricolfi, 'Quanti voti ha spostato al tv' (note 13).

19. On the theory of agenda-setting, see, e.g. M.E. McCoombs and D.L Shaw, 'The Agenda Setting Function of the Mass Media', *Public Opinion Quarterly* 2 (1972) and M.E. McCoombs, and L. Mastel-Walters, 'Agenda-Setting: A New Perspective on Mass Communication', *Mass Communication Research* 2 (1976). For a critical account, see G. Mazzoleni, *Televisione elettorale e televisione politica. Materiali per un bilancio della ricerca sugli effetti* (Milan: Unicopli 1984).

20. The idea that certain aspects of the mind's functioning can be seen in terms of information elaboration is not simply metaphorical, but forms the basis of much cognitive psychology. See the monumental text by P.H. Lindsay and D.A. Norman, *Human Information Processing: An Introduction to Psychology* (NY: Academic Press 1977). The Italian translation is *L'uomo elaboratore di informazioni. Introduzione cognitivista alla psicologia* (Florence: Giunti Barbera 1983).

21. Prime Minister Dini presented the logo of his party (*Rinnovamento Italiano*) on 28 Feb. 1996. Both in polls prior to this date and in those immediately afterwards, support for the Dini list was estimated at 6–8 per cent (Abacus, Cra-Nielsen, Unicab polls) with a potential electorate of over 10 per cent. In the following weeks, support dropped

noticeably to 4 per cent. It cannot be ruled out that this decline was in part due to the huge number of negative statements Dini had been subject to on the right (Trojan horse, traitor, Pinocchio) and on the left (toad, lizard, villain), and the notable relish with which these labels were used in the television news. According to a study by the Studio Frasi, five times the amount of time was devoted to negative statements about Dini than to negative views of leaders such as Berlusconi and D'Alema. Only Romano Prodi bettered Dini's score (*La Repubblica*, 19 April 1996).

22. The Mediamonitor group in Rome is directed by Professors Mario Morcellini and Sara Bentivegna, to whom credit is due for some of the material in this text on the differences between the 1994 and 1996 campaigns.

23. Morcellini, (note 10).

24. I owe this observation to Professor Carlo Marletti, who formulated it during a CATTID (Centre for Communications) conference of opinion poll and mass media experts in Rome on 8 June 1996.

25. The electronic panel survey by Cra-Nielsen is a panel of families whose members are interviewed every week by modem, via a computerised interview system. On the differences between modem and telephone interviews, and on the advantages of the former, see L. Ricolfi, 'Fra incertezza e verità', in F. Di Spirito, P. Ortoleva and C. Ottaviano (eds.) *Lo strabismo telematico* (Turin: Utet 1996).

26. The index has not been calculated for the last week before the election, when references to the 'future government' could have provided misleading results. Even if the explicit occurrence of this phrase is low, it seems reasonable that with the immediacy of the vote, political parties' references to the future government might increase. In Figs. 4a and 4b, the two groups of electoral support and of the weekly shifts in the index are out of phase by one week (support at time t, as against the shift in the index in the week falling between time t-1 and t-2).

27. Among the experiments that I carried out is an analysis of those who watched and those who did not watch the debate between Prodi and Berlusconi transmitted on *Canale 5* (the largest Fininvest channel). A comparison of the two groups shows that the main effect from watching the programme was one of reinforcement: changes in electoral orientation in the last week before the election were small for those who watched, and broader for those who did not. The direction of change was the same (favourable to the centre-left) in the two groups.

28. The effects were analysed using a regression model similar to that used for 1994. The dependent variable was taken from the choice of centre-right or centre-left (with the exclusion of LN voters and those who abstained). The independent variables were estimates of exposure time to RAI and Fininvest channels. Included in the control variables were socio-demographic characteristics (treated as dummies); electoral orientation at the beginning of the campaign, measured on a 10-step proximity scales, submitted for each of the 13 parties; and exposure to other mass communications media (radio, daily press, periodicals). The $R^2$ of the regression was equal to 69 per cent.

29. I owe this conjecture to a conversation with S. Bentivegna.

30. This concerns judgement no.420, 7/12/94. See *Giurisprudenza Italiana* (1995), I, C.129 ff., and in particular the note by S. Ambrosini, 'Anti-trust e informazione radiotelevisiva: incostituzionalità della norma sulla concentrazioni'.

31. See e.g. G. Almond and S. Verba, *The Civic Culture. Political Attitudes and Democracy in Five Nations* (Princeton UP 1963), R. Putnam, *Making Democracy Work: Civic Traditions in Modern Italy* (ibid. 1993) – translated into Italian as *La tradizione civica nelle regioni italiane* (Milan: Mondadori 1993) – and R. Cartocci, *Fra Lega e Chiesa* (Bologna: Il Mulino 1994).

32. On this issue, see M. Ricolfi, 'La convergenza tra telecommunicazioni, informatica e mass media e sistema giuridico', *Mediario* 62 (1995).

# The Judiciary in the Italian Political Crisis

## CARLO GUARNIERI

*In post-war Italy the judiciary has played an increasingly significant role in the political system. The roots of this development have to be traced to the Constitution of 1948 and to the way in which it was implemented. The institutional setting of the Italian judiciary has been radically altered, in an attempt to make it as independent as possible from the political branches of government. However, for many years judicial power was somewhat constrained, with political parties exploiting the internal divisions of the judiciary. After 1992, the collapse of traditional governmental parties, partly brought about by judicial actions, has made Italy a example par excellence of judicialised politics.*

### THE TRADITIONAL SETTING AND ITS TRANSFORMATION

For a long time the Italian judiciary was structurally very similar to those elsewhere in the European continent. Especially during the period of Unification (1859–70), the influence of Napoleonic models of government organisation was very strong. Even later, notwithstanding some minor adjustments, the basic structure did not change very much, at least until the period following the Second World War. For this reason, the Italian judiciary displayed the well-known characteristics of civil law judicial bureaucracies:

- Applicants for the judiciary were selected on the basis of their general institutional knowledge of the law, as tested by written and oral exams and guaranteed by a university degree.
- Professional training and experience was to be acquired inside the judicial organisation, starting from the bottom of the pyramid-like hierarchy, since candidates for the judiciary were encouraged to enter the competition soon after graduation.
- Promotions to higher positions were granted, according to the traditional criteria of seniority and merit, by hierarchical superiors enjoying considerable discretion, with the government playing an important role in appointments to higher positions.
- The approach to work performance and role assignment was of a 'generalistic' type, whereby members of the judiciary were supposed to

be able to perform equally all organisational roles formally associated with their rank: for example, adjudicate a criminal case, a bankruptcy case, a family case or to perform as a public prosecutor.[1]

The role played by the judiciary in the political arena more or less conformed to the classical stereotype of the civil law tradition, according to which judges are – and have to be – the *bouche de la loi*, merely giving voice to the will of the legislator. However, notwithstanding the fact that judicial independence was guaranteed, a vast array of hierarchical controls and continuous oversights by Justice Ministers ensured that this role had to be performed in such a way that it did not conflict with government policies.

Immediately after the Second World War, in 1946, as a first reaction to past abuses – occurring, although with different intensity, during both the Liberal and the Fascist regimes – the guarantees of judges and public prosecutors *vis-à-vis* the executive were somewhat reinforced, even though the hierarchical character of the judiciary was left untouched. But much more important reforms were contained in the Constitution enacted in 1948.[2] Indeed, the Constitution triggered a long process which has led to a deep transformation of the political role of the Italian judiciary. In the Constituent Assembly the memory of the past contributed to a general attitude of distrust towards executive power, often seen as a potential threat to democracy. Therefore, the Constitution envisaged the institution of a self-governing body of the judiciary, the Higher Council of the Judiciary (*Consiglio Superiore della Magistratura*), two-thirds of which was composed of magistrates elected by their colleagues and one third of lawyers or law professors elected by Parliament, to which all decisions concerning the status of magistrates had to be referred.

However, after the sweeping victory of the Christian Democrats (DC) at the 1948 legislative elections, the constitutional design in the realm of the administration of justice was, at first, not implemented. At least until the end of the 1950s, the Italian judiciary was governed mainly by the higher-ranking magistrates, acting very often in full agreement with the Minister of Justice. Thus, direct pressures by the executive in judicial affairs were rare, since the hierarchical setting allowed more discrete interventions through senior magistrates. Apart from some minor cases, there were no serious tensions in this period between the higher judiciary and Christian Democratic governments.

Only after 1959 did things begin to change, leading to a great increase in both the internal and external independence of Italian judges. In that year, the constitutionally-mandated Higher Council of the Judiciary was instituted, progressively taking away the powers of the executive in the administration of judicial personnel, namely, of judges and public prosecutors. Since 1975, this body has had 33 members:[3] in addition to the President of the Republic, and the President and Prosecutor General of the Court of Cassation, ten are elected by Parliament (the electoral quorum – 60 per cent – is such that representation has been guaranteed for parties of the left, i.e. Socialists and Communists) and 20 are elected via proportional representation by all magistrates. Its main institutional function is to make all decisions concerning judicial personnel: recruitment, promotions, transfers from one judicial office to another, disciplinary sanctions, and so on. Even this summary of the functions and composition of the Higher Council suggests how it broke with the traditional bureaucratic structure of the judiciary, in so far as lower- and middle-ranking magistrates participated for the first time in decision-making processes regarding the distribution of organisational awards and sanctions, not only with respect to their peers, but higher-level magistrates as well.

The reforms of the post-war period also affected the position of public prosecutors. From Unification until 1946, the public prosecutor was considered to be the representative of the executive inside the judiciary. The prosecuting officers were members of the judiciary, following the same career path as judges, but could be transferred into the ranks of the latter group – at least formally – only under special circumstances. The prosecution offices were structured according to hierarchical principles. The prosecutor-general attached to each court of appeal had powers of direction and supervision over all subordinate offices of its district. At the top of the pyramid was the Minister of Justice. In 1946 the traditional dependence of the public prosecutor on executive instructions was abolished. The Constitution of 1948 recognised the principle of compulsory prosecution of criminal offences by the public prosecutor, reaffirmed that prosecutors had to be members of the judiciary, and proclaimed their equality of status with judges, guaranteeing their autonomy from every other branch of government, a goal that was fully achieved after the institution of the Higher Council in 1959.

The institution of the Higher Council, therefore, brought about a remarkable increase in the independence of the Italian judiciary *vis-à-vis* the executive, the traditional point of reference of its so-called 'external' independence. However, another major modification in the organisational set-up of the judiciary concerned the system of promotion. The traditional system was sharply criticised by the majority of lower-ranking magistrates, strongly organised inside their professional association – the *Associazione Nazionale dei Magistrati* (ANM) – which claimed that promotions contradicted the principle of judicial independence (or at least its 'internal' aspects) as sanctioned by the Constitution. In the face of this pressure, Parliament passed a series of laws, between 1963 and 1973, which dismantled step by step the traditional system of promotions and with it the traditional power of the higher ranks. The consequence is that, today, those candidates with the seniority required to compete for promotion at the different levels of the judicial hierarchy are no longer evaluated – as they were until the 1960s – either by written and oral exams, or on the basis of their written judicial works, but rather by a 'global' assessment of their judicial performance. Once promoted, even in excess of existing vacancies, they enjoy all the material advantages of the new rank, even though they may continue to exercise the lower judicial functions of their previous rank. In fact, all candidates who fulfil the seniority requirements are promoted to the highest ranks. It is a phenomenon that can be explained to a great extent by the way in which the composition of the Higher Council is determined, its judicial members being elected by the very colleagues they have to evaluate.[4]

By the end of this process, in the mid-1970s, the Italian judiciary had assumed considerable political significance. Its guarantees of independence, both external and internal, are considerable. Moreover, it is the only case, among democratic polities, in which the same corps of career magistrates performs both judicial and prosecuting functions in conditions of full independence.

THE GROWTH OF JUDICIAL POWER IN THE 'FIRST REPUBLIC'

As we have seen, deep changes have been brought about inside the judiciary by reforms of the status and the career of magistrates. An important phenomenon related to this development has been the emergence of organised factions (*correnti*). Due to the internal conflict over career structure, since the late 1950s, the professional associations of Italian magistrates have been officially divided into ideological factions, each with a stable, although limited, organisational structure. After a long history of divisions and reunifications, the most important today are, from left to right: *Magistratura Democratica, Movimento per la Giustizia, Unità per la Costituzione*, and *Magistratura Indipendente*.

The *correnti* have played a remarkable role in furthering the interests of the magistrates. After realising that not much could be obtained from the government – which, at least until the end of the 1960s, supported the highest ranks – they turned their attention first to public opinion, trying to enlist its support for their cause, and later to political parties. In fact, the laws dismantling the traditional career structure were passed thanks to the support of the parties of the left, and especially of the Socialist Party (PSI), during the years when it became part of the new centre-left governing majority. The Socialists were obviously interested in developing contacts with a strategic body like the judiciary and in strengthening its guarantees of independence from an executive branch they could not hope fully to control. In this situation, the traditional party of government, the DC, found itself confronted by new and powerful competitors. Its internal fragmentation, with growing competition among various factions, gave the judiciary ample opportunities for finding allies within its ranks. In the process, new and stronger relationships developed between association leaders, political parties and public opinion, as represented by the media. At the same time, the traditional pro-active definition of the judicial role came under fire. The more 'progressive' groups – like *Magistratura Democratica* – began to stress the need for a 'less positivistic' approach to the interpretation of the law by judges and the duty to take into account the principles – above all, that of equality – set out in the Constitution. The result was the development of more activist conceptions of the judicial role which, although shared only by a minority, nevertheless began to exert a slow but steady influence on judicial decisions.

As already mentioned, the demands put forward by the judicial groups were well received, above all, in the PSI. The other important party of the left – the Communist Party (PCI) – supported the reforms, but at the time had a much more cautious attitude towards them. Inside the party, there was still considerable mistrust of the judiciary, since it was perceived, according to traditional Marxist ideology, as a 'bourgeois', repressive institution. Things began to change after 1968. In that year, the eruption of mass movements nearly everywhere in Italian society triggered a new, and deeper conflict inside the judiciary as well. Some left-wing magistrates – grouped around *Magistratura Democratica* – further developed the activist conceptions of the judicial role (which were by now widespread within the profession) and began sharply to criticise traditional judicial policies. This critique was much more than doctrinal: it produced concrete judicial decisions, frequently defying the traditional jurisprudence of the Court of Cassation, and often involved the direct participation of 'progressive' magistrates in mass meetings and demonstrations. One of the consequences of these new developments inside the judiciary was a slow shift in the attitude of the Communist Party. The judiciary came to be considered a profession in which 'democratic' magistrates were also at work and whose decisions could be supportive of the workers movement.[5] This changing position of the PCI was accelerated by its electoral successes of 1975 and 1976 and by its growing involvement in the policy process.[6] Indeed, the law which introduced the principle of proportional representation with competing lists of candidates for the election of judicial representatives in the Higher Council, and which erased the last prerogatives of the judicial hierarchy, was enacted, with Communist support, at the end of 1975.

The changes in the institutional setting of the judiciary have also strengthened the role of the Higher Council. The very growth of judicial associations – a phenomenon that can also be found elsewhere, for example, in France, Portugal and Spain – has acquired a greater relevance in Italy because of the unparalleled role played by the *correnti* in the Higher Council of the Judiciary – an important decision-making body. The changes in that institution's electoral rules, especially the reform of 1975, have made the *correnti* stronger: since 1976, all magistrates elected to the Higher Council have belonged to one or another corrente (see Table 1). In fact, with this last reform the possibility of being represented in the Council has been offered to all the main groups.[7] Yet, the significance of the *correnti* cannot be understood without taking into account the fact that, by *de facto* associating rank exclusively with length of service, the dismantling of the hierarchical structure has deprived the Council of the criteria with which to evaluate magistrates when making appointments to higher positions or deciding on transfers or when many applicants compete for the same position. In these cases, since the Council finds itself in a position to choose among candidates of the same rank, – all of which, at least formally, are equally qualified – the links between a candidate to a faction or a party could become highly relevant. In other words, the transfer or 'promotion' to a given position occurs, when not on the basis of the simple seniority, very likely as the result of a deal among the factions and parties, which often support one another in a process reciprocal exchange. On the other hand, the relevance of the Higher Council is also supported by the fact that, thanks to the decline of the powers of the Ministry of Justice, it has become the most effective institutional link between the judiciary and the political sphere.[8]

In this new context, there was a slow but steady growth of judicial interventions in politically relevant matters, which were greeted with varying degrees of enthusiasm by the political class. In fact, part of it was not enthusiastic at all. Some examples are particularly interesting. The part played by the judiciary in the fight against political terrorism was, without doubt, very important. Government and Parliament granted extensive powers to the judiciary, allowing public prosecutors and investigating judges to direct criminal investigations. This trend was especially strong in the years of 'National Solidarity' (1976–79) when the PCI lent its support to the governing majority. This could be seen in the PCI's expanded participation in the criminal policy process, since many of the magistrates in charge of these affairs were well-known PCI sympathisers or, at least, sympathetic to the left. On the other hand, the PCI strongly supported the fight against political terrorism, both left and right, at the institutional level – for example, in Parliament – and at the mass level, mobilising its organisation in support of the judiciary and the police forces.

TABLE 1

ELECTIONS TO HIGHER COUNCIL BY CORRENTE (1976–1994):
VOTES, PERCENTAGES AND SEATS

| Left | | <===> | | Right | | |
| Year | Magistratura Democratica (MD) | Movimento per la Giustizia[9] (MG) | Unità per la Costituzione (UC) | Magistratura Indipendente (MI) | Others[10] | Voters |
| --- | --- | --- | --- | --- | --- | --- |
| 1976 | 755 13% 2 | | 2526 42% 9 | 2156 36% 8 | 506 9% 1 | 5943 |
| 1981 | 803 14% 3 | | 2557 43% 9 | 2263 38% 8 | 297 5% | 5990 |
| 1986 | 1107 19% 3 | | 2517 41% 9 | 2078 34% 7 | 402 6% 1 | 6159 |
| 1990 | 1337 22% 4 | 714 12% 3 | 2236 36% 8 | 1828 30% 5 | | 6115 |
| 1994 | 1620 24% 5 | 1133 16% 4 | 2854 42% 8 | 1230 18% 3 | | 6837 |

*Note*: Superscript figures 9 and 10 refer to the endnotes on p.173.

One of the most important consequences of this period was the build-up of investigative capabilities inside the judiciary, well exemplified by the growing influence of public prosecutors and investigating judges over the police forces. In the 1980s, these capabilities began to be employed in another important field, the fight against organised crime. We cannot deal here with the well-known historical strength of organised crime in some Italian region, such as Sicily, Calabria or Campania.[11] It is sufficient to note that, for different reasons, the beginning of the 1980s saw a resurgence of organised crime in these regions and their spread to the more industrialised regions of the North. Some parts of the judiciary – often, but not only, those which had already played an important part in the fight against terrorism – began to conduct important investigations in this field as well. This time, the attitude of the political class was less straightforward. While it cannot be said that it fought against judicial initiatives, its attitude was much more passive than in the case of terrorism. This statement however, applies mostly to government parties since, broadly speaking, the PCI also supported this new judicial trend, which in any case led to defining the maintenance of public order as the responsibility of the judiciary, rather than, as was traditionally the case, the executive.

The first part of the 1980s witnessed a definite growth in judicial power. Another, striking example is the case of judicial salaries. Between the end of the 1970s and the middle of the 1980s, judicial salaries were increased substantially, thanks to favourable legislation and to the even more favourable interpretations of it by higher courts, like the Court of Cassation, the Council of State and the Court of Accounts. What must be emphasised is, first, that judicial salaries have become the highest in the state sector, outpacing their traditional point of reference, the higher civil service. Second, all parties more or less willingly supported judicial demands – including the Communists who broke with their traditional stance of not supporting salary increases for higher-ranking state officials.[12]

However, as we have already noted, not all the political class welcomed this expansion of judicial power. Indeed, some groups were strongly opposed to it. The most important was the PSI, under the leadership of Bettino Craxi, even though opposition towards judicial interventionism was not confined to this party but could also be found in minor centrist parties as well as among the Christian Democrats. The tensions between the PSI and the judiciary, or at least that part of it more prone to intervene in politically relevant matters, erupted in the early 1980s in the course of the Ambrosiano scandal.[13] The aim of checking the expansion of judicial power led the PSI and its allies to back proposals for a system of civil liability for magistrates, who had hitherto been more or less exempt from it. Capitalising on widespread dissatisfaction with the performance of the judicial system and on some miscarriages of justice like the Tortora affair,[14] the proponents of the referendum were able to attract wide popular support. The move was an astute one, since those parties usually much more sympathetic to judicial interests, like the Communists, had to give in and advise their electors to vote yes in the popular referendum as well. But the Socialists were also helped in achieving their aim by the stubbornness of the leadership of the ANM, which refused any kind of compromise on the matter and asked the electorate to vote no. Therefore, the results, with more than 80 per cent of votes in favour of introducing some form of civil liability for the judiciary, was seen as a defeat of the judiciary as a whole, as it was unable to enlist the support of the majority of the voters.

The weakening of the judiciary, and especially of its associational leadership, opened the way to a more important reform: that of criminal procedure. Since 1930, Italian criminal procedure has been governed by the code enacted by the then justice minister, Rocco, which more or less followed the traditional Napoleonic inquisitory model of an instructing judge in charge of the investigation, at least for serious cases. Even though its more authoritarian aspects were removed in the 1950s and 1960s by legislative reforms and by the Constitutional Court, criminal procedure was thought to contradict the values of the new democratic regime. However, attempts at reform came up against the careful, but always strong, obstruction of the judiciary, which was afraid of losing some of its powers. Only after the referendum of 1987 was the situation ripe for the reform to be introduced, under the aegis of the justice minister, the Socialist jurist, Vassalli. A new, more accusatory code was introduced with the intent of reducing the powers of the judiciary and abolishing the role of the instructing judge. But, as we will see below, the results have not been those anticipated by the reformers.[15]

Thus, the end of the 1980s was characterised by an attempt, especially by Socialists, to resist the expansion of judicial power. The Socialist leadership found an ally in the President of the Republic, the Christian Democrat, Francesco Cossiga (1985–92), and the tension thereby created spread inside the Higher Council. But this attempt also met with the opposition of the Communists, who remained the most faithful, long-term, ally of the judiciary, and of a large part of the DC.[16]

Summing up, from the 1970s onwards, Italy has witnessed an intense process of political judicialisation.[17] The growth of judicial power was confronted by the political class in different ways. Some parties, like the PCI and, in part, the DC, have supported the trend while others, like the Socialists, have tried different means to undermine it. However, the growing political significance of Italian magistrates has given a strong incentive to the political class to cultivate the judiciary. Personal ties are difficult to document in full but they have often been reported and are based, above all, on the flourishing of extra-judicial duties, assigned with remarkable frequency to many magistrates by the political – and social – environment.[18]Furthermore, another sign of the development of such connections and of their ramifications in other institutions is, without doubt, the growing number of magistrates elected to Parliament and not-so-rare cases of rapidly advancing political careers. Personal ties often supported more complex relationships among groups, or factions, of magistrates and parties. In the latter case, there are naturally some connections of an ideological nature – the most visible, but not the only one, being that between *Magistratura Democratica* and the parties of the left.[19] But there are also different ties which might be called 'opportunistic'. In any case, such connections – that have not been without the occasional tensions and conflicts – have allowed an exchange of reciprocal favours between magistrates and parties, with the Higher Council providing a useful institutional setting for these exchanges. As a result, the growth of judicial power has in some ways been balanced by this set of informal checks.

THE POLITICAL CRISIS AND THE ROLE OF THE JUDICIARY

This 'equilibrium' has been radically altered by the political crisis brought about by the set of *'Mani Pulite'* ('Clean Hands') or *Tangentopoli* ('Bribe City') corruption investigations. The investigations leading to *Tangentopoli* began in Milan in February 1992,[20] but they acquired momentum only in May, after the April parliamentary elections. The result of the elections – a setback for the Socialists and Christian Democrats and a victory for the Northern League, scoring very good results in Milan and in all of Lombardy – triggered a major crisis among the traditional governing parties, further aggravated by the resignation of President Cossiga. In a context marked by tragic events, such as the assassination of Giovanni Falcone by the Mafia, and with executive power weaker than ever (the Presidency of the Republic was vacant and there was no government with full powers) the Milan prosecutors profited from the weakness of the traditional political class and began progressively to expand their investigations, reaching by the end of that year the national leader of the PSI, Bettino Craxi.

As is well known, as a result of judicial investigations, the traditional party system was completely overhauled in less than two years. The parties which had most participated to government – the so-called, *pentapartito* – were those hit most: some of them disappeared altogether (the Social Democrats); others were drastically weakened and lost any importance (Liberals and Republicans); others, after heavy electoral losses and several schisms, finally decided to change their names (Socialists and Christian Democrats). The most important consequence has been the sudden and radical dissolving of the most important political forces of post-war Italy, producing a crisis of the traditional networks of party power. Since the parties were no longer able to exert influence on the policy processes, the old complicities – for example, in the assignment of public works – declined in importance, facilitating the investigative efforts of the judiciary. At the end of the process, the only parties surviving were, besides the extreme right, the heirs of the Communists, that is, the *Partito Democratico della Sinistra* (PDS) and *Rifondazione Comunista* (RC) – in other words, those traditionally more responsive toward judicial demands. As a consequence of this change in the political environment, the informal mechanisms of checking judicial powers lost their effectiveness. A sign of this has been the much smoother functioning of the Higher Council since the resignation of President Cossiga – with President Scalfaro taking a more conciliatory line – and of the Socialist justice minister Claudio Martelli, in February 1993, because of his involvement in the Ambrosiano scandal. Moreover, judicial investigations into political and administrative corruption were greeted with much enthusiasm by public opinion. The popularity of the judiciary increased, with the media supporting judicial actions as well as amplifying their consequences.[21]

The context was ripe for the expansion of judicial power. It has already been emphasised how the institutional independence of the judiciary has been steadily strengthened since the end of the 1950s. We have also seen that this evolution has been followed by the development of more activist conceptions of the judicial role. However, it is the structure of the criminal process that has been the crucial factor in enabling the judiciary to so effectively prosecute political and administrative corruption. As already noted, public prosecutors are part of the judiciary and have enjoyed, at least since the end of the 1950s, the same status as judges. The growth of the prosecutors' independence has been made easier by the fact that, unlike the case in all other democratic countries – with the possible, partial exception of Germany – in Italy criminal initiative is mandatory. In other words, the Italian criminal process is governed by the principle of compulsory prosecution, as required under the Constitution itself: 'the public prosecutor has the duty to institute criminal proceedings' (Art.112). The concrete meaning of the principle of compulsory prosecution is far from clear. It 'is currently interpreted in Italy as denying to the public prosecutor any discretion in deciding whether or not to start a criminal prosecution. It is maintained, at least by the great majority of Italian jurists, that in every case where a suspicion arises that a crime has been committed the public prosecutor must request a decision from the judge, even if he is convinced of the innocence of the accused'.[22] The Italian legal system – with more than 100,000 laws on its books and frequently vaguely-defined criminal offences[23] – entrusts the prosecutor with wide margins of discretionary powers. Therefore, by requiring prosecutors to start a prosecution and to ask for a judicial decision every time there is *some* evidence that a crime has been committed, it assigns to the prosecuting authorities a task which is impossible to perform. However, the principle seems to have been very often interpreted in a formalistic way: that is, when the prosecutor finds some evidence of a crime she or he must open a file. Nothing more is required and often criminal initiatives lag behind until the statute of limitations has to be applied.

Thus, the lack of substantial controls on prosecutorial activity, which arises from the way the principle of compulsory prosecution has been interpreted, has made the prosecution virtually unaccountable for the choices it has inevitably to make. Moreover, the general structure of the prosecution is characterised by a high level of decentralisation, since the old hierarchical relationships no longer work and every prosecutorial office is autonomous from the others.[24] On the other hand, the weak accountability of public prosecutors has to be coupled with the powers they actually enjoy.

As we have seen, especially since the 1970s, the fight against terrorism and organised crime has steadily increased the role of magistrates – (prosecutors and investigating judges) – in the criminal process. The trend has not been reversed by the 1989 reform of the Code of Criminal Procedure which, introducing, at least on paper, an adversarial-style process, has given investigative powers to public prosecutors. Subsequent legislation, issued after the assassination by the Mafia of the public prosecutors, Falcone and Borsellino, and rulings by the Constitutional Court further reinforced this trend, entrusting the prosecutor to a large extent, with the power of instructing the process. Currently, the wide powers enjoyed by the prosecution and the organisational connection between prosecutor and judge, both belonging to the same corps, tend to strike an uneven balance between the two conflicting parties, openly disadvantaging the defendant, whose rights do not seem to be well guaranteed. In this context, even apparently minor elements can become significant. For example, according to Italian procedural law, a person under investigation must be notified by the prosecution. The prosecutor has some discretion over when to send the notification: at the beginning of the investigation or just before the first court appearance. This discretion, which in ordinary cases can have only a limited impact, can have a tremendous effect in politically significant cases, especially in connection with media intervention. Notwithstanding the fact that notification should not be made public, the media are invariably able to find out about it. Given the strong inquisitorial tendencies of Italian political culture,[25] a notification – which *per se* does not signal any criminal responsibility – is often interpreted as a guilty verdict and in any case cannot but damage the public image of politicians.

Thus, after 1992, free from previous restraints, the judiciary, or at least those parts willing to act, began to put to use the formidable weapons accumulated hitherto. The main field chosen was political and administrative corruption, with extremely effective results. For example, the Amato government (July 1992–April 1993) came under heavy fire: seven of its ministers resigned after having been notified of being under judicial investigation. But also much more serious charges were raised. As is well-known, one of the most important politicians of the 'First Republic' – Giulio Andreotti – is presently standing trial because of his alleged connections with organised crime.

The victory of the right-wing coalition at the 1994 election did not bring to power a group particularly welcomed by the judiciary. Just before the elections, the Milan prosecutors had started to investigate Silvio Berlusconi's financial company, and arrested his brother Paolo for corruption. In fact, the judiciary seemed to have campaigned for other groups, as can be seen from the fact that as many as 18 magistrates were elected in the leftist alliance and only four on the right.[26] Moreover, many inside the winning coalition were openly in favour of curbing judicial power. Senator Previti, for example – thought likely to be appointed minister of justice in the Berlusconi government, who ended up in charge of Berlusconi's defence – openly advocated a reform of the Higher Council in order to 'depoliticise' it and make it more in tune with governmental majorities. However, Berlusconi initially tried to appease the judiciary. He offered the interior ministry – a key portfolio since it is in charge of the police – to Antonio Di Pietro, perhaps the most popular of the Milan magistrates. Moreover, Berlusconi was the first – and, so far, the last – head of government in post-war Italy to formally meet the judicial association in order to explain his programme. In the course of the meeting Berlusconi promised that judicial independence – and, above all, the independence of public prosecution – should not be endangered by the policies of his government.

But the honeymoon was short-lived. In July the government issued a decree-law[27] granting, among other things, a form of conditional amnesty to people involved in corruption investigations and making preventive detention more difficult. This was perceived as a kind of political solution to *Tangentopoli*, as a way of stopping judicial investigations into the matter. The Milan prosecutors vociferously opposed the decree, using television to promote their cause, and mass demonstrations followed in their support. The governing coalition began to vacillate. The 'post-Fascists' in the *Alleanza nazionale* and the Northern League expressed their, at least partial, disagreement. Eventually, the government was forced to withdraw the decree, although this did not end the conflict. The investigations led by the Milanese magistrates into the financial activities of Berlusconi continued, with Berlusconi being publicly notified of his judicial investigation when attending the UN Conference on the fight against crime in Naples, in November 1994. Even though the Milan investigations cannot be said to have brought about the fall of the Berlusconi government the following month, it did much to tarnish his image. Investigations by the Milan prosecutor's office into Berlusconi's affairs continued throughout 1995 and the first trial in the case opened in January 1996.

PERSPECTIVES: TOWARD JUDICIAL DEMOCRACY?

The political significance of the Italian judiciary seems likely to endure. As already emphasised, institutional arrangements give Italian magistrates significant scope for intervention in the policy-making processes. More-over, this expanded participation is still finding a welcoming response in academic doctrine, whose legitimising role in civil law countries should not be discounted. Despite some disagreement, the overwhelming majority of

Italian lawyers tends to support judicial intervention: only the 'excesses' are sometimes reprimanded, and they are attributed to individual faults rather than to the institutional setting.

Judicial interventions will also be encouraged by the relative support enjoyed by the judiciary in public opinion, especially when compared to that of the political class. However, the support for the judiciary is a relatively new phenomenon and its strength should not be overestimated, as the results of the 1987 referendum showed. But the Italian judiciary does have some other weak points. The most important is a consequence of the virtual abolition of the career structure in the 1960s and 1970s. Since the recruitment process has remained unchanged, after entering the corps in their late twenties, young magistrates today, after a short and casual apprenticeship of more or less one year, are entrusted with judicial – or prosecuting – functions and their professional competence is not subject to further assessment, while salaries increase automatically with seniority until reaching the highest level. Therefore, the selection process is still providing the corps with inexperienced young people, while the abolition of the traditional career – with its deep, even if debatable, socialising effects – has not been replaced by other equally effective methods. In other words, institutional identification among Italian magistrates seems to be rather low, since there are no organisational mechanisms at work to ensure it[28]. Therefore, capture by outside interests is always possible, if not probable, because of the political salience of many judicial – and especially prosecutorial – decisions. Having little to gain – or fear – from the organisation, it is likely that at least some magistrates will be ready to listen to those interests, especially those able to provide them with some reward. On the other hand, the dismantlement of the career structure has further accentuated the already lax working habits of the majority of magistrates, harming the performance of the judicial system.[29] Since the poor performance of the system affects directly or indirectly large groups of citizens, they may sooner or later blame the judiciary, even though, so far, the judiciary has been able to transfer this dissatisfaction on to the political class.

Potentially most damaging for the power of the judiciary is its internal divisions. We have already pointed to the decentralised structure of the corps, where traditional forms of control are no longer in use and institutional socialisation is extremely weak: every unit – and, to some extent, also every magistrate – is autonomous from the other. This structural fragmentation is compounded by ideological and political divisions. As we have seen (see Table 1), the corps is presently divided into four organised groups, each with a small organisational structure enjoying a share of the Higher Council's seats, and, therefore, participation in the government of the corps. Even though the factions tend to coalesce strongly when common interests come into play, their divisions are rather deep and offer to external political groups opportunities to influence the corps, pitching one *corrente* against the other, for example, when appointments to key positions appear on the Higher Council's agenda. However, rectifying this situation requires the emergence of a strong external actor, which is unlikely under current political circumstances.

On the other hand, the judiciary seems to have stronger relationships with groups on the centre-left, even if it seems to be the dominant partner. The participation of many magistrates as candidates in the leftist lists at the elections of March 1994 has already been noted. The election of the vice-president of the Higher Council in July 1994 pointed in the same direction: the magistrates in the Council split their vote between the candidate of the left and that of the centre (who was elected), while no magistrate voted for the candidate put forward by the right.[30] Also, the recent case of former Justice minister, Mancuso, seems to indicate at least a tactical convergence between the judiciary and the political left. Mancuso, a retired magistrate appointed minister in the Dini government, was dismissed in October 1995 after a no-confidence vote in Parliament, which censured his policy of sending inspectors into magistrates' offices which, as in the case of Milan, were engaged in anti-corruption or anti-organised crime investigations. The votes censuring Mancuso, who was also criticised by the ANM, came from the parliamentary groups of the centre and left. However, the decentralised structure of the judicial corps, as well as its ideological divisions, prevents the development of a homogeneous judicial policy. Judicial decisions can therefore still have negative consequences for individuals or interests normally identified with the left.[31]

As has been noted elsewhere,[32] there is a trend towards judicialisation in contemporary democratic regimes. However, the extent and nature of this expansion of judicial power seems to differ from case to case and depends much on their political context. In the Italian case we should remember the importance of the authoritarian legacy. The experience of Fascism led the founding fathers of the Constitution to reinforce constitutional guarantees and, above all, the checks on executive powers. Consequently, the independence and the role of the judiciary was strengthened. Thus, the Constitution of the 1948 had *in nuce* represented an important step in the development of the relationships between justice and politics. As the Constitution was gradually implemented in the 1950s and the 1960s, the traditional Napoleonic model of judicial organisation underwent a radical transformation leading to its substantial demise. While in other civil law countries, the political branches tend to exercise influence on a judiciary organised along bureaucratic, hierarchical lines through their powers over higher-ranking judges, in Italy, even though the selection of judicial personnel is still made through public examinations at a youthful age, the internal hierarchy has been dismantled. The power of higher-ranking magistrates, as well as of the government, has been dramatically reduced, even though the political system has been able to exercise some influence through its representatives in the Higher Council.

The Italian model has also exerted a strong influence – via academic doctrine and judicial associations[33] – in other Latin democracies such as Spain, Portugal and, to some extent, France.[34] But it has been implemented fully only in Italy, thanks to the consensual or proportionalist trend in Italian politics since the end of the 1950s.[35] The decisions which step by step dismantled the traditional institutional arrangements cannot be understood outside a context in which judicial demands receive a receptive political response. As we have seen, the new relationship between the judiciary and politics, together with the growth of Socialist and, above all, Communist influence on parliamentary decision-making, resulted in the approval of those reforms that fully satisfied magistrates' demands. However, if political trends helped to reinforce the role of the judiciary, the Constitution had already provided an institutional setting conducive to a higher degree of judicialisation.

If the process of judicialisation cannot be divorced from deeper trends in the political system, what are the likely consequences of the new majoritarian trend which has emerged in Italy, at least since the electoral referendum of 1993? We have to point out that the current state of judicialisation of Italian politics is an obstacle *per se* to such a development. However, it is likely that the emergence of a stronger executive could exploit the weak points of the judiciary outlined above and lead to a containment, and even reduction, of judicial power. But, so far, the influence of the majoritarian trend, if it exists at all, has still to be felt, at least in the field of the administration of justice.

## NOTES

1. The general traits of the judiciary in civil law countries are presented in John H. Merryman, *The Civil Law Tradition* (Stanford UP 1985) pp.35–9. For a fuller account of the characteristics of Italian judicial personnel see Giuseppe Di Federico and Carlo Guarnieri, 'The Courts in Italy', in Jerold L. Waltman and Kenneth M. Holland (eds.) *The Political Role of Law Courts in Modern Democracies* (London: Macmillan, 1988), pp.161–70.
    In Italy, as in France, the term – *magistratura* – refers to personnel who are able to perform both prosecuting and judicial roles. It goes without saying that Italian magistrates must not be confused with English magistrates, i.e. lay judges.
2. For a fuller account of these developments see Carlo Guarnieri, *Magistratura e politica in Italia* (Bologna: Il Mulino 1993) pp.87–108. For an analysis of the political and

institutional developments of post-war Italy see David Hine, *Governing Italy* (Oxford: Clarendon Press 1993).

3. Between 1959 and 1975 the body was composed of 24 members: besides the three *ex-officio*, there were 14 magistrates and seven members elected by Parliament. The judicial component was elected with a majoritarian electoral law which tended to overrepresent the higher ranks.

4. For these developments, see G. Di Federico, 'The Italian Judicial Profession and its Bureaucratic Setting', *The Juridical Review* 1 (1976) pp.40–57; Giorgio Freddi, *Tensioni e conflitto nella magistratura* (Bari: Laterza 1978); Di Federico and Guarnieri (note 1).

5. Judicial decisions applying the Workers' Statute, a law issued in 1970, were highly influential in this change of perception. *Magistratura Democratica* has played a very important role in ensuring the full implementation of the rights established in the Statute. See Tiziano Treu (ed.) *Lo Statuto dei lavoratori: prassi sindacali e motivazioni dei giudici* (Bologna: Il Mulino 1976).

6. In the same years the party organised throughout Italy a series of meetings – attended by many lawyers, politicians and, above all, magistrates – on the reform of judicial organisation. See *La riforma dell'ordinamento giudiziario* (Roma: Editori Riuniti, 1977).

7. The electoral law was slightly modified in 1990, but with no important implications for this analysis.

8. We have to remember that the Higher Council is presently composed, outside of the 20 magistrates elected by the corps, of 10 lawyers or law professors chosen by Parliament, usually along strict party lines. See G. Di Federico, 'Le qualificazioni professionali del corpo giudiziario: carenze attuali, possibili riforme e difficoltà di attuarle', *Rivista trimestrale di scienza dell'amministrazione* 32/4 (1985) pp.21–60; Giorgio Rebuff, *La funzione giudiziaria* (Torino: Giappichelli 1993) pp.91–8.

9. MG was formed by splinter groups of MI and UC.

10. Includes some short-lived moderate and conservative factions.

11. See Salvatore Lupo, *Storia della mafia* (Roma: Donzelli 1993); Romano Canosa, *Storia della criminalità in Italia dal 1946 a oggi* (Milano: Feltrinelli 1995). On organised crime in Sicily, see, e.g. Pino Arlacchi, 'Mafia: The Sicilian Cosa Nostra', *South European Society and Politics* 1/1 (Summer 1996) pp.74–94.

12. See Francesca Zannotti, *La magistratura. Un gruppo di pressione istituzionale* (Padova: Cedam 1989); and 'The Judicialization of Judicial Salary Policy in Italy and the United States', in C. Neal Tate and Torbjörn Vallinder (eds.) *The Global Expansion of Judicial Power* (NY UP 1995) pp.181–203.

It is interesting to note that the ANM was able to get the support of the trade unions movement for its demands for higher salaries. See Guarnieri (note 2) p.144.

13. In 1981 Roberto Calvi, the chief executive of the Ambrosiano bank – one of the major private banks in Italy – was arrested for violating the currency control law. The Socialists sharply criticised the magistrates of Milan in charge of the case and advocated a reform of the status of public prosecutors. The following year Calvi was found dead in London and the Ambrosiano ended up bankrupt. See Vladimiro Zagrebelski, 'La polemica sul pubblico ministero e il nuovo Consiglio superiore della magistratura', *Quaderni costituzionali* 1 (1981) pp.391–9; Canosa (note 11) pp.195–203. We can speculate that Craxi saw a judicial investigation which was undermining one of his financial supporters as an interference with his attempts at reinforcing Socialists' assets in their competition with the other two big parties: the PCI and the DC.

14. Enzo Tortora, a well-known television entertainer, was arrested in 1983 and accused of drug trafficking and association with Neapolitan organised crime. He was later condemned by the court of Naples but, in 1986, the court of appeal cleared him of all charges, the court declaring that none of the original accusations had any basis in fact, but were based only on hearsay collected mainly from career criminals. See G. Di Federico, 'The Crisis of the Justice System and the Referendum on the Judiciary', in Robert Leonardi and Piergiorgio Corbetta (eds.) *Italian Politics: A Review*, Vol.3 (London: Pinter 1989) pp.25–49.

15. For an enthusiastic account of the reform see Ennio Amodio and Eugenio Selvaggi, 'An

Accusatorial System in a Civil Law Country: The 1988 Italian Code of Criminal Procedure', *Temple Law Review* 62 (1989) pp.1211–24.

16. It is difficult to define in one sense or another the DC's policies since, as it is well-known, the party was divided into different and conflicting factions. However, broadly speaking, leftist factions, being also in favour of a closer collaboration with the Communists, were more supportive of judicial positions. For example, Galloni, vice-president of the Higher Council and a prominent member of the left of the party, was always in disagreement with President Cossiga.

17. By which, following Vallinder, 'When the Courts Go Marching In' (note 12), we mean 'the expansion of the province of the courts or the judges at the expenses of the politicians and/or the administrators' (p.13).

18. The range of extra-judicial duties of Italian magistrates is extremely wide. Among them is an important role as well-paid arbitrators, possibly in disputes between state-owned companies, or by appointment as consultants for various governmental departments. For more details see F. Zannotti, *Le attività extragiudiziarie dei magistrati ordinari* (Padova: Cedam 1981) and the introduction by Di Federico.

19. See Zannotti, *La magistratura* (note 12) pp.70–155; and Sergio Pappalardo, *Gli iconoclasti. Magistratura Democratica nel quadro dell'Associazione Nazionale Magistrati* (Milano: Franco Angeli 1987).
The number of magistrates in Parliament began to rise in the second half of the 1970s: in 1992 there were 13 and, by 1994, 22. There have also been some cases of magistrates becoming ministers or deputy ministers.

20. The investigations started even before 1992, but in Feb. the first arrest was made of a lower-level Socialist politician. In the 1980s the Milanese magistrates had already tried to investigate cases of corruption, but with insignificant results. On the growing intensity of judicial investigations into the political class, see Franco Cazzola and Massimo Morisi, 'Magistratura e classe politica. Due punti di osservazione specifici per una ricerca empirica', *Sociologia del diritto* 22/1 (1995) pp.91–143.

21. See Andrea Lavazza, 'La toga e la verità', *Il Mulino* 44/362 (1995) pp.1045–58. However, in the 1980s, the degree of trust in the judiciary did not seem very high. See Roberto Cartocci, *Tra Lega e Chiesa* (Bologna: Il Mulino 1994) p.23.

22. See Di Federico and Guarnieri (note 1) p.172; and also Di Federico, 'Crisis' (note 14) esp. pp.28–35. For the general problems involved in the implementation of this principle see C. Guarnieri, *Pubblico ministero e sistema politico* (Padova: Cedam 1984) pp.125–52.

23. There are no precise data on the number of statutes presently in force. However, according to conservative estimates there are no less than 100,000 (*Il Sole-24 Ore*, 6 July 1994). An example of a crime, whose definition is rather vague, is the 'abuse of power' (art.323 of the criminal code), according to which a public official who 'in order to provide for himself or others an unjust benefit, or to damage another unjustly, is guilty of an abuse of her or his office' and still be punished. The crime has been used to prosecute many public officials.

24. Only in the field of organised crime has disappointment with the lack of co-ordination in the fight against the Mafia has led to the establishment, in 1992, of a special structure – the Anti-Mafia District Offices, at the regional level, with the National Anti-Mafia Office at the top. The latter's senior personnel is appointed by the Higher Council and is in charge of all the investigations against the Mafia and organised crime. However, the power of the National Office should not be overrated.

25. For example, since they are members of the same corps, very often prosecutors are referred to by the media as 'judges', generating a dangerous confusion between two functionally very different roles.

26. See Giuseppe Di Federico, *Il Tempo*, 3 July 1995.

27. Namely, a decree with temporary value of law, but which must be approved before 60 days by Parliament. See Hine (note 2) p.149.

28. As Edward Gross and Amitai Etzioni, *Organizations in Society* (Englewood Cliffs, NJ: Prentice-Hall 1985), have pointed out, '... the degree to which an organisation selects ... its participants affects its control needs ... [since] the same level of control can be

maintained by high selectivity and a low level of organisational socialisation as by low selectivity and high level of organisational socialisation' (pp.125–7). The Italian judiciary has a low level both of selectivity and organisational socialisation.

29. See Di Federico and Guarnieri (note 1) pp.168–70. The unsatisfactory performance of the Italian judiciary was stressed once again by the Prosecutor General at the Court of Cassation in his annual report for 1995 (*Il Sole-24 Ore*, 19 Jan. 1996).

30. The Constitution prescribes that the vice-president must be chosen from among the lay members of the Council. However, on the right, *Alleanza Nazionale* seems to be the group on the best terms with the judiciary.

31. An example is provided by the investigations in Venice into the use of public funds by many co-operatives traditionally affiliated to the PCI and the left. A new phase of investigations from the autumn of 1996 has implicated a number of left-wing figures and provoked the ire of influential left-wing politicians.

32. See Kenneth M. Holland (ed.) *Judicial Activism in Comparative Perspective* (London: Macmillan 1991); Lawrence M. Friedman, 'Is There a Modern Legal Culture?', *Ratio Juris* 7/2 (1994) pp.117–31 and Tate and Vallinder (note 12).

33. Especially strong are relations between progressive groups of European magistrates. They have recently founded an international association – Magistrats Européens pour la Démocratie et la Liberté (MEDEL) – which advocates the adoption of the Italian model of judicial organisation.

34. See Carlo Guarnieri and Patrizia Pederzoli, *Pouvoir judiciaire et démocratie* (Paris: Michalon, forthcoming).

35. See Maurizio Cotta 'Il Parlamento nel sistema politico italiano. Mutamenti istituzionali e cicli politici', *Quaderni costituzionali* 11 (1991) pp.201–23.

# Sub-National Governments in the Long Italian Transition

## BRUNO DENTE

*This analysis examines how the territorial dimension in Italian politics has changed since the fall of the Socialist regimes in eastern Europe in 1989 and the beginning of the corruption scandals in the early 1990s. Institutional changes and trends at the regional and local levels are outlined, before a study is made of the current distribution of power and resources between centre and locality. This analysis allows a more realistic assessment, than current political debate offers, of the likelihood, and possible nature, of constitutional (federalist) reform which many hope to see during the 13th legislature of the Republic.*

The territorial dimension in Italian politics has undergone considerable, but not uniform, change during the 1990s. Yet, whether these changes, and the underlying trends they reflect, are as radical, in portent, as the current political debate about constitutional (federal) reform suggests is open to question. This account analyses these changes, and evaluates their significance, in five sections. The first section provides an interpretation of the territorial dimension of party politics, before analysing, in the second and third sections, the institutional changes and trends occurring at the regional and local levels. The fourth section evaluates the current distribution of power and resources between centre and locality. The final section assesses the difficulties confronting the fundamental (constitutional) changes proposed for centre–periphery relations in the next century.

### THE TERRITORIAL DIMENSION OF PARTY POLITICS

The change in the territorial dimension of party politics in Italy has been characterised primarily by the birth, development and apparent permanence of the Northern League (*Lega Nord*). This requires some requires explanation. Much has been written on the electoral fortunes of the Lega. What is important, however, is the permanent nature of the support it has developed, despite apparent setbacks. In Lombardy, the party's historical stronghold, the proportion of votes it obtained rose from 19 per cent to 24 per cent between 1990 and 1996. It has reached nearly 30 per cent in the region around Venice and has settled at a comfortable 18.5 per cent in Piedmont. The fact that the Lega is the largest party north of the river Po is symptomatic of the significance of the phenomenon.

The reasons for this success are well known: a growing protest against the old party system that had remained basically unchanged since the end of the war; and a vague, but nevertheless radical, public awareness of the need to transform relations between central and local government, above all because of the inefficiencies of the former. It is equally well known that the electoral fortunes of the Lega have been greatly helped by growing abstentionism in northern regions, something which created a potential reservoir of votes for any political force with anti-party and radical, alternative policies. The skill of Umberto Bossi, the leader of the Lega, lay in his ability to appeal primarily to this area to consolidate an electoral consensus for his new party.[1]

From a more structural viewpoint – and this is more important to the argument developed in this essay – the electorate represented by the Lega (and, it should be added, by the other political forces of the centre-right, and specifically *Forza Italia* – FI) constitutes an important sector of society and the economy made up of small and medium-sized firms, which are most highly concentrated in northern Italy. This sector, which is responsible for a considerable percentage of the Italian Gross Domestic Product (GDP), and an even larger proportion of total exports, has never developed a strong sense of identification with Italy as a state, and above all, with the politics of Rome. However, this lack of identification was unproblematic as long as three conditions existed: (1) widespread awareness of continued economic expansion; (2) little interference by central government in the affairs of companies; and (3) a relatively strong identification of this sector with sub-national governments (and municipalities in particular). All three of these conditions have, in the 1990s, gradually disappeared.

First, it had already become clear, by the end of the 1980s, that the economic boom of the mid-decade was over and that the problem was less that of achieving further economic expansion than of simply avoiding falling behind in international competition. Second, the new demands of public finance, which were largely a result of the progressive growth of welfare spending decided on between the end of the 1960s and the middle of the 1980s, resulted in increased tax burdens on firms and individuals. When the progressive growth of regulatory policies – environment regulations provide a good example[2] – is also taken into account, it is evident that the second condition – little interference by government in the life of companies – has also given way.

The third condition was perhaps the most important, even though it has often been overlooked in political and academic debate. In the past, relations between this large and important sector of Italian society and the state had, to a large extent, traditionally been mediated by local governments. These not only provided basic services, but, from the beginning of the 1960s onwards, expanded their activities by setting up networks of social services and developing policies and infrastructures of direct concern to industry. The progressive politicisation of local government, encouraged by fiscal policies which abolished any form of local fiscal autonomy, interrupted this direct link between the world of small firms and public institutions. The development of a *partitocrazia* (the dominance of parties over all aspects of political and civil society) and the accompanying instances of generalised corruption, were significant because when a business enterprise or an individual has to bribe a party representative or public official in order to obtain something (whether legal or illegal) from a local authority, identification with the local authority inevitably declines. Furthermore, in a situation where there is even less identification with higher levels of government, there occurs a dangerous delegitimisation of the state as a whole.[3]

Italian political scientists, and political commentators, in general, have tended to underestimate the political importance of local authorities. This is because of a tendency to overestimate the importance of political parties as a channel for the transmission of society's demands and as a means by which society is organised. This has, amongst other things, made it difficult to understand the role played by strategies to develop local services in maintaining political support for the parties of the left (PCI/PDS) in those areas where it has traditionally been in power. Space does not permit a detailed treatment of this question. What should be emphasised, however, is that the disappearance of the three conditions outlined above released small and medium-sized companies as an autonomous voting block, allowing them to use their economic muscle to influence the political and electoral agenda. The consequences were threefold.

First, there were large differences in the way this vote was used in different areas of the country. In particular, the Lega emerged as decisively important in three key regions: Piedmont, Lombardy and Veneto. Second, there was a basic acceptance (verbally at least) by political parties at the national level of the political agenda of the world of small business: reduction of the tax burden, reduction of the welfare state, anti-trust legislation, privatisation, etc. Third, reform of the constitution – and particularly change in a federalist direction – became a prominent political issue.

It is legitimate, therefore, to ask whether there has not been a permanent change in the Italian polity during the course of this long transition and whether a new cleavage has not emerged, one which sets the world of small business in northern Italy against a block consisting of the worlds of big industry, finance and the unions, the latter of which identify themselves with central government institutions. Is there in fact an international comparison to be made between the path that Italy is currently following and that which led to federalism in Belgium and Canada? True, these are countries which are very different from Italy, but they share one (often largely overlooked) factor, namely a huge public debt.

Answering this question is difficult, although some factors certainly weigh in favour of an affirmative answer. The Lega's vote has obtained a certain permanence, and was, indeed, reinforced by the April 1996 elections, when the party stood on a platform which, for the first time, clearly stated separatism of some of the regions of the north as a prime objective. A related development was the formation of a mayors' movement (the so-called 'Mayors' Party') in north-eastern Italy, with the participation of members of various parties.

However real or unreal the threat of separatism may be, what is certain is that the 'northern question' is now firmly on the national political agenda. Furthermore, one should not assume that, because the centre-left coalition which won the 1996 national elections is a minority party in northern regions, the problem can be ignored. The Prodi government faces the same challenge as that facing all previous governments: that of healing the deep rift between North and South, something which – as suggested above – can be interpreted as a cleavage between the world of small business and the rest of the country.

What are the likely consequences of this state of affairs for sub-national governments? To answer this question, the recent history of institutional changes at the regional and communal levels needs first to be considered.

REGIONAL GOVERNMENT: TOWARDS FEDERALISM?

This is not the place for a detailed history of regional government, on which much has already been written. For the purposes of this article, it is sufficient to review what might be described as the principal factors which originally undermined the role of the regions, and to explore the interaction between these factors and the political, institutional and financial crisis of the 1990s.

First, the birth of the new level of government was entirely 'political'.[4] Leaving aside the role played by ideology, there is no doubt that the provision made for regional governments in the 1948 constitution (Title V, which remained unimplemented for over 20 years), and their subsequent creation in 1970, can be explained in terms of party politics. The support of the Italian Communist Party (PCI) for the inclusion of regions in the constitution was a consequence of its exclusion from the government of national unity (1945–47). The fact that Title V remained a dead letter for so long can be explained in terms of the ideological polarisation between the parties during the Cold War, and the fear of the Christian Democrats (DC) and their allies that the regions of central Italy (where the PCI's vote was strong) would fall into the hands of the Communists.

The final introduction of the regional governments in 1970 can also be explained in political terms, since it was prompted by the crisis of the DC-led centre-left coalition and the need to involve the PCI in government. This 'political' birth played a part in determining how the regions functioned, and this proved to be different, in more ways than one, from the way in which central and local government functioned at the time. The regions functioned primarily on the basis of strong ties with pressure groups and on the mediation of political parties rather than on the existence of strong and autonomous bureaucracies.

Viewed from this perspective, one can begin to understand the particular fragility of the regional governments when the *Tangentopoli* investigations were unleashed. From 1992 onwards, many regions found themselves politically decapitated due to the number of elected members incriminated. This resulted in the formation of anomalous majorities by groupings of individual councillors. In contrast with the large local authorities, the judicial earthquake did not cause the dissolution of regional legislatures and new elections; and, in contrast with central government, it proved impossible to create governments composed of technical experts, or formed from a 'reserve team' of political leaders. The result was paralysis, and the effective disappearance of the regions from the political scene. The regional elections of 1995 appear to have initiated a process of 'normal' functioning again, but to what extent this is so is still too early to tell. What is clear is that the regions have been effectively absent from the political scene during the period when the transformation of government in Italy has been under discussion.

The second factor is that the essentially 'political' birth of the regions resulted in an internal constitutional structure with an abnormally enlarged role for the legislatures. The regional constitutions, passed in the first half of the 1970s, created a situation in which an able opposition could block almost any decision – not only legislative, but also administrative – and oblige a majority to negotiate the support of the minority. Obviously this second characteristic was perfectly in keeping with a political system based on proportional representation, wide-ranging coalition governments and 'consociational' politics. But it is hardly suitable for a two party system which many commentators would like to see emerge in Italy. Hence, there is, currently, a certain reluctance to discuss the role of the regions; they are regarded almost like a poor relative of whom one is a little ashamed.

The third factor is that the regions were set up in a period dominated by policies for expanding the welfare state. In particular, they were seen as the main instruments for economic planning. It is natural, therefore, that in a period in which the concept of welfare is being subjected to redefinition and one in which planning is in crisis, the regions tend to constitute both a cumbersome and inconvenient presence, needful of a conversion that will be neither easy nor painless. This is especially so because the planning role of the regions had been made virtually impossible by the fact that the powers they had been given were only partial (because central government often continued to hold on to control over the same sectors), heterogeneous (because article 117 of the Constitution reflected a backward vision of state responsibilities) and unevenly distributed (items as different as health, agriculture, local transport and occupational training account for more than 90 per cent of regional expenditure).[5]

The fourth factor is that the regions' financial structure was, and still is, essentially based on transfers. Almost all of their income comes from central government and almost all their expenditure consists of transfers to local government (municipalities and area health authorities above all) or companies (especially agricultural enterprises). This role of financial broker constitutes one of the prominent features of the regions and has prevented them from developing a strong technical bureaucracy (which is normally formed for the direct management of public sector services).

Other factors could be added. The original territorial design for the regions was irrational (e.g. the region of Lombardy has a population of 9 million, while Molise has only 300,000 inhabitants) and there is little identification with the regions on the part of citizens. There is also a tradition of conflict in relations with local governments, which hardly ever use regional governments to represent them in dealings with central government. It is consequently not difficult to conclude that the road to strong regional autonomy, to a 'new federalist-type of regionalism' (to use current jargon), is hardly straightforward or easy.

Nevertheless, despite the above scenario, parties across the whole political spectrum – with the exceptions of *Rifondazione Comunista* (RC – Communist Refoundation) to the far left, and an element of the far right *Alleanza Nazionale* (AN – National Alliance) – apparently aspire to federalism, or at least something that resembles it, and various plans for constitutional change have been drafted. These plans, generally speaking, are based on three ideas: first, regional governments should be given responsibility for all matters not explicitly reserved to central government (a sort of reinforced 'subsidiarity' principle); second, the Senate should be transformed into a regional chamber with responsibilities similar to those of the German Bundestag; and third, the acceptance, more generally, of a co-operative federalist model for Italy. There is much less agreement, however, on the need to change the political borders of the regions and on the need for financial autonomy.

Should one conclude, then, that the transformation of the Italian state is imminent? Although moves will certainly be made in this direction (if, for no other reason, than the need to segment the huge problem of the public deficit), there are several factors which suggest that a radical transformation is unlikely.

First, the regions have scarcely participated in the debate on federalism; with a few exceptions, the majorities that emerged from the 1995 regional elections either do not want to, or are unable to, speed up development in the direction of federalism. This suggests that a transformation, when seen from the viewpoint of local government, is much more difficult than the scenarios painted by newspaper headlines. Second, even though there are conflicting tendencies in the objectives of the two main coalitions (*Ulivo* – Olive Tree coalition – on the centre-left and *Polo delle Libertà* – Freedom Alliance – on the centre-right), both favour a decentralised, but not really *federalist* system. When political leaders declare, as they have done, that 'federalism must start with the local authorities' (and in particular with the large cities), what is actually intended is less a real division of powers than a more co-ordinated institutional framework. Third, the electoral manifestos of the two main political coalitions are contradictory. On the one hand, they include decentralisation as a part of their institutional proposals, yet, on the other hand, when they tackle the problems of other social or economic sectors they tend to propose (and make promises of) central government intervention.

It can be concluded that, despite almost ten years of constitutional designs and conferences, the situation is not yet conducive to a radical transformation of the state in a federalist direction. The key issue, moreover, is less what is said about the regions and more what is said (or not said) about central government reorganisation. As has been noted by others, any federalist proposal which does not involve a radical reform of central government and, more generally, of the style of government and administration, is bound to fail.[6] In reality it is in the arena of the reform of public sector administration as a whole, and of central government administration in particular, where the federalist battle will be won or lost. There does not, however, seem to be much awareness of this fundamental point, something which will be returned to later.

COMMUNAL RENAISSANCE?

Historically, the communes (*comuni*) have constituted the most important level of local government in Italy. They are significant administrative and political institutions in terms of their functions, work force, political visibility and roots in society. Citizens have a considerable degree of trust in them and they constitute a level of government which is flexible in adapting and responding to the changing demands and needs of society.[7]

A consequence of this historical importance is that, during the course of the political and institutional crisis of the early 1990s, the municipalities adapted more quickly than other institutions, anticipating certain trends in the rest of the institutional system. Their ability to adapt was reinforced by the fact that, in 1990, the long-awaited reform of the law governing local authorities and provinces was finally passed, after almost twenty years of proposed bills and debates. The first reaction of many commentators was, in fact, disappointment.[8] Law no.142/90 changed very little, leaving the main problems unresolved (territorial jurisdictions, the electoral system, local finance, the role of the provinces, etc.). The few elements which seemed genuinely to break with the past – for example, provisions for the introduction of some form of metropolitan government – seem to have been wishful thinking: six years later they have not seen the light of day. With the benefit of hindsight, it can be said that some of the changes anticipated developments which were already in train, notably in three areas:

- The virtual abolition of external control (until then entrusted to a regional body, the *Comitato regionale di controllo*) for the large majority of local decisions, which resulted in increased autonomy and, above all, the speeding up of bureaucratic processes. Some years later the same thing was achieved for central government administration by abolishing the need for approval of decisions by the *Corte dei conti* (National Audit Office).
- Strengthening the executive by allowing most (and particularly the most important) decisions to be made by the executive (*Giunta*) rather than by the Council. Curiously, during the 1960s local authorities were in the vanguard of a tendency towards stricter control by legislatures through the setting up of district councils; now they are leading a trend towards more executive-led government.
- Strengthening of bureaucracies by giving the secretary general and senior officials considerable powers of veto. They are required to express an opinion on the legitimacy and merits of proposals made by the executive. This route was subsequently followed by all government administration through legislative decree no.29/93 which assigned powers directly to permanent civil servants.

The origins of all these changes was a growing mistrust of politicians leading to greater powers being given to the executive (and the majority supporting it) and permanent staff. Yet, as already noted, if the changes which occurred had been solely those provided for by law no.142/90, the functioning of local government would not have been that different from before. It was subsequent developments which invested the formal changes with much more importance.

The local authorities were much faster in making changes in the early 1990s than the regions (which, as already noted, despite the judicial investigations which decimated the political class, did not experience a renewal of personnel until the regional elections of 1995). In contrast, many towns and cities were, by 1993, already dissolving local councils and holding new elections under a new electoral system which not only tackled the problem of unstable majorities but also that of reforming the mechanisms of government. Law no.81/1993 provided for direct election of mayors in two rounds of voting, only the first two candidates proceeding to the second ballot, and the winning coalition being rewarded with a 'bonus' (thus ensuring it an absolute majority). Furthermore, the members of the executive were henceforth to be appointed directly by the mayor and therefore accountable directly to him/her (and necessarily chosen from outside the Council).

The result of these changes was spectacular. Between 1992 and 1993, the class of municipal politicians was completely renewed through the election of mayors who were either new to politics (e.g. Castellani in Turin, Sansa in Genoa, Illy in Trieste and Di Cagno in Bari) or different to the usual politicians (e.g. Cacciari in Venice, Rutelli in Rome, Orlando in Palermo and Bianco in Catania). Furthermore, the composition of the executives ('personally selected' by the mayors), combined with the transfer of power away from local authority legislatures, completely transformed local policymaking by substantially depoliticising it. This has had the effect of allowing people with professional experience from outside politics to be appointed to positions of responsibility – namely, to membership of the executive – inside local government, thus enriching policy-making capabilities.

Finally, a partial remedy was introduced for one of the most glaring structural weaknesses of Italian local government: finance. The financial and currency crisis of 1992 necessitated an increase in the tax burden on private individuals, and this allowed a greater degree of financial responsibility to be re-established by the development of local taxation. The introduction of the ICI tax, a local authority property tax, for which the rates can be set by individual local authorities, constituted a key change. Revenue from this tax and other minor taxes, together with income from the sale of services, has resulted in many northern cities obtaining a degree of financial autonomy that varies between 60 per cent and 70 per cent, with dependence on regional and central government transfers for the remaining amount. In short, autonomy from Rome, and accountability to the public, has been enormously strengthened.

Seen together, these changes – the abolition of external controls and the strengthening of executives (law no.142/90), the direct election of mayors and the appointment of executive officers who are not councillors, the introduction of a local property tax and the financial autonomy provided by the power to tax – have led to a new style of government in Italy. Municipalities (and provinces too) have confirmed their reputation for flexibility and a capacity to adapt to the changing demands of the public. They have been profoundly renovated and their prospects are optimistic.

This is not to suggest that there are no remaining problems. For example, bureaucratic procedures (i.e. the rules to which both local and central government must adhere) have not changed and continue to be dogged by red tape. Centralised administration and legislation remains prevalent, and consequently, local authorities find themselves obliged to obey complicated, confused and often irrelevant laws. Even elements of the recent reforms are inconsistent and have created new difficulties. For example, the celebrated separation of political and executive powers – which, as noted, was first achieved by local authorities – will have little effect while (despite the change in politicians), many senior bureaucrats remain those who gained promotion under the old regime. Moreover, the introduction of fiscal autonomy has not solved all of the financial problems of the poorest local authorities or, more importantly, the major cities. The latter provide services for a very large public and find it difficult to support these entirely out of revenues collected from residents.

Nevertheless, despite these caveats, a measure of optimism is justified, particularly in view of the current public prominence of mayors, and the fact that they seem to represent a drive for further reform in Italy. The 'Mayors' Party' (referred to earlier) is a dynamic force for change in the confused transition which Italy is currently undergoing. While, to a large extent, the mayors represent the orientations of the centre-left coalition that predominates in urban areas, it is also true that they have so far been careful not to make partisan use of their role and power. In contrast, for example, with the trade unions (which have not undergone reform), the mayors did not engage in a head on battle with the Berlusconi government; and their participation in national debate has consisted of a non-partisan case for autonomy, federalism and change. Significantly, in this respect, Massimo Cacciari, the mayor of Venice and one of the national leaders of the centre-left coalition, also leads a movement of north-eastern mayors containing members of Forza Italia and the Lega.

Much will depend on the next round of local elections in 1997, which will confirm whether the changes have been consolidated or whether the political parties have recovered the ground they have thus far been obliged to surrender. It is sufficient, at this point in time, to note that a transformation has occurred of a positive nature, in the sense that it has, generally speaking, been welcomed by the Italian public.

### CENTRAL–LOCAL RELATIONS: A REAPPRAISAL

If the developments outlined above represent real change, what implications do they have for the Italian state from the perspective of central–local relations? Answering this question does not involve identifying the precise degree of autonomy wielded by local governments. This sort of approach is not very fruitful in the context of the fragmentation of government and policy making in contemporary political systems. The real question is, in fact, more complex. Given the changes that have occurred – above all with regard to local authorities – have the terms of the relationship between central and local government shifted? Has there been a permanent re-allocation of certain resources or have the changes simply reinforced existing trends? An answer to this is important because it will reveal the degree of difficulty (or ease) involved in a move towards federalism, at the same time as revealing the limits of a 'Jacobin' approach to the problems of governance. A broadly centralised approach to governance has certainly characterised the action of 1990s governments (Amato, Ciampi, Berlusconi, Dini and Prodi).

It is important to approach the question through the issue of *resources*, a concept which has generated considerable confusion and caused many observers difficulties in evaluating the degree to which Italian government is centralised. It is worth, at this point, summarising an analysis made before the 1990s, one which examined the different types of resources which could be deployed in Italian central–local relations, and then identified the strengths of central government on the one hand and local government on the other.[9] The following picture emerged.

- *Legal resources* favoured central government. As far as the division of powers was concerned, central government had carefully limited the powers of local government, denying it any significant room for manoeuvre. Moreover, government action in general was so heavily controlled by national legislation that the main problem facing local governments which wished to initiate something was whether they were permitted by law to do so (with the likely result of being prevented from taking any action by controlling bodies).
- An analogous situation existed with regard to *financial resources*. The almost total dependence of local government on central government for

both current and capital account spending (through the *Cassa depositi e prestiti*, the state bank for local investments) meant that the position of local government was extremely weak. In addition, central government exercised close control over manpower resources; not only was the total number of employees for each local authority decided by Rome, but also each individual appointment had to be approved by the Minister of Public Works (a power which represents an important combination of legal and financial resources).

- *Political resources*, on the other hand, favoured local government. Various studies of intergovernmental policymaking found that the high degree of politicisation of local government had led to the formation of channels of influence through which mayors and other local political leaders could bring their vote-pulling powers into play. The political parties, on the other hand, seemed neither capable of, nor interested in, imposing policy-making decisions on local government from above.
- Local government monopolised *information resources*. Central (and also regional), government lacked the resources for collecting data at grassroots level, with the result that local authorities, partly because of their close contact with the general public, but also because they had control of the census and registry offices, monopolised the possession of the data required for policymaking and administration at higher levels of government.
- The situation regarding *technical resources and know-how* was more complex. The extremely heterogeneous nature of local governments, and the variety of fields in which they operate, made it difficult to assess whether these resources (which essentially refer to the quality of local government bureaucracies) were more important than those that central government was able to deploy. It was concluded that these resources were probably decisive, and that it was the better know-how and skills of the northern Italian local authorities which explained their stronger position *vis-à-vis* central government, when compared with local authorities in the South.

To what extent has the situation described above changed after the political upheaval of the early 1990s?

- As far as *legal resources* are concerned, the distribution of powers has not changed significantly. Although the delegation of some powers to the regions is currently underway, they are not expected to have a significant effect. The only real changes concern the abolition of external controls (already noted), which has been important in terms of speeding up bureaucratic procedures, and the partial liberalisation (recently threatened) of personnel appointments. Centralised collective bargaining procedures, however, continue to constitute a heavy constraint on the development of management policies by municipalities and provinces.

- With regard to *financial resources*, the introduction of local fiscal autonomy, by means of the property tax, has reversed the previous situation. Today, local authorities (especially medium-sized ones) depend much less on transfers from central government. Furthermore, the recent freedom to issue bonds is reducing dependence on the *Cassa depositi e prestiti*. True, this reversal of outlook originated in the need to increase the general tax burden, and, as a consequence, the use of tax-levying powers by local authorities is heavily constrained by the likely unwillingness of the public to bear further taxation. Nevertheless, this control over funds, which in the past constituted a fundamental resource of central government, now lies much more in the domain of local government.

- There have also been changes with regard to *political resources*, which, as noted, already favoured local government. On the one hand, the crisis of the national political parties eliminated one of the channels through which local government gained access to Rome; yet, on the other hand, this development has finally put an end to the very idea that local policies can and should be decided elsewhere. What matters here is not so much the disappearance, transformation and fragmentation of various parties, such as the Socialists (PSI) and the DC, but the fact that the abandonment of the old financial practices (swept away by the *Tangentopoli* investigations), has weakened party bureaucracies enormously, thus preventing them from acting as the channel for processing and monitoring decisions at the sub-national level. When combined with the weakening of legislatures (through directly elected mayors who are able to attract votes from opposing factions), the overall effect is a strengthening of the local level as a political force, capable of better resisting the intrusion of the national level. The development of the 'Party of the Mayors', both at a national level (the mayors of the major cities) and at a regional level (the mayors of the North-East) is an effect, not cause, of a further accumulation of resources at local level.

- The advantage which local authorities previously enjoyed with respect to *information resources* has, to a large extent, been lost. This is due to two factors. The first is the general paradox of the information society (i.e. an overabundance of data with respect to the ability to process them), and the second is the improvement and modernisation of central government administration, which has managed to create reasonably efficient information systems (starting with the reform of the National Statistics

Institute). The result is a more balanced distribution of technical resources between the local and central levels than was the case in the past.

- Finally, the situation regarding *technical resources and know-how*, and the capacity to mobilise competent professional bureaucracies, is complex, although there are several factors which seem to give local government the edge. Although local authority bureaucracy is essentially no different from what it was ten years ago (and, in any case, these changes take time) there are nevertheless some indications that the quality of senior personnel has improved. This is partly a consequence of the new election law which allows mayors personally to select members of the executive. While in the past they were members of the parties belonging to the winning coalition, and consequently did not tend to consider the effectiveness and efficiency of policies as a priority, today members of the executive are often selected on the basis of their professional career experience. They are selected primarily as people who are capable of putting order back into local government administrations often shattered by judicial investigations, and to give an impetus to reform of local policies.

This is one area, however, which remains under-researched. On the little evidence available, the impression is that there has been a distinct improvement in the capabilities of local government élites and that this gives them an advantage over central government. Moreover, the new personnel (who remain 'politicians' because of their method of appointment and the posts they occupy) have had to find assistants from both inside and, more importantly, outside local government bureaucracies, thus introducing private sector managers and professionals from the outside world into the administrations. This is not to suggest that local government bureaucracies are now completely different from what they were ten years ago. Nevertheless, there seems to be little doubt that, as a result of changes and renovation, local governments now have better management and administrative resources, and this puts them in a stronger negotiating position with respect to central government.

The result of all these changes is clear. While a few years ago, the thesis of central government dominance could only be doubted, today it can be unequivocally refuted. The long Italian transition has, among other things, generated a better intergovernmental balance, and one which is more consistent with the trend (which some would like to accelerate), towards federalism, or at least a more accentuated form of decentralisation. What at the legislative level and those concerning taxation would be difficult to change. For example, reintroducing external control would seem improbable, and, proposals currently under discussion regarding taxation would strengthen further the powers of regions and local governments. With respect to political changes, it is possible (but unlikely) that political parties would be able to resume their traditional role since this would involve changing the leading part played by mayors both at a local and a national level.

It would seem, therefore, that a genuine break with the past has been enacted, and that one of Italy's paradoxes – a nation without a strong central government but with a strongly centralised system of government – is on the road to resolution. Yet, one final qualification should be noted. The changes outlined in this article have involved not only a redistribution of resources from central to local government, but a fundamental (and possibly permanent) change in the focus of government activity. If Italy's development was anomalous it was partly because the growth of the welfare state was not supported by a concomitant strengthening of local government. Paradoxically, a strengthening of local government is now occurring in a context of retrenchment of the welfare state. Consequently, the increased freedom of local governments seems to correspond with a decrease in the importance of the services they are called upon to manage.

## CONCLUSION: CENTRE–PERIPHERY RELATIONS INTO THE NEXT CENTURY

The future development of centre–periphery relations in Italy remains uncertain. On the one hand (at least from a reading of the manifestos of the major parties which fought the 1996 elections) Italy would appear to be on the threshold of federalism, the Lega's surprisingly good results reinforcing this impression. On the other hand, this development cannot be taken for granted, if for no other reason than the fact that fundamental constitutional change of the existing territorial entities is a very difficult task. Consequently, future changes in the relationship between the national and sub-national levels of government would, in all likelihood, favour the regions, currently the weakest link in the institutional chain.

In any case, even if it is assumed that Italy *is* on the road to constitutional reform, what type of federalism would result? Here too, the certainties are few and the difficulties many. It would seem almost impossible to achieve a rigid division of powers between centre and periphery (i.e. 'dual federalism'). There would be considerable difficulties in defining and redistributing competencies during a period of a more general (and complex) change in governmental responsibilities. Rome would also fear having to renounce all authority in some areas. A more likely outcome would be a mix of 'co-operative federalism' (on German lines) and competitive federalism in which the main levels of government would be free to intervene on the same issues. This would probably be the model on which the various political forces could reach a compromise. This type of debate, however, cannot be conducted in a vacuum. On the contrary, it will be infused by more concrete aspects which raise their own set of problems and will thus shape the final outcome. The most significant of these are: the question of the South, the fate of the welfare state, the public deficit and administrative reforms.

First, with regard to the south, central government has, in a certain way, been fortunate that the European Union (EU) has virtually forbidden any form of national subsidies to underdeveloped areas. If nothing else, this has defused the question of special aid for the south and the issue of central (rather than regional) government responsibility. The question of whether, in a federalist set-up, relations with Brussels would be conducted directly by regional governments or would still pass through central government is an open question. The main argument for leaving central government's role intact is the extreme weakness of regional government administrative structures. This could lead to arguments in favour of 'federalism with a variable geometry' (on Spanish lines) in which northern regions would have direct relations with Brussels while southern regions would continue to deal through Rome. Whether this would be politically acceptable, however, is another matter.

Second, in any list of responsibilities with which local governments should be entrusted in a federalist system, there are at least two that typically fall into the welfare state category: health (already partly decentralised in Italy), and education. In the context of a progressive reduction of government intervention, federalism could be a form of Trojan horse, used to make the abandonment of the welfare state model a painless (or at least less painful) process. In Italy, however, this would involve a spectacular redistribution of resources between north and south. Put simply, while northern regions could maintain current levels of service without increased taxes, in the south taxes would either have to be increased considerably or a reduction in free schooling and health services would follow. Having said this, the maintenance of current levels of inter-regional transfers would only make sense in a context in which central government – or at least Parliament – defined the degree, and method of provision, of services. Would such a solution be compatible with a federalist system? If not, would a solution which left the regions free to decide on the extent of the provision of services be politically acceptable and compatible with the notion of equality laid down in the constitution in its present form?

Education is a more limited, but no less thorny, problem. Is the regionalisation of education compatible with a single national corps of teachers? If it were to be abandoned, what effects would this have, not just on union relations, but on the job market for southern university graduates who see teaching as one of the main career opportunities open to them?

Third, the problem of the national debt is linked to the question of the welfare state. Even if it is admitted that the financial situation is now more stable than it was, and that the burden of debt is destined to improve, who will carry responsibility for it? The level of debt can partly be explained by the high level of subsidies transferred from North to South, but, at the same time, the holders of Treasury bonds (who finance the debt) generally live in the South. The solution would, therefore, seem to be to leave the debt with central government, but that would also mean that a large proportion of taxes would continue to be levied by central government.

Fourth, what sense would constitutional reform have if it did not involve an administrative revolution? Despite its significance, this issue tends to be overlooked in relation to central–local relations. Here too, there are difficult problems to tackle, the main one being that of safeguarding the subsidiarity principle which favours local authorities (and other independent institutions such as the universities, chambers of commerce, etc.). Does the protection of the autonomy of these organisations require central government to act as an arbiter or is the constitution and judicial protection sufficient? This issue is one which would have to be resolved in the event of the creation of a true federal state.

Yet, behind the administrative issue lurks a further question. The administrative problem is probably the chief obstacle to achieving genuine institutional reform.[10] An inefficient and unresponsive public bureaucracy constitutes the largest gap separating Italy from other industrialised countries, and, until this gap is reduced, institutional reform will fail to meet expectations. All the political forces are in agreement on this, yet actually making progress on the issue is difficult because, in a tight economic situation, any moves towards administrative restructuring would be confronted by fierce opposition from employees, who are themselves represented by both the main political coalitions.[11]

Furthermore, even if it were possible to overcome resistance to change, the question would remain of the type of administrative reform which should be enacted. Unfortunately, as studies of the most recent processes of reform have shown, the dominating theories of administrative reform are, to a large extent, based on welfare state theory and practice, and are, therefore, probably inadequate for Italy (and other industrialised countries), in the 1990s.[12] Any reform of sub-national government in Italy must come to terms with this problem above all others. Like all late comers, Italy is faced with a difficult task, that of preparing its government for the next century without having made it function properly in this one.

NOTES

1.  For this interpretation of the origins of the Lega Nord see P.Feltrin, 'La struttura politica' in CINSEDO, *II Rapporto sulle Regioni* (Milan: Franco Angeli 1994) pp.351–95.
2.  See R. Lewanski, 'La politica ambientale' in B. Dente (ed.) *Le politiche pubbliche in Italia* (Bologna: Il Mulino 1991) pp.281–314.
3.  For the importance of trust in local authorities on the part of individuals, see R. Putnam, *Making Democracy Work – Civic Traditions in Modern Italy* (Princeton UP 1992) pp.54–5.
4.  See B. Dente, 'Il governo locale' in G. Freddi (ed.), *Scienza dell'amministrazione e politiche pubbliche* (Florence: La Nuova Italia Scientifica 1989) pp.126–9
5.  Ibid. p.132.
6.  See, for example, M. Cammelli, 'Sistema politico bloccato, Stato accentrato', *Il Mulino* 3 (1994) p.478.
7.  B. Dente, 'The Fragmented Reality of Italian Local Government' in J.J. Hesse, *Local Government and Urban Affairs in International Perspective – Analyses of Twenty Industrialised Countries* (Baden Baden: Nomos 1991).
8.  See M. Cammelli, 'La politica di riforma locale', in Dente, *Le politiche pubbliche* (note 2) pp.173–4.
9.  B. Dente, 'The Fragmented Reality of Italian Local Government' (note 2) pp.544–9. It is worth adding that this chapter argued that the regions represented the weakest link in the chain of government, something which remains unchanged, as suggested earlier in this article.
10. B. Dente, *In un diverso stato – come rifare la pubblica amministrazione italiana* (Bologna: Il Mulino 1995).
11. But not, significantly, by the Lega, something which explains the more radical nature of its proposals.
12. *Riformare la Pubblica Amministrazione* (Turin: Edizione della Fondazione Giovanni Agnelli 1995).

# The Reform of Finance and Administration in Italy: Contrasting Achievements

## GIACINTO DELLA CANANEA

*This assessment reviews the changes which have affected Italian financing and the administration in recent years. In particular, it considers why public administration is in a worse state than finance, and why this issue has been relatively neglected. An assessment of the extent to which the questions of finance and administration are linked is made first. The evolution and current state of both issues is then analysed, before explaining why moves have been made towards greater financial rigour when, by contrast, the public administration remains largely unreformed.*

The poor state of Italian finances and the inefficiency and ineffectiveness of the Italian administration have been well-known since the 1970s, as have the difficulties in achieving an improvement in either. In recent years, however, there has been a marked divergence in the paths followed by financial and administrative reform. This discussion analyses the changes which have affected both areas. In particular, it considers why public administration is in a worse state that finance, and why the former issue has not been adequately addressed. The evolution and current state of both areas is analysed before an attempt is made to explain why the 1990s have witnessed moves towards greater financial rigour, while the administration remains largely unreformed.[1] Before doing so, however, it is necessary to examine the extent to which the two areas of finance and the administration are linked.

### THE LINK BETWEEN FINANCE AND THE ADMINISTRATION

There are three reasons for treating the questions of finance and administration together.[2] The first is that both have grown considerably in importance with respect to the Constitution and the political system. Financing and administration, as basic components of public power, received little attention from the Constituent Assembly which was responsible for drafting the Italian constitution of 1948, and this state of affairs continued until the early 1970s, when there was a move to expand the competencies and scope of both. Public finance, according to recent estimates, now absorbs more than half of Gross Domestic Product (GDP), with the deficit amounting to about 10 per cent. Moreover, decisions affecting financing – such as major funding legislation – have risen to the top of the political agenda. The administration, meanwhile, has witnessed an increase in both its normative powers and personnel. Today, it is Italy's largest employer. Furthermore, its reputation depends much more than in the past on satisfying citizens' interests. In the course of this century, fundamental interests have developed which cannot be satisfied without state intervention to provide such things as a good educational system and an efficient health service.

The second reason is that both finance and administration have been subject to clientelistic party interference, which has had undesirable effects. The fact that from 1950–90 political parties assumed a greater role in state and society than was in the general interest has been well-documented. It is important, however, to note the effects of this expanded role on finance and the administration. Public spending sustains political power through the distribution of group benefits, and is regulated by the constitutional rule governing finance limits (Art.81, last sub-section) and other constitutional principles of impartiality and administrative efficiency (Art.97, §2). Yet, the huge intake of public employees who have not passed the requisite competition – as required by the Constitution (Art.97, §3) – and the lack of selection by merit has caused a crisis in public finance and reduced efficiency in the administration. In effect, the administration has come to perform the social function of guaranteeing employment, rather than providing services. Moreover, as protection of its personnel has become more important, so responsibility for performance has declined. As a result, there have been hostile confrontations between politicians and bureaucrats over efficiency controls. The bureaucracy has accepted an undermining of its independence and role through party interference, and has willingly subjected itself to stringent controls, which are often based upon fulfilling the requirements of individual laws. This has produced numerous levels of co-decision making between politicians and the bureaucracy, which, while in accordance with the law, tend nevertheless to overlook the main objectives behind the collection and distribution of public resources, for which the administration is responsible.[3]

The third reason for considering finance and the administration together is that the reform of one has an effect on the other. The extent to which the reform of public finances is contingent on overhauling the administration became increasingly clear during the 11th legislature (1992–94). In order to begin the reorganisation of public finances, the governments of Giuliano Amato (1992–93) and Carlo Azeglio Ciampi (1993–94) initiated a comprehensive reform of the administrative system. The Amato government effected a major reform of the main public spending sectors – (health, social security, employment and local financing) and, after years of debate, began to privatise public enterprises. The Ciampi government, for its part, paved the way for the modernisation of public administration, in all of its dimensions – organisation, procedure, personnel and controls.[4] But then the reform of finance and administration began to diverge.

## THE REFORM OF PUBLIC FINANCE

From the mid-1970s onwards, there were increasing demands from various institutions and public opinion for a restructuring of the public accounts. A succession of reforms gradually changed the profile of financial institutions. Two sets of changes were particularly noteworthy: (1) clearer links were established between the various sectors of public finance (the state, the regions, and local and other public bodies); and (2) the instruments for intervention at the disposal of public institutions were modified.[5]

To understand the importance of the first set of changes, it should be noted that the state, while being almost exclusively responsible for collecting resources, redistributes them via the budget which passes them on to other bodies. These are either sub-national authorities (at the regional or local level) or auxiliary institutions (such as social security or local health agencies). The separation of the collection and distribution of finances has tended to make the different spending bodies or agencies largely irresponsible, resulting in dysfunction and waste. To remedy this, laws were introduced to control public financing *in toto* during the yearly cycle of financial decisions: the economic and financial planning act (law of 14/8/1988, no.362) and the finance law (law of 5/8/78, no.468, amended under law no.362/1988). Moreover, fixed spending levels were established for all bodies in the enlarged public sector (a figure for public administration costs was provided by the protocol on excessive deficits linked to the Maastricht Treaty). These aimed to conform to regulations on keeping individual accounts, to provide information for the Ministry of the Treasury and to keep treasury capital near to the state Treasury in order to reduce the costs of obtaining funding on the financial markets.[6] Finally, controls were introduced which applied to public financing in general. These were entrusted to the Court of Accounts which, as the body controlling state accounts, became the Court of Public Accounts (the National Audit Office).

The second set of changes concerned the instruments of intervention at the disposal of public institutions:

- Whilst the Constitution (under Art.81, §4) requires single items of spending to be covered by revenue (which has often had to be ignored by legislators), ordinary law requires that projected medium-term spending (over three years) is also covered by revenue. Law no.384/91 extends constitutional law and demands that medium-term spending should also be adequately covered.

- Whereas previously the budget could restrain areas of spending, but could not modify the norms established, this capacity has now been included in the annual Finance Bill. At the level of quantitative regulation, the finance law now assesses the total cost of financing, and determines what the maximum level of market funding should be (thus establishing a ceiling for spending). It also determines the commitments to longer-term spending and modification to the rates of taxation. The laws linked to the Finance Bill, which contain many norms, have also modified previously existing arrangements, and were used during the eleventh legislature to reform the organisation of public administration.
- The system of procedures affecting public finance have been modified. These are now divided between two consecutive sessions (spring and autumn) and concern almost exclusively economic and financial measures (excluding decree laws) in order to guarantee a fixed calendar for parliamentary debate. Furthermore, limitations were placed on the modifications which the Chamber of Deputies (the Lower House) can make to proposals submitted by the government. Amendments can no longer be considered if they alter the total cost of the proposed Finance Bill. Finally, the order of voting is such that it now gives priority to the vote on the revenue side of the Bill which subsequently sets the limits on spending.
- Finally, five measures were introduced to allow the identification and measurement of the negative effects arising from fixed and proposed spending. On the one hand, because a law can increase spending or reduce income, an appropriate technical report must now be made which measures the law's effects. This report is submitted to the State Accounts Department (*Ragioneria generale dello Stato*) for scrutiny. On the other hand, the Ministry of the Treasury must inform Parliament of the actual costs as compared with the initial forecasts; it should also propose solutions to overcome the discrepancies between the two. Furthermore, the Court of Accounts carries out checks on the limits on spending and where these fail, before referring them to Parliament.

The reform of the financing system, summarised above,[7] has certainly not resolved all of the problems of public finance inherited from previous legislatures. Among the unresolved problems there is the sheer scale of the public debt, which has deterred more productive investment and has left Italian finances vulnerable to fluctuations in the financial markets.

Furthermore, it has not solved the (still legal) legislative and administrative evasion of fixed levels of spending and public debt. Legislative evasion stems from the reluctance of the government and Parliament to respect the rules; it also derives from the weakness of the existing limits, which, being established under ordinary, rather than constitutional, law, can be altered by another ordinary law.[8] Administrative evasion is the result of the accounting regulations by which the Treasury ensures the formal respect of limits, artificially determining the distribution of certain resources (for example, those destined for the regions or tax returns demanded by citizens). Moreover, some activities which increase spending have not been changed, such as the mechanisms which are incorporated into the laws governing social welfare, which are still divided into approximately 6,000 sections, and which prevent the setting of clear financial limits.[9]

There are also problems created by the reforms themselves. Although state expenditure has been reined in, this does not mean that spending is disbursed according to need (rather than the pressure of interests) or that it is managed in an efficient and economic manner. Furthermore, financial centralisation has reduced the autonomy of the regions and of local bodies. At the same time, the reform of public finance has brought the conflicts between different groups and interests over state funding into the very heart of the process by which financial decisions are made and adopted.

That said, placing financing at the centre of the institutional and political agenda has also had many positive effects. The growth of spending has been stemmed and fiscal pressure alleviated.[10] The deficit – the substantial reduction of which is fundamental to Italy's future role in the European Union (EU) – has been brought down to within more manageable limits. Italy's primary surplus has risen faster than that of any other member of the G7. In other words, tax receipts are now higher than public spending. Mention should be made, however, of the presence of high interest rates demanded for servicing the debt. These are the result of errors made in the past, which pushed the state into debt, and of financing from current expenditure (family benefits and funding public companies).

These changes have also had an effect at the institutional level. Since 1988, the Finance Bill has been approved within the time schedule set by budgetary policy, whereas in the previous decade, there were instances when provisional budgets were used (twice in 1985 for example). The new law, if correctly employed (i.e. on the basis of realistic estimates) allows for an effective control of spending. During the first few years of using the new rules, the number and quality of technical reports has grown. Parliament has been able to produce more considered decisions, thanks to the new budgetary reports which it has received. The government, for its part, has managed to avoid changes to established budgetary targets, although there

TABLE 1

PUBLIC SECTOR DEBT: 1970–95 (AS PERCENTAGE OF GDP)

| Year | % | Year | % |
|------|------|------|-------|
| 1970 | 34.2 | 1983 | 68.4 |
| 1971 | 38.4 | 1984 | 73.3 |
| 1972 | 42.7 | 1985 | 81.1 |
| 1973 | 44.0 | 1986 | 85.3 |
| 1974 | 44.1 | 1987 | 89.9 |
| 1975 | 49.9 | 1988 | 92.7 |
| 1976 | 48.7 | 1989 | 96.0 |
| 1977 | 51.2 | 1990 | 98.7 |
| 1978 | 57.0 | 1991 | 101.9 |
| 1979 | 56.6 | 1992 | 108.6 |
| 1980 | 54.8 | 1993 | 115.9 |
| 1981 | 57.7 | 1994 | 124.3 |
| 1982 | 62.7 | 1995 | 123.8 |

*Source*: Bank of Italy

has still been the problem of compensatory parliamentary amendments which do not alter the level of spending but which nevertheless can significantly affect the government programme.

Finally, there has been a strengthening of independent financial powers. Since 1981 the Bank of Italy has been relieved of its obligation to buy public paper not purchased during sales of ordinary Treasury bonds. This has allowed it to improve its capacity to function autonomously in the monetary sphere, as required by the agreements instituting the European Monetary System (EMS). More recently, the law of 26 November 1993, no.483, implementing the Treaty on European Union, has severed the remaining links between the Bank of Italy and the Treasury. Monetary policy has thus been separated from budgetary policy, with the stabilisation of prices as its primary objective.[11]

THE MIXED FORTUNES OF ADMINISTRATIVE REFORM

Thus, despite its inconsistencies, the reform of public finance has followed a relatively coherent and progressive course. In contrast, administrative reform went through three phases which were so disjointed that they hardly amount to a single, coherent programme of reform.

In a first phase (until the end of the 1970s) there was a move away from the idea that administrative reform should be 'global' in nature towards *ad hoc* reform. In the 1980s, whilst the conviction that major institutional reform was necessary spread, the administration at the lower levels became – wrongly, as it turned out – the object of *ad hoc*, organisational changes with no clear, overall plan (for example, the introduction of a general law for administrative procedures, under law no.241/1990, and of new regulaions for local autonomy, in law no.142/1990). Consequently, while there was an obvious path to be followed in financial reform, there was no clear vision of comprehensive administrative reform. For example, the government of Giovanni Goria (1987–88) instigated measures in disparate areas with no common thread: the Prime Minister's office, public works, local autonomy, civil protection, simplification of administrative procedures, and administrative justice. Moreover, even where some of these reforms were achieved by successive governments at the legislative level, they had little concrete effects. For example, in 1988, the Parliament approved, under law no.400, the reform of the Prime Minister's office and the normative powers of the government. Yet, the directive in the law on the removal from the legal sphere of areas only partially governed by law was not implemented; as a result, many areas became subject to legal intervention, despite being matters originating in other spheres (public investment, for example). Nor did the government instigate the reorganisation of interministerial committees, something which happened only some years later under the Ciampi government.

The contradictions became even clearer in the period after 1989, when a general move towards improving the exercise of public power emerged. The demand for the separation of centre and periphery led to the statutory empowerment of autonomous bodies, such as universities (law no.186/1989) and local bodies (law no.142/1990), but these remained linked to the financial decisions of the central agencies. The demand for the separation of administration and politics produced new institutions, divided according to function and organisation, in the areas of radio and publishing (law no.223/1990), competition (law no.287/1990) and strikes in essential public services (law no.146/1990). The demand for the simplification of administrative procedures pushed the legislators to provide relevant instruments, such as the services conference and programme agreements (law no.241/1990); but in other cases they preferred simply to suppress controls or defer their implementation (e.g. in matters of public works).

Between 1992 and 1994, however, there was a noticeable change of tack, due to several factors. First, the state of public finances made more rigorous measures inevitable. Second, the political and institutional crisis resulting from the investigation of political and administrative corruption reduced the scope of action of political parties. And third, the completion of the Single Market tightened the margins between the public resources which could be targeted at unproductive investment and the level of goods and services (resourced by the administration) which could be restricted to national firms. These were to be at the centre of the abrogative referenda of April 1993. Seven out of the eight referendums held that month concerned the administration (further referendums being avoided only through legislative reforms); so this might be described as a form of public reappropriation of the administration. These developments lay at the heart of a series of structural interventions without parallel in recent Italy history, and which can be grouped into six areas or themes, dealt with during the Amato and Ciampi governments:[12]

- *Separating the political and administrative spheres.* This included measures to separate the executive (the domain of the political organs) from the administration (entrusted to the 'managers'), as set out in the legislative directive no.29/1993, and prohibiting politicians and trade unionists from sitting on jury panels for public office appointments (directive of the Prime Minister, 17 December 1993, instigated by judgement no.416/ 1993 of the Constitutional Court). New, semi-independent, bodies were also created, such as the *Agenzia per l'ambiente* (Environmental Agency) and the *Autorità per l'informatica* (Information Technology Agency) (legislative directive no.39/1993).
- *The reduction of the scope of the public sector.* The number of ministries was reduced, some by referendum, some under law no.537/1993. Further reductions, envisaged by this law, were prevented by conflicts inside the executive and the hostility of Parliament towards any kind of 'Jacobean' reform. Many public bodies and local organisations were also eliminated. The legal status of other groups was altered, to make way for privatisation. The first step towards privatisation was taken through law no.356/1990 for state-sector banks. This was followed by law no.359/1992, relating to the large state-holding groups, such as IRI, ENI and ENEL. Some privatisation was achieved, but it did not have the desired effect, namely the creation of a wider shareholding base. Instead, it produced a rapid consolidation of control by a limited number of private groups.
- *A change in status of personnel* who, except for certain categories (magistrates, directors, university professors), became employed mainly on a contractual basis, and subject to private-sector type efficiency norms. This did not, however, solve the problems in the upper echelons.
- *The reorganisation of administrative procedures*, initiated by law no.241/1990, but still on the drawing board. Only a few modifications have, thus far, been adopted into law. Nevertheless, more than 50 regulations for the simplification of procedures originated with this law, including some dealing with the regulation of financing and supplies. Other regulations were focused on liberalising economic activity previously under state control (d.p.r. Nos.407 and 411/1994).
- *Modifying the system of controls.* In the same way that law no.142/1990

limited the number of controls on the decisions of local bodies, this also occurred at the regional level (legislative directive no.40 and 476/1993) and at the level of the state (law no.20/1994). Furthermore, controls on public administration management were widened, and entrusted to the Court of Accounts. Finally, controlling bodies were introduced into all administrative agencies, under the secondary supervision of the Court.

• *Altering the links between the administration and citizens.* Norms governing access to administrative documents were introduced, the first being rather restrictive (d.p.r. no.352/1992), but its successor being far more open (d.p.r. no.130/1994). With the Public Services Charter, laws protecting the rights of users of public services were promised both in specific sectors, such as health (legislative directive no.502/1992), and more generally (directive of the Prime Minister, 21 February 1994).

This phase of reform was interrupted in 1994 by an event of the utmost constitutional and political importance. A primarily majoritarian electoral system was introduced for the Chamber of Deputies under laws no.276/1993 and no.277/1993, following a similar change enacted for the Senate via a referendum held in April of that year (the rules on electoral campaigning were also changed under law no.515/1993). However, the form of government was not amended in any way. This partly explains why, in the first attempt at a 'majoritarian' government, Prime Minister Silvio Berlusconi was forced to bargain and compromise as much as previous governing coalitions. Furthermore, this government witnessed a retreat from the ideal of separating clearly the executive from the administration, not only in the sectors traditionally most affected by political influence (such as the RAI broadcasting agency), but also for autonomous or nominally independent groups, such as the Bank of Italy.

At the same time, the priority given to administrative reform by previous governments was downgraded. There was no mention of administrative reform in the government's 'one hundred day programme', save one ambivalent reference: the revision of the new norms governing contracts, whose aim was to reduce 'contractual obstacles', produced instead a reduction in the administration's power and an increase in conflict through judicial action. Moreover, the commitment to economic liberalisation was contradicted by the introduction of controls and permits by the government control agency, *l'Osservatorio.* The goal of reducing the public sector had some success. Certain bodies were reorganised, although the restructuring of ministries under law no.537/1993 was abandoned. The main preoccupation of the governing coalition was, instead, with the acquisition and occupation of existing institutional positions, rather than their rationalisation and reduction.

The subsequent government, led by Lamberto Dini, set itself a few objectives: further financial reorganisation (if possible), reform of the regional electoral system; the reorganisation of the pension system; and the guarantee of equal access to the media during electoral campaigns. Administrative reform, therefore, was not at the centre of its programme. Nevertheless, some measures were taken of relevance to the administration. For example, certain steps were taken regarding the regulation of public services (law no. 483/1995) as already required by law no.537/1993. Furthermore, under decree no.163/1995 (converted into law no.273/1995), the introduction of charters of public service was made obligatory in certain sectors of public service (schools, health, electrical energy for example).

In short, there was no systematic reform of the public apparatus – in particular the administrative sector – either before or after the 11th legislature . Instead, there was a series of initiatives (such as law no.241/1990 on administrative procedure) put together with varying degrees of effectiveness. However, these were still isolated cases, in so far as they were not co-ordinated with other structural reforms, and were not followed up by a period of committed implementation, either at the regulatory or administrative level. Thus, even if the Italian system has experienced the introduction of a large number of innovative norms, aimed at improving the functioning and transparency of administrative activity, the effects have not been as positive as expected.[13] In particular, a lack of incisive action in the political sphere has reduced the savings envisaged under law no.537/1993 (which accompanied the 1994 finance law), resulting in an increasing call for investment by subscribers in government bonds as of the summer of 1994.[14]

## WHY IS PUBLIC ADMINISTRATION IN A WORSE STATE THAN FINANCE?

At this point, it is worth returning to our initial question: why, if public administration is in a worse state than finance, has this not been remedied, particularly when it is precisely in this area that one of the fundamental forces for financial restructuring is to be found? There are various possible answers to this question, some more convincing than others.

To begin with, it is not convincing to argue that, while the costs arising from problems in public accounts are quite evident, it is difficult to calculate the costs caused by the absence of administrative reform. Leaving aside the parameters set by the EU, this argument is doubtful for two reasons. First, there are two types of administrative cost analysis available today: direct economic costs (which derive from taxes) and indirect costs, such as non-paid taxes, time-wastage, failure of services – in short, any dysfunction which forces citizens, if they have the means, to resort to private alternatives to the public sector (which continues to incur costs regardless). Second, the belief that the Italian administration is less efficient than those in other EU states has been frequently demonstrated through institutional comparison. This view has become increasingly prevalent amongst Italians, as shown by the abrogative referendums of 1993, where a clear majority called for the abolition of parts of the administrative apparatus. Furthermore, initial attempts to measure the attitudes of public service users have all unearthed considerable dissatisfaction.

Explanations which highlight the exceptional nature of the governments of the eleventh legislature are more convincing. Indeed, in contrast with previous governments, there was only minimal intervention from political parties in the distribution of ministerial posts. That this was an aspect common to both governments was confirmed by their respective prime ministers who both reaffirmed 'the decisional autonomy of governing bodies in relation to the role that parties exercised earlier in surpassing all reasonable bounds that might be deemed to be within the sphere of the public interest'. Another communication, of 26 May 1993, from Ciampi to his ministers, underlined his desire for a united government, in the face of 'a delicate and difficult context ... [for] this government, and one which is different from the coalitions which preceded it'.

Yet, this argument is of too general a nature to explain satisfactorily why particular attention has been paid to administrative reform only under certain governments, and why the consequent solutions have been such that the same fate awaits them as the temples of Central America: of gradually becoming covered in the very vegetation that they had briefly replaced. To explain this phenomenon, two factors need to be considered: the first derives from the difference in costs and benefits in the reforms of finance and the administration; the second relates to the interests of those respon-sible for protecting the general interest.

As for the first, it is arguable that the administration is difficult to reorganise, and the effects of reorganisation are hard to see, because it is a structure with many centres, inevitably leading to fragmentation, whereas finance is a unitary phenomenon, with centralisation of its instruments of function and control. The source of revenue is singular (national wealth), as is responsibility for the financial balance and the deficit (which the EU assigns to central governments). Moreover, it is possible – as was demon-strated by the Ciampi government – to reduce and rationalise public spending 'without implementing cuts, at least in terms of eliminating waste in public services', in other words 'by making each lira spent on public services more efficient' (Declaration of Programme, 6 May 1993).

As for the second factor, any attempt at administrative reorganisation confronts two major obstacles. First, changing the criteria for the organisation and functioning of these bodies will inevitably conflict with vested interests, especially those – widespread in Italy – which view public posts as sinecures. This can be seen in the case of the recruitment of people to jobs without open competition (running counter to Art.97 of the Constitution, which requires a meritocratic and egalitarian system). In general, the opposition of a large number of public employees – or at least the better organised of them – to changes in their employment status has deflected the process of reform and changed the terms of reference (something to which the mass media has also contributed): instead of *administrative* reform, people now speak of *bureaucratic* reform.

Second, while the inefficiency of public services has adverse consequences for most people, it nevertheless has advantages for those responsible for providing those services, and whose utility would be reduced were the administration able to function efficiently. The best example (although others could be cited, such as commercial licensing) was the press campaign promoted by the National Union of Driving Instructors (*Unione nazionale delle autoscuole*) against the simplification of the driving test, on the basis of the (claimed) negative effects that would be caused by the proposed measures. This is a case of intransigent hostility to reform caused by vested interests, which have made decision-making procedures more complex and arduous.

It remains to be explained, however, why a reform so likely to damage individual interests, such as financial reform, met with so little opposition. The majority of recent governments, rather than reforming finance for the purpose of governing, have given the impression of governing for the purpose of reforming finance, in order to resolve the crisis in the state accounts inherited from previous governments. This focus depended a great deal, to borrow a phrase from Giuliano Amato, on a climate of 'obvious financial crisis ... as a consequence of a lack of control', but also on two other factors: the emphasis placed on the renewal of public institutions, and the symbolism attached to such reform in the context of pressures from the EU.

## The Changing Role of Public Institutions

In Italy, interest in the functioning and impartiality of public offices has never been strong. The Ministry of Public Administration has, in fact, been more responsive to the needs of its employees than to those of the administration and public service administration. Examples abound of it behaving more as an advocate for spending than as an agent of the Treasury, with requests for increases in salaries irrespective of the efficiency of the personnel and the quality of services provided to citizens and other users.

This situation changed under the Ciampi government, when the Minister for Public Administration, Sabino Cassese, targeted the interests of the 'clients' rather than those of the employees, something which was noticed immediately by the trade unions. Moreover, he reorganised the department so that its prime concerns were with its internal organisation, procedures and controls, rather than simply its staff. This altered role also emerged through an internal requirement of the Cabinet (directive of 30 November 1993) that the presentation of government amendments for discussion in Parliament should be preceded by a meeting of the Ministers of Public Administration and of the Budget if the amendments refer to the organisation and functioning of the administration (Art.17, §1). The Prime Minister, however, can defer analysis of measures which impinge on the government's general policy (Art.18, §1).

There has, therefore, been a change in role of the Ministry of Public Administration. which, 'for the first time has aligned its own objectives with the reduction of administrative costs'.[15] Nevertheless, as a ministerial task without portfolio, administrative reform has depended a great deal on the importance given to it by the Prime Minister, whatever the intentions of public administration ministers may have been. This probably explains the differing performances of the ministers who succeeded Cassese (Giuliano Urbani and Franco Frattini) because there was a decline in interest in administrative reform during the 12th legislature.[16]

The monitoring of public finance is rather different, resting, as it does, with the Ministry of the Treasury. The Treasury must check the coherence of government decisions and their effects across different sectors. To this end, every measure that incurs costs must receive its assent (Articles 17 and 18 of internal regulations). At the political level, the extent of the Treasury's importance is reflected in the number of times a Minister of the Treasury has been called upon to lead a government.[17]

Nevertheless, the Treasury has, in the past, often yielded to pressure from particular interests. For example, it has often allowed non–accountable spending to occur, or has used resources acquired through debt as an instrument to finance direct aid (rather than investments). The detrimental effects of this laxity, however, have been offset by the role played by a stricter guardian of public finances, the Bank of Italy. The Bank of Italy has never failed to convey to political institutions and the public the seriousness of the state of the public accounts. A glance at the *Considerazione finali* of the Governor of the Bank of Italy during the 1980s reveals demands for the relocation of financial procedures under the auspices of Art.81 (1981), and references to the chronic imbalance between income and spending and the need to balance the various items of current spending in the budget (1983). The financial rigour of the Bank has been greatly valued. The draft law presented by Giuliano Amato (Prime Minister 1992–93) which proposed the delegation of emergency economic and financial powers to the government, gave a prominent role to the Governor of the Bank of Italy. Following this, in 1993, the Governor of the Bank, Carlo Azeglio Ciampi, was asked to form a government, as was, in 1995, Lamberto Dini (who had been Director-General of the Bank before becoming Minister of the Treasury under Berlusconi in 1994).

A significant contribution to maintaining more rigour in public finance has also come from the Court of Accounts. In spite of widespread hostility to this new regime of control (based on the primacy of public accountability and management efficiency), the external controlling bodies gradually modified their perception of their own role. Proof of this can be seen through the consolidated orientation on the basis of which it sought the intervention of the Constitutional Court, in order to confirm the constitutional legitimacy of the spending laws approved by Parliament, but which the Court of Accounts considered to be lacking the necessary financial cover.

## External Influence on Public Finance

The reorganisation of public finances cannot be explained purely by the widespread belief amongst institutions and broad sections of public opinion of its urgency, or by the high profile of the institutions responsible. External factors also played a role, especially pressure from the EU.

The launch of the EMS in 1979 – in which the Bank of Italy played a supporting role[18] – reimposed an external constraint on national monetary policy which had been in decline since the crisis of Bretton Woods in 1971. This clearly had far-reaching political implications. The discipline imposed on excessive deficits placed considerable pressure on member-states if they wished to enter the third phase of European Monetary Union (EMU). In the process, the power of central banks and bankers was increased. Convergence with the Maastricht criteria has also had considerable symbolic value. If one considers that adhesion to European integration has been one of the few constants in Italian foreign policy in the post-war period, and that the Maastricht Treaty offers the possibility of measuring governmental financial activity according to fixed parameters, the importance of European influence on Italian public finance becomes clear. The political and economic costs of exclusion from the single currency would be devastating for Italy, not only symbolically but possibly also for future financial rigour.[19] The financial markets make daily judgements on the policies of government which are no longer able to protect themselves from such external pressures by regulating the flow of capital. As Guido Carli has confirmed, the policy constraint imposed by the EU fulfils 'a positive function with respect to the revitalisation of public finance'.[20]

None of this, however, is applicable to the administration, even it is crucial that its problems are resolved if Italy is to enjoy the benefits of European integration, without coming into conflict with other countries which are better organised and have a more developed capacity to support the interests of their citizens in the European arena. It follows that, if support from the public administration is absent, it is improbable that financial reorganisation will be sufficient to ensure a satisfactory government of the *res publica*. For this reason, a session on the functioning of public administration might be usefully included in the EU's intergovernmental conference.

## NOTES

Giacinto della Cananea would like to thank Professor Sabino Cassese for his helpful comments on a draft version of this article, but as the author, G. della Cananea, takes full responsibility for any errors and omissions.

1. For a fuller analysis of these issues, see G. della Cananea, *Indirizzo e controllo della finanza pubblica* (Bologna: Il Mulino 1996).
2. The link between finance and administration is explored in M. T. Salvemini, 'Riforma dell'amministrazione e riduzione del disavanzo nella politica di bilancio del governo Ciampi', *Politica economica* 11/1 (1995) p.4.
3. See S. Cassese, 'L'inefficienza della pubblica amministrazione e i suoi costi', *Rivista trimestrale di scienza dell'amministrazione*, 1989, p.71ff. On the role of political parties see P. Scoppola, *La Repubblica dei partiti. Profilo storico della democrazia in Italia* (Bologna: Il Mulino 1992). Also of use are D. Della Porta, *Lo scambio occulto. Casi di corruzione politica in Italia* (ibid. 1993) and M. D'Alberti and R. Finocchi (eds.) *Corruzione e sistema istituzionale* (ibid. 1994).
4. See Carlo Azeglio Ciampi, *Un metodo per governare* (Bologna: Il Mulino 1996) pp.105ff.
5. The legal instruments adopted to keep spending and the deficit under control are examined in S. Cassese, *La nuova costituzione economica* (Bari: Laterza 1995) pp.142ff. On controls, the most recent and accurate study is U. Allegretti (ed.) *I controlli amministrativi* (Bologna: Il Mulino 1995).
6. The law creating a single budget line for the public administration (law of 29 Oct. 1984, no.702) was also spared being subject to the abrogative referendum. Art.75 of the Constitution grants immunity from this only for financial acts, fiscal laws and the budget. However, the Constitutional Court extended this privilege to financing laws and 'related' laws (judgement no.2/1994 in *Giurisprudenza costituzionale*, 1994, pp.9ff., with a comment by G. Gemma), and subsequently to law no.702/1984, because – in the Court's view – these laws also affected the use of available resources (judgement no.12/1995, ibid. 1995, pp.54ff.).
7. For further details, see D. Franco, *L'espansione della spesa pubblica in Italia* (Bologna, Il Mulino 1992), G. Morcaldo, *La finanza pubblica in Italia* (ibid. 1993), L. Bernardi (ed.) *La finanza pubblica italiana. Rapporto 1995* (ibid. 1995) and A. Monorchio (ed.) *La finanza pubblica italiana dopo la svolta del 1992* (ibid. 1996) (which includes the U-turn of the Amato government).
8. An example of the overlapping competences of the government and the Treasury is provided by the U-turn effected by the law of 30 June 1994, no.423 (A.S. no.526, 12th legislature) in which financing was traced using a global figure, without taking into account the limit set by the finance law on the rate of redemption of loans, and the limits to such engagements.
9. Giuliano Amato, *Due anni al Tesoro* (Bologna: Il Mulino 1990) provides a good account of the work of the Treasury minister.

10. Public spending reached 56.6 per cent of GDP in 1993, then fell to 52.5 per cent in 1994; at the same time, fiscal pressure (taxation as a proportion of GDP) dropped from 44.3 per cent to 43.9 per cent. On the progress of the deficit, see Table 1. In the programme for Italy's presidency of the EU (Jan.–June 1996) the Prime Minister, Lamberto Dini, drew on the forecasts of the Dpef (the government's rolling medium-term financial strategy) from 1995 to 1997, which predicted a reduction of the national deficit from 5.8 per cent to 4.4 per cent of GDP in 1997, and to 3 per cent in 1998, a figure which would prevent Italy from joining the third phase of EMU.

11. The autonomy of the Bank of Italy with respect to the Treasury is described in M.T. Salvemini, *Le politiche del debito pubblico* (Bari: Laterza 1994) pp.178ff.

12. The administrative reforms undertaken during the eleventh legislature are described in N. Lupo, 'Le deleghe del governo Amato in Parlamento', *Rivista trimestrale di diritto pubblico*, 1994, pp.85ff.; and in C. Lacava and G. Vecchi, 'L'amministrazione nella XI legislatura', *Riformare la pubblica amministrazione* (Turin: Fondazione Agnelli 1995), pp.157ff. For a critical account, see S. Cassese, 'La riforma amministrativa all'inizio della quinta Costituzione dell'Italia unità', *Il Foro italiano*, 1994, V, p.9 and G. della Cananea, 'Reforming the State: The Policy of Administrative Reform in Italy under the Ciampi Government', *West European Politics* 19/2 (April 1996) pp.321ff.

13. For further analyses of administrative reform, see S. Cassese, 'Hypotheses on the Italian Administrative System', *West European Politics* 16/2 (April 1993) pp.316ff, G. Capano, *L'improbabile riforma* (Bologna: Mulino 1993) and S. Cassese and C. Franchini (eds.) *L'amministrazione pubblica italiana. Un profilo* (ibid. 1994). On the independent authorities see, S. Cassese and C. Franchini (eds.) *I garanti delle regole* (ibid. 1996).

14. On the 12th legislature, the analyses provided by the 'Osservatorio sull'attività normativa del Governo' are quite useful, coordinated by G. Vesperini, and published every two months in *Giornale di diritto amministrativo* from 1995. The report on the six months of the Berlusconi government is in *Vita italiana. Documenti e informazioni*, 1994, nos.8–12 (on p.15, the programmatic proposals are outlined, and p.60 contains a section on actions relevant to personnel).

15. E. D'Albergo, 'Rendimento istituzionale e logiche di azione organizzativa nella politica di bilancio', in F. Bassanini and S. Merlini (eds.) *Crisi fiscale e indirizzo politico* (Bologna: Il Mulino 1995) p.744.

16. See S. Cassese, 'Il difficile mestiere di Ministro della funzione pubblica', in *Riformare la pubblica amministrazione* (note 12) p.135ff; and P. Marconi, 'Gli interventi di riforma delle amministrazioni pubbliche nella politica di bilancio per il 1994–96', *Politica economica* 11/1 (1995) p.99ff.

17. These have, in the past, included Giovanni Goria, Bettino Craxi and Amintore Fanfani. More recently, Giuliano Amato, Minister of the Treasury under Goria, was Prime Minister 1993–93; and Lamberto Dini, Minister of the Treasury under Berlusconi, was Prime Minister 1995–96, while remaining at the Treasury.

18. The commitment of the Bank of Italy to the formation of the EMS was shown by its then governor Paolo Baffi, 'Il sistema monetario europeo e la partecipazione dell'Italia', in P. Ciocca (ed.) *La moneta e l'economia. Il ruolo delle banche centrali* (Bologna: Il Mulino 1983) pp.261ff.

19. On the importance of the European constraint, see A. Manzella, 'Il 'vincolo europeo' sul governo dell'economia', in *Studi in memoria di Franco Piga*, Vol.2 (Milano: Giuffrè) p.1491ff.

20. This phrase is taken from the memoirs of Guido Carli, according to whom external influence plays a greater role in Italy than in other nations. This is because 'the market economy, open to the outside, is always in a precarious position, fragile, exposed to the continual effects of an autarchic mentality. External influence has maintained Italy's position amongst the free nations. Our choosing this influence is a constant that has lasted throughout the post-war period.' This choice was 'born out of pessimism based on the conviction that the basic instincts of Italian society, left to develop naturally, would have carried our country elsewhere'. See Guido Carli, *Cinquant'anni di vita italiana* (in collaboration with P. Peluffo) (Bari: Laterza 1993).

# Employers, Unions and the State: The Resurgence of Concertation in Italy?

## MARINO REGINI and IDA REGALIA

*In the 1990s a series of events has signalled the resurgence of concertation between governments and the social partners. Two tripartite agreements on incomes policies and the collective bargaining system, and 'negotiated' laws designed to reform pensions and the civil service, have provided the basis for the economic recovery which took place despite the turbulent phase of political transition. Concertation appears to be broader and more stable than it was in the early 1980s, and it also seems to run counter to the prevailing trend in other European countries. It is argued that this outcome is mainly due to changes that have taken place in the nature and strategies of the actors involved.*

*For years you've been walking along a razor's edge, and the unions could have given you the fatal push. They didn't do so. Perhaps you don't realise it, but the unions are the jewel in your crown.*

(Paul Samuelson, interview in *La Repubblica*, 3 May 1996)

CHANGING RELATIONS BETWEEN EMPLOYERS, UNIONS AND THE STATE

*From the Unstable Social Pacts of the 1980s to the Re-Emergence of Political Bargaining in the 1990s*

In the early 1980s relations between unions, employers' associations and governments were characterised mainly by a search for an 'anti-inflation social pact'. The outcome of this long and laborious political negotiation was a tripartite agreement signed in January 1983. In exchange for a jointly-agreed revision of the *scala mobile* (inflation-linked wage escalator) and a more flexible use of the labour force, the government offered state-financed benefits to the social partners: subsidies for social security contributions were offered to employers, and the neutralisation of fiscal drag and an increase in family allowances to workers. The role of the government, therefore, was to offset the costs incurred by employers and workers in complying with the agreement.

Although that agreement was hailed by many observers as marking a crucial stage in relations between industrial relations actors and the political system, it did not in fact give rise to stable concertation. An attempt was made the following year to repeat the experience, but this was less successful. Neither the government nor the unions could in fact replicate the role they had performed the previous year. After being widely criticised for using public expenditure to gain consensus, and faced with a huge public deficit, the government found it more difficult to offer compensation to the social partners for the 'sacrifices' required of them. The unions, for their part, were undergoing a crisis of representation, and they were especially vulnerable to internal splits created, amongst other things, by the divergent policies pursued by the political parties with which they were associated. The Craxi government sought to acquire social legitimation by means of a new tripartite agreement which the majority block of the *Confederazione Generale Italiana del Lavoro* (CGIL), closely linked to the Italian Communist Party (PCI), was unwilling to accept. The government's proposal, therefore, was accepted by the two minority unions – *the Unione Italiana del Lavoro* (UIL) and the Italian *Confederazione Italiana Sindicati Lavoratori* (CISL) but not by the majority one – the CGIL. The outcome was a flawed agreement which the government sought to remedy by introducing its contents in a decree law.

The importance that the parties attributed to the issues regulated by the agreement, and even more to its symbolic value, was made plain by the PCI's decision to promote a referendum against the decree. Although the result of the referendum, held in June 1985, proved to be a defeat for the PCI, it aborted any further attempt at an anti-inflationary social pact for the rest of the decade. The economic content of such pacts was now secondary to their symbolic function as an exchange of legitimation between organised interests and the government. Divergent political goals thus came to predominate again within trade union cultures which grew increasingly unable to agree on the concrete issues to bring to the bargaining table. Moreover, the government's ability to offer compensatory measures was drastically restricted by the size of the public debt, which precluded any increase in welfare benefits, and also by restructuring processes that made promises of increased employment hard to believe.

The attempted social pacts of the early 1980s can, with hindsight, also be viewed as a determined effort to institutionalise Italian industrial relations by means of a mix of associative and state regulation. Although, as mentioned, the specific concern was with inflation, employment and welfare benefits, this method of political bargaining had the more general aim of replacing the antagonism and informality that typified relationships among the social partners with rules for stable and centrally institutionalised co-operation. The objective was thus to create a model that would be imitated by a 'knock-on' effect at more decentralised levels. But these informal aims were even less successfully achieved than the explicitly stated goals.

However, while relations between unions, employers' associations and government were paralysed and adversarial at the central level, in the periphery of the system a practice of 'secluded micro-concertation' became increasingly widespread, especially in large companies seeking to reorganise themselves and in small-business districts.[1] This was a voluntarist and negotiated solution to the problem of making the rules governing the employment relationship more flexible; in many cases, even a genuine, although informal co-management of industrial adjustment was achieved. In several companies, in fact, industrial restructuring was carried forward, not in open conflict with the unions, but in a sort of permanent discussion on solutions to problems as and when they arose: whether to resort to *Cassa Integrazione* (the wages guarantee fund), for example, or use early retirement or other instruments to manage redundancies, or how to keep the effects of technological innovation under control and whether to pay for overtime or to adopt forms of compensation with longer vacations, etc.

There thus emerged in the 1980s a tacit acceptance of the existence of two distinct spheres of action: the central and official level (which continued to be dominated by difficult and often adversarial relations), and the local level of the company or the industrial district, where instead a search for joint regulation, if only informal and voluntaristic, prevailed. The lack of institutionalisation, however, implied a certain amount of instability in relationships, and uncertainty over rules and outcomes. It is only in the 1990s that political bargaining – which ceased after the failed tripartite agreement of 1984 – has been resumed with vigour, and that a solution has at last been found for the problem of incomplete institutionalisation. The most significant events of this re-emergence of concertation have been the following: the laws informally negotiated with the unions in 1990 and in 1992–93 to bring the civil service into line with the Italian model of industrial relations in the private sector; negotiation over incomes policy and the collective bargaining structure, which concluded with two tripartite agreements in 1992 and 1993; and negotiation over pension reform, which gave rise first to the most severe social conflict of the last 20 years and then to an agreement between government and unions on a law which was strikingly innovative for the Italian policy-making system.[2]

The revival of concertation is a crucial feature of the political system and the management of the Italian economy during the transition from the first to the second Republic. It is also an essential factor in its stability. It is even more significant because it stands in sharp contrast to both the crisis of centralised bargaining on incomes policies in countries with long neo-corporatist traditions like Sweden;[3] and the failure of similar attempts to reform the pension system conducted unilaterally by the French government. It is on this revival that the attention of this essay largely focuses.

*Incomes Policies and Collective Bargaining Reform: The New Tripartite Agreements*

The absence of formal political bargaining in the second half of the 1980s did not mean that relationships among the three major actors were entirely non-existent. Various governments continued the practice of consulting the social partners separately before they introduced important economic policy measures (in particular, prior to preparation of the annual *legge finanziaria*, or Finance Act for the budget). They even occasionally reached bilateral agreements, an example being the tax agreement signed with the unions in 1989. However, besides the factors discussed above, any genuine revival of tripartite concertation was obstructed by the major and unresolved issue of the *scala mobile*. Although it effectively shielded wages from the risk of inflation (until the mid-1980s, wages were automatically adjusted to cover about 80 per cent of the inflation rate), the *scala mobile* was the principal problem in employers' labour costs and competitiveness, but also for collective bargaining, given that it left very narrow margins to negotiate wage growth and differentials. For the unions, on the other hand, the *scala mobile* had great symbolic significance, since it was the outcome of previous waves of collective mobilisation and the main indicator of their ability to resist changes in the balance of power between themselves, employers and the state.

Hence, when negotiation over the cost of labour and the collective bargaining structure was resumed in 1989, the issue of the *scala mobile* prevented any progress. The two new tripartite agreements signed in 1990 and 1991 also acknowledged this deadlock by restricting themselves to declarations of principle while postponing reform of the indexation system. However, the political situation changed radically in 1992, the year in which the *Mani Pulite* ('Clean Hands') investigation was launched.[4] The April elections brought the collapse of the old political system, and the new 'technocratic government' headed by Giuliano Amato found itself faced with a dramatic fiscal and monetary crisis. It was this climate of national emergency that enabled the government to mobilise the consensus necessary for the most drastic attempt to balance the state accounts since the late 1940s.

The tripartite agreement reached in July 1992 which abolished the *scala mobile* was also the product of this climate. The aim was to reduce the inflation rate from the then 5.4 per cent to 3.2 per cent in 1993, to 2.5 per cent in 1994, and to 2 per cent in 1995. For this purpose, not only was the *scala mobile* abolished, but company-level bargaining was frozen for the entire period of 1992–93. The core of the agreement was, therefore, the curbing of wages growth without the compensatory measures that had traditionally accompanied political trade-offs in the early 1980s. Despite the resignation (later withdrawn) by the leader of the CGIL, who had signed the agreement notwithstanding considerable pressure from his union members, and despite numerous wildcat strikes in the most unionised factories, the agreement was generally hailed as the first true, albeit incomplete, turning-point in the relationships between the three actors – incomplete because it did no more than set a temporary halt on company-level bargaining, while failing to introduce rules and procedures into the overall system of collective bargaining.

The problem was tackled the following year by the new 'technocratic government' led by Carlo Ciampi. In fact, the agreement signed by this government with the social partners in July 1993 was less obviously an emergency measure with short-term solutions. Instead, it set out a stable architecture for incomes policies and collective bargaining. First of all, as well as confirming the abolition of the *scala mobile,* the agreement set out an incomes policy based on the joint but autonomous commitment of the parties involved to peg wage rises to the expected inflation rate. For this purpose, two annual meetings were set up in order, respectively, 'to define common objectives concerning the expected inflation rate, the growth of GDP and employment' and 'to verify the coherence of behaviour by the parties engaged in the autonomous exercise of their respective responsibilities'.

Second, the bipolar character of the Italian collective bargaining system – consisting of a national industry level as well as of a company or local one – was confirmed. At the same time, however, the roles of the two levels were specified, and the relations between them better defined, in order to prevent the overlapping that had occurred in the past. The national industry contract (of two-years' duration for wages and four years for other matters) was given the function of adjusting pay scales to the expected rate of inflation and, if possible, to productivity increases in the industry. The company contract (for large companies) or the local contract (for small ones) were instead expected to redistribute further productivity increases, as well as to deal with the consequences of technological and organisational innovation, although they were not to overlap with concessions obtained at the national level. In order to render this second level of collective bargaining viable, a new system of workplace representation was envisaged – a system later sanctioned by an agreement between the unions and the employers' associations in December 1993. For the first time, 'collective bargaining, and especially the relationship between the social partners and the government has become the core of economic and social regulation'.[5]

## Negotiation over Pension Reform

The Italian pension system grew rapidly after the Second World War, but in an incremental and confused manner, with the progressive extension of insurance to different occupational categories, each with a diverse relationship between contributions and benefits and often with separately managed funds. Reform of this chaotic system had long been on the policy agenda for reasons of cost cutting, rationalisation and equity. The latter objective was an enduring component of concertation in the 1970s and 1980s. For example, it shaped the bill negotiated by the government with the unions in 1978 during the period of 'national solidarity', although it was blocked in Parliament by the pressure groups that it penalised.

In the 1990s, the problem of curbing expenditure on social security has grown especially dramatic. Although in Italy the percentage of overall social spending to GDP is below the European average, the proportion of that spending allocated to pensions far exceeds the average.[6] When this fact is set against the background of a huge public debt on the one hand, and of a constant decline in the population and labour force on the other, it is evident why reform of the pension system has become a central concern of the country's policy makers and the keystone of Italy's strategy for economic recovery.

The first to get to grips with the problem with any degree of success was the Amato government, which issued a decree in 1992 that raised the age of retirement and increased the minimum number of years of contributions necessary to qualify for a pension. Among other changes, it was also made more difficult to combine a pension with other work-related income. But a 'structural' reform which would replace earnings-related pensions with a contributions-related scheme, and abolish the 'seniority pensions' (which enabled employees to retire at any age as long as they had completed 35 years of contributions) was still lacking. These issues were closely bound up with the 'acquired rights' of many categories of workers, as well as the role and the power of the unions, since these hold the majority in the board of directors of INPS (the institute that manages the pensions of wage and salary earners in the private sector). It was, therefore, extremely difficult to deal with these problems without building some consensus among the interest organisations concerned.

The Berlusconi government installed in May 1994 initially seemed to support the latter project when it set up a committee of experts and representatives from the social partners with the task of formulating proposals for reform. However, given the inability of this committee to go beyond agreement on generic principles and suggest shared and specific measures, the government decided to act unilaterally by including provisions in the Finance Act that would effectively eliminate seniority pensions. The first centre-right government of the post-war years, therefore, tried to change the unwritten rules of the game that had regulated the Italian social security system. The government decided, that is, to use the pension reform issue – for which there was broad political consensus combined with strong pressure from the financial markets – to test what it perceived to be an altered state of power relations. It also wished to see if it was possible to cut public spending without the consensus of the unions.

However, it was precisely the nature of this initiative that gave particular impetus and incisiveness to trade union mobilisation. Although the reform proposals that the unions themselves drew up were not greatly dissimilar to those of the government, a general strike was immediately proclaimed, and it achieved notable success. The protest was vociferous and spread to every part of the country. Wildcat strikes were staged in many workplaces, even prior to the general strike; nation-wide demonstrations by pensioners had a major impact, and the bulk of public opinion apparently supported the mobilisation. The protest culminated in a national rally in Rome organised by the unions in November 1994. With a million and a half people taking to the streets in protest, this was the largest demonstration in post-war Italian history, and its inevitable effect was to weaken consensus for the government's policy. Even the Confindustria (the main employers' confederation), which had explicitly supported it, and some parties in the government coalition, watched these developments with disquiet. The result was a defeat for the government, which, in an agreement signed with the unions, was forced to remove the provisions on pensions from the Finance Act and postpone them until the following year.

At the beginning of 1995, the centre-right Berlusconi government was replaced by a further 'technocratic government', led this time by Lamberto Dini, which included pension reform among the four points of its programme to be fulfilled before new elections. Although Dini had been treasury minister in the previous government and, therefore, one of the architects of the failed attempt at reform, his technocratic government was based on parliamentary support from the centre-left. The new project to reform the pension system, therefore, had once again to seek the support of the trade unions.

In fact, in marked contrast to the situation under Berlusconi, the government and the unions were now able to engage in bargaining, based on a plan for reform drawn up by union experts. Agreement was reached in May 1995. Although the employers' associations were involved at various stages of the long and difficult talks, the Confindustria was generally critical of the reform, deeming it insufficiently radical while regarding the planned spending cuts as excessively diluted over time. The agreement was therefore signed only by the government and the unions. The government converted the text of the agreement into a bill submitted to Parliament, while the unions put it to referendum in the workplaces, where they obtained a hard-won but significant majority backing.

The bill was finally approved by Parliament in July, and, together with the tripartite agreements of 1992 and 1993, the new 'negotiated' law was hailed as one of the cornerstones of Italy's economic recovery. There is no doubt that this was one of the most radical reforms in the history of the Italian welfare state, although its immediate effects on curbing expenditure on pensions were not particularly pronounced. The key condition for obtaining trade-union consensus was, in fact, retention of the previous pension system as far as more elderly workers were concerned, with the introduction – total or partial – of a new and more rigorous system for workers with lower seniority. This obviously meant that savings would only accrue gradually. But the key point was the assent given the reform by the unions. Backed by the more or less convinced approval of their members, this support yielded a result quite different both from the previous year's setback and from the social conflict generated by the Juppé reforms in France. Moreover, in an incrementalist policy-making system like Italy's, the social security reform represented a quite unusual policy innovation.[7]

ACTORS AND PROCESSES IN THE RE-EMERGENCE OF CONCERTATION

At the beginning of the 1990s, the features and strategies of Italian interest organisations appeared by and large to be a continuation of past practice, namely a pluralist and voluntarist one combined with some aspects of institutional involvement on the part of industrial relations actors.[8] Numerous actors, on both sides of industry, were engaged in complex games of co-operation and confrontation, not only between the two alignments of capital and labour but also within them as well. The level of formalisation and institutionalisation of relations between the two sides continued to be low; and this restricted their degree of predictability and reliability and hampered the growth of explicit co-operation. On the other hand, the veto power of trade unions was still strong enough to discourage any attempts to ignore them, as had occurred in other countries. Finally, the marked differentiation of rules and practices between the public and private sectors should be noted, since these gave rise to several distortions.

In the 1980s, each of these aspects – the segmentation and dispersal of representation, the informality and scant co-ordination of relations

between actors, the differences between the normative frameworks of the
public and private sectors – prompted the various parties concerned to
undertake numerous projects for rationalisation. However, these attempts
at reform were thwarted by the difficulty of dealing with the complex games
among actors and the peculiar mix of informality and institutional
regulation in industrial relations. If innovations were to be successful,
strong external pressure and/or government intervention were apparently
required. As we shall see, it was precisely this that occurred in the early
1990s, bringing profound changes to the industrial relations' framework.

*Dealing with Trade Union Weakness: The Reform of Works Councils and the
Debate on Union Unification*

At the beginning of the 1990s, Italian confederal trade unionism appeared
weaker than it had been ten years previously, although a proper assessment
of union strength reveals it to be less transformed than is commonly claimed.
A first signal was the decline in membership of the CGIL, CISL and UIL
among active workers from 7,376,000 in 1980 to 6,149,000 in 1990, with a
consequent reduction in the unionisation rate from 48.6 per cent to 38.6
per cent.[9] This decline, however, seems to have stemmed more from the
effects of structural changes in the economy rather than any explicit worker
disenchantment with trade-union strategies. And in any case the rate of
unionisation in Italy remained rather high by European standards.[10]

Another sign of growing weakness was the deterioration in the confederal unions' relationship with their rank and file as symbolised by the
growth of the *Cobas* (the 'base committees' or independent unions) and by
expressions of discontent such as the so-called, 'self-convened' councils.
However, while this discontent was certainly evident in areas of the public
sector, it was much more sporadic in the private sector, where confederal
unionism continues to predominate at the company level. In fact, at this
level the unions have been actively engaged in the micro-concertation
processes mentioned earlier.

There were also negative effects from the division and competition
among trade-union organisations that followed the breakdown of the
*Federazione Unitaria* (the federative pact between the three confederal
unions) in 1984 and which repeatedly blocked attempts at organisational
reform. However, although this competition made the decision-making
process more sclerotic, it did not substantially impede united action.
Indeed, after several previous attempts, in March 1991 the three union
organisations managed to reach an important agreement on rules of
reciprocal behaviour and on a new pattern of workplace organisation (see
below).

More generally, until the early 1990s, the role of the unions at the company level remained scattered, scarcely visible and socially unrecognised. Distinctions and tensions among the three confederations, especially at the central level, created space for direct intervention by the state in resolving controversial issues, while also systematically impeding implementation of the various projects for organisational self-reform (including that of 1991 mentioned above). Subsequently, however, changes in relations between unions and workers and among the three union organisations were finally introduced with the tripartite agreement of July 1993. This strengthened confederal unionism and enhanced its role and influence.

A first and most crucial change was the reform of workplace representation in 1993. Under the tripartite agreement of July 1993, the social partners decided that a single pattern of workplace representation was to be introduced for the whole economy.[11] This new system was called *Rappresentanza sindacale unitaria* (RSU), a name coined in the 1991 agreement between CGIL, CISL and UIL to stress the unions' commitment to creating unitary organisations in workplaces. Actually, much like the 'old' works councils, this new body was to be elected by all workers (and not only by union members), and would represent the trade-union organisations, since they had priority in nominating candidates. The novel aspect was rather that, following the reorganisation of the collective bargaining system by the 1993 agreement, the employers realised that it was also in their interest to place in-company representative bodies on a sounder footing, to provide a reliable partner for decentralised bargaining.[12] Accordingly, in December 1993 the employers' associations and the trade unions signed a national-level agreement on the RSU, the first to regulate such matters after 30 years of informal arrangements.

Although there were still ambiguities in interpretation and resistance from those who feared losses in workplace elections, in 1994 and 1995 the workplace representative bodies were renewed and revitalised to an extent unknown since the end of the 1970s. The results were striking. According to data from the 'National Observatory on RSU', more than 70 per cent of those entitled to do so turned out to vote. Everywhere, confederal unionism obtained large majorities of votes and of representatives (95 per cent and 96 per cent respectively).[13] This led to a broad, and perhaps unexpected, turnover of workplace representatives. In Milan alone, 5,000 new delegates, that is without previous experience, were elected over these two years. In consequence, efficient channels for voice (from below) and for consultation initiatives (from above) have been created, as confirmed by support for the pension reform in May 1995. This is all the more significant if one bears in mind that, after an interval of many years, the RSU elections have been widely coverage in the press, which has helped strengthen the public image of the confederal unions.

Another new feature has been the resumption and acceleration of debate on union unification. This is a change which has been contemplated ever since the breakdown of the federative pact in 1984. It was partly anticipated by the joint action undertaken by the unions in the second half of the 1980s, as well as by the decision taken by the CGIL in the early 1990s to dissolve its internal party factions. But the intention is now to unify confederal unionism: that is, to create a single union organisation after half a century of either splits or *ad hoc* pacts (whether of non-belligerence or alliance). For this purpose, several meetings have been held among the union leaders, and the schedule formally established, although the outcomes are, as yet, unclear.

Overall, then, in the mid-1990s various changes have taken place in the relationships between representatives and represented, and among the labour organisations; changes which have consolidated confederal unionism while also strengthening its role *vis-à-vis* employers and the government. In this new context, even the results of the referendum of June 1995, which abolished several statutory provisions particularly favourable to the confederal unions, have not – at least to date – had the damaging effects that one might have expected in other circumstances. This depends in part on the fact that these matters were also regulated by collective bargaining, which the referendum did not affect. But it is certainly significant that the employers have not used the results of the referendum to launch a campaign against the confederal unions, taking advantage of their decreasing popularity.

All of these successful reforms had been attempted in the past but failed. This raises the question as to which factors are responsible for this change – a question that cannot be answered solely by reference to the actors themselves, namely, to shifts in their strategies and choices. The decisive factor has instead been the impact of external variables, which have functioned as catalysts of change. The first variable relates to changes that have occurred in the parties of the left since 1989, which have gradually eliminated the historical reasons for divisions in the labour movement. A second factor has been the explosion of corruption scandals involving parties, commercial enterprises and institutions, the unexpected outcome of which has been to make a break with the past socially desirable. The third factor has been the constraints imposed by the process of European unification, especially since the ratification of the Maastricht Treaty.

*The Dilemmas of the Employers' Associations. Between Laissez-Faire Pressures from Small Employers and a Strategic Interest in Consensus*

For the employers' associations, too, the early 1990s continued the pattern of the 1980s: that is, diverse strategies and marked segmentation among organisations. During these years, the emergence of new associations in the service sector, together with a widespread tendency by industry-level employers' associations to sign uncoordinated agreements with the unions, confirm the impression of a pluralist system of representation devoid of effective co-ordination.[14]

However, the strong external constraints (stemming from the turbulence of the international markets, as well as the increasingly stringent requirements of European unification) placed common pressures on businesses and created common, cross-sectoral objectives for collective entrepreneurial action. Common to all employers was the crucial problem of mounting labour costs which were increasingly difficult to pass on to consumers. There was a common concern to curb public spending and alleviate the fiscal burden, or at least to distribute it in a manner more favourable to commercial operators. Also, there was a common call for the improvement and rationalisation of the public services, and for aligning the treatment of public-sector companies with that of their private-sector counterparts. Finally, there was a unanimous demand for a more flexible labour market, albeit flanked by adequate social shock absorbers. These shared demands provided the basis for a process of simplification and rationalisation of the employers' representation, at least in negotiations or in alliances with unions and governments, which ran counter to traditional practices.

These two aspects (the 'game' of drawing distinctions and the 'game' of interest aggregation) gave rise to a rather inconsistent pattern of positions and initiatives regarding the strategies to be adopted in dealing with commonly shared problems. The main issue for employers was their relationship with the unions: whether and to what extent they should embrace consensus and the involvement of the trade unions – the strategy preferred by the large and innovative companies – or whether to engage in a more *laissez-faire* strategy of relaxing external restraints on companies, an option backed by small-company employers.

Initially, the positions adopted tended to replicate the traditional standoff between the Confindustria and the public employers' associations (*Intersind* and *Asap*).[15] In 1990, both the Confindustria and Intersind sought an alliance with the unions against the government in order to obtain a reduction in the welfare contributions paid by employers and their partial transfer to taxation. At the same time, both of them, albeit separately, signed agreements with the union confederations backing the macro-economic parameters set by the government. Nevertheless, faced with a bill to defer abolition of the wage indexation system until the end of 1991, and union demands for the renewal of labour contracts which it deemed excessive and contrary to the previous understanding, the Confindustria declared in June that year that it would withdraw from the 1986 agreement on the *scala mobile*. This action predictably led to major deterioration in industrial relations. Intersind, however, did not follow suit, since, as an association of mostly large firms, it believed that keeping good relationships with the unions was preferable.[16] Similar distinctions emerged in the same year during the renewal of the engineering workers' contract, when the private industrialists, unlike their public counterparts, adopted an intransigent posture which led to acrimonious confrontation, the proclamation of several strikes and difficult intervention by the minister for labour. Only in 1993–94, as an outcome of the government's programme for the privatisation of public enterprises, did Intersind and Asap enter the orbit of a Confindustria now in expansion. In the process, this diverse array of interests was absorbed by the Confindustria itself.

After the tripartite agreement of 1993, the priority aim of the new '*grande Confindustria*' – now representative of an increasingly heterogeneous base – became the co-ordination and harmonisation of its affiliates' bargaining policies.[17] In fact, during negotiations over the renewal of the many contracts that lapsed in 1994, conformity with the principles enshrined in the 1993 agreement became the acid test for the success of concertation. A central body was set up to monitor the progress of collective bargaining, although its direct intervention did not prove necessary. For with the implementation of the new rules, the negotiations over the 1994 contract renewals proceeded rapidly and smoothly, within agreed-upon parameters, and without the outbreak of the traditional, almost ritualistic, conflict. The renewal of the engineering contract, which for the first time in its history was achieved in five days and free from strikes, was emblematic of this new state of affairs.

On the other hand, the Confindustria found itself having to deal with the tensions provoked first by the corruption scandals, and then by the entry into the political arena of Berlusconi – an entrepreneur with markedly *laissez-faire* leanings and unlikely to sympathise with the principles of concertation. The strategy chosen was one of explicit autonomy from the parties and from politics in general. As a consequence of this choice, the Confindustria took up a neutral position during the electoral campaign of 1994, and then a pragmatic one of case-by-case critical appraisal of decisions taken by the Berlusconi government. Despite numerous difficulties and tensions, both internally and in its dealings with the government, the Confindustria kept to this strategy in order to hold together a highly heterogeneous entrepreneurial front, and protect its co-operative and stable relationship with the unions, the importance of which it repeatedly stressed.

By the mid-1990s the employers' associations were organisationally more cohesive and stronger than at the beginning of the decade. There were therefore numerous items in the credit column of the metaphorical balance sheet presented by the Confindustria at its general meeting of October 1995. These concerned the reform of industrial relations and the containment of labour costs, the satisfactory results of collective bargaining, and the positive outcomes and stabilising effects of the new pattern of workplace representation.

However, many problems still persist. The most problematic area, one in which government intervention (and trade-union support) has been called for, is the labour market, in particular employers' flexibility to hire and fire. Actually, from the employers' point of view, some positive steps have been taken, including measures to facilitate recruitment and dismissals, and the interconfederal agreements of 1993 and 1995 on work-and-training contracts. But there are still excessively tight constraints which prevent matching labour demand to supply. Arrangements such as temporary contracts, part-time work, and in-company *stages* are unsatisfactorily regulated and the vocational training system is inadequate. These are matters on which, to date, only partial agreements have been reached with the unions. And they are issues which, internally to the employers' associations, are prioritised by small employers and the expanding service sector.

*Coping with the Anomaly of Public Employment*

In the area of public employment, changes in the regulatory framework and in the organisation of the actors tended to anticipate rather than accompany the turning point of the tripartite agreement of July 1993. Indeed, they constituted one of its major preconditions. In June 1990 a law was introduced to regulate the right to strike in 'essential' public services. In October 1992, another law empowered the government to begin the so-called privatisation of public employment. Accordingly, the following year, the government issued a decree implementing the privatisation process, as a consequence of which the July 1993 agreement became the first simultaneously to apply to both private-sector workers and public employees.[18] The laws on privatisation and public sector strike regulation clearly facilitated the July agreement, for they provided some sort of government guarantee to private sector employers that the disruptive power of public employees would be reduced and that public spending would be curbed.

In both cases, the changes in the public sector have come about after systematic consultation/negotiation with the unions. This was obviously essential given high levels of unionisation (it is estimated that confederal unions alone organise just under 50 per cent of employees) and a powerful presence of 'autonomous' and rank and file unions. The law regulating the right to strike in the 'essential' public services has been the outcome of prolonged negotiation based on a proposal drawn up by a group of legal experts appointed by the unions. Although this law breaks with the more than 40-year-long tradition of non-intervention by the state, it builds on the trade union practice of self-regulation and it does not affect the constitutional principle of the right to strike. It introduces a number of rules (prior announcement of the form and duration of industrial action, compliance with measures that ensure the delivery of essential services), the implementation of which is contingent on agreement between the parties, thereby strengthening their role and promoting their co-operation. Finally, a new actor *super partes* has been created – *the Commissione di garanzia dell'attuazione della legge* – which consists of experts appointed by presidential decree and accountable to parliament with the task of non-mandatory mediation. To be sure, this reform has many weaknesses and numerous correctives have been proposed since it was first introduced.[19] None the less, it is probably no coincidence that there has been a pronounced decline in labour disputes since its approval, not only in industry, where strike action has been in decline for more than ten years, but also and especially in public services, reversing the anomalous trend of increasing conflict in that sector during the 1980s.[20]

The jointly-agreed legislation on the 'privatisation' of the employment relationship in the public sector also stems from proposals made by a group of legal experts appointed by the unions. These were harshly critical of a previous law reforming the sector (the 'framework law' of 1983) whose effects have been extremely disappointing. The latter law had, in fact, introduced some collective bargaining alongside the traditional mechanism of regulation by decree. But it did so in a manner that simultaneously encouraged the uncontrolled growth of expectations and demands, pushed public spending up to excessive levels, created grievances among the categories of public-sector workers most able to apply pressure, and provoked these categories into rebellion against confederal unionism.

Under the new system, on the other hand, civil servants find their employment relationship entirely regulated by collective bargaining. This bargaining freedom, however, has been constrained within a legal framework that places controls on public spending and redefines the bargaining parties, on both the workers' and the government's side. The greatest innovation in this respect has been the creation of the *Agenzia per le relazioni sindacali*, a technical agency with legal status which takes the place of the traditional committees nominated by ministries to represent the government as employer. The twofold objective has been the central co-ordination of negotiations and the separation of political from administrative responsibilities, in order to reduce clientelism and curb public spending.

## CONCLUSIONS

### Why Has Concertation Re-Emerged?

In the 1990s, both the priorities of employers and the agendas of economic policy makers have changed in all European countries. Although labour flexibility – the most pressing need in the 1980s – is still important to companies, increased international competition means that it is imperative for them to curb costs while simultaneously securing greater co-operation from the work force. For policy makers, cutting state deficits and controlling inflation have become an external and more powerful condition to fulfil in order to participate in European Monetary Union, while the problem of unemployment has everywhere grown to such proportions that it can no longer be ignored. As a consequence, incomes policies, the functioning of the welfare state, and job-creation policies – all typical subjects of traditional tripartite concertation – acquire a new importance. However, closer analysis of recent experience in Italy provides further clues about the conditions determining the success of such concertation in the new environment.

First, the tripartite agreements and the negotiated laws of the 1990s have been based on the immediate 'exchange' of benefits and on the compensatory role of governments to a much lesser extent than were the relatively unsuccessful attempts of the early 1980s.[21] In fact, recent negotiations over collective bargaining procedures, incomes policies and pension reform have implied a devolution of policy-making functions to organised interests (especially to trade unions) in a framework of regulative rather than redistributive policies. In other words, negotiations have seen an assertion of economic policy authority in a context of 'emergency' in which objectives are largely shared, rather than an exchange of the resources available to each party.

This suggests that, contrary to received wisdom, concertation involving a devolution of policy-making functions to interest organisations, aimed at solving urgent and shared problems, is more likely to succeed when such organisations cannot hope for selective benefits in exchange. Governments may then structure their agendas by giving priority to the shared problems over others, by devising alternative solutions to them, and by involving the interest organisations so that they may bring their values and preferred solutions to bear, without building up expectations for specific advantages.

Second, contrary to the assumptions of neo-corporatist theory, such 'concertation without explicit political exchange' does not seem likely to succeed to the extent that interest organisations are centralised and gain representational monopoly. On the contrary, it may acquire stability precisely because it strengthens workplace representation and gives it a more prominent role. Whereas the tripartite agreements of the late 1970s and early 1980s were made highly unstable by, among other factors, the excessive distance created between the unions' top leadership and the rank and file, the 1993 agreement, as well as the pension reform negotiations of 1994–95, have been accompanied by the creation of a new system of workplace representation (as discussed above) which enabled the unions to consult their rank and file and receive legitimation in return.[22]

Consequently, the potential crisis of representation has been channelled and controlled not by securing legal monopoly over representation but by creating mechanisms for the expression of 'voice' within, rather than outside, the trade unions. Moreover, the elections of workplace representatives held during this period have revealed unexpected and overwhelming consensus for the confederal unions engaged in concertation (see above), and this has also indirectly given them greater legitimation to proceed in this direction.

Finally, 'the three partners involved were weak and needed to lean upon each other'.[23] This shared weakness may go a long way towards explaining the ease with which traditionally intransigent internal oppositions have been overcome. Not all actors find themselves in the same position, however. To be sure, the public image and self-confidence of the employers have been damaged by their involvement in *Tangentopoli* (the corruption scandals). And the legitimacy of a political class either identified with the old regime or possessing technocratic credentials not ratified by democratic elections has perhaps been even more severely diminished. The 'technocratic governments' (those headed by Dini in 1995, by Ciampi in 1993 and by Amato in 1992) have been those most in need of the external support and social legitimation provided by organised interests as a substitute for elections. At the same time, however, they have been able to play on their image of being 'neither pro- nor anti-labour' but instead entrusted with the task of coping with a national emergency. Not surprisingly, therefore, these governments have been able to find the consensus with which to achieve such goals as reforming pensions, regulating collective bargaining, and abolishing the wage indexation system, that their predecessors found impossible, regardless of their wider parliamentary majorities.

As for the unions, however, although hit by growing unemployment and by internal fragmentation, they have not been fundamentally weakened; or at least not to the extent of their counterparts in most of the other European countries, where the employers have instead grown far stronger. This difference in relative strengths helps to explain the greater prominence acquired by concertation during the early 1990s in Italy. It is the medium-strength trade unions, in fact, those which do not possess the high power resources of the Scandinavian ones but are at the same time well-rooted in the workplaces and embedded in networks of more or less institutionalised co-operation, that in the current situation provide, perhaps, a 'precondition' for successful concertation. Such unions can be simultaneously a constraint and a resource for their partners: they may discourage both governments and employers from taking unilateral action which would risk confrontation, while they may convince their rank and file that existing power relations will not allow them to obtain more than the joint regulation of wages and some economic policies.

## The Institutionalisation of Relations Between Employers, Unions and the State

The Italian industrial relations system has traditionally been described as having a low level of institutionalisation, with only a weak formalisation of the rules which regulate relations among actors. Compared with the two polar models of European labour relations – the Anglo-Saxon system based on broad voluntarism in the parties' behaviour, and the German one based instead on a high degree of legal regulation – the Italian model has certainly resembled more closely the former, although it has not possessed its stability and coherence.[24]

The resurgence of concertation in the 1990s has radically changed this scenario. Interaction between unions, employers' associations and governments has not only yielded a large number of formal, bilateral or trilateral, agreements, but, more importantly, unlike in the late 1970s and early 1980s, these actors have explicitly addressed the task of imposing order on the collective bargaining structure, of introducing rules into the relations among them, and increasing their degree of formalisation. These objectives were achieved with the tripartite agreement of July 1993. This drive for the institutionalisation of relationships was by no means inevitable, since it conflicted with the tradition of voluntarism, with the climate of profound uncertainty that surrounded ongoing political transition, and partly with the interests of the actors themselves.

Indeed, informality may have significant advantages, as demonstrated by the good performance of the Italian industrial relations system during the phase of economic adjustment in the 1980s. An informal system offers the possibility of flexible and adaptive industrial relations in a phase of intensive change; it allows the solutions adopted in the periphery of the system to be diversified according to local conditions; and it enables experimentation with innovations that would be more difficult to introduce if they entailed institutional change. Moreover, whenever general rules and therefore new standards are established, those who fall below these standards are forced to adjust or to exit, while those who already overfulfil them are encouraged to lower their standards. Finally, the formal regulation of relationships may have the unintended effect of restricting the space for interaction by removing issues not subject to regulation from the agenda.

Nevertheless, the choice of imposing order on relations among actors by institutionalising industrial relations eventually prevailed, probably because its benefits were deemed to outweigh the disadvantages. But informality also has its drawbacks, in particular the scant predictability of industrial relations and their vulnerability to shifts in power relations. Secondly, in the current phase, the unions considered it more likely that, in the absence of rules, sub-standard situations would multiply more than those in which power relations would secure higher standards. Finally the normative framework provided by the tripartite agreement of 1993 was designed so that it would favour the growth of interaction in the periphery of the system (i.e. collective bargaining at the company or local level) rather than suffocating it.

*The Early 1990s: a Transition Period or the Beginning of a New and Stable Pattern of Relationships?*

The revival of concertation in the 1990s stems from the renewed importance of public policies – not as the traditional source of welfare benefits but as a crucial factor in national competitiveness. Incomes policies, like the reform of social security, are regarded as an important factor in the ability of firms to compete in international markets, as well as being mandatory for European governments constrained by the 'Maastricht parameters'. Moreover, although the processes of micro-social regulation of the economy that developed during the 1980s are still able to secure a certain amount of wage co-ordination and other collective benefits for companies, the new economic context requires greater stability and a greater predictability of outcomes. These objectives can be more easily achieved by means of incomes policies and concertation.

Finally, the globalisation of markets and the intensification of international competition make it more difficult for companies which compete principally on flexibility and product quality to restrict themselves solely to these. Curbing labour costs has become once again important for these organisations as well. And since medium-strength trade unions obstruct the pursuit of this goal with market instruments, while also being a key resource for concerted policies of wage restraint, many employers have now become the most convinced proponents of an incomes policy.

These features of the external context are important factors in the stabilisation of concertation. But it is still not clear to what extent actors are willing to regard concertation as a permanent, institutionalised state of affairs, one not to be called into question whenever the economic situation or power relations change. The request formally submitted by the Confindustria to the head of state prior to the 1994 elections, urging that whatever the winning coalition, it should commit itself to maintenance of the tripartite agreement signed the previous year, is certainly a signal of profound change in employers' attitudes. But this shift in behaviour has still to develop into a shared view of how the economy should be regulated.

Although extremely important, the tripartite agreement of 1993 was an agreement on rules; it was not a social pact which committed the parties to common views on economic development and its priorities. To be sure, in the contemporary period, agreement on the rules may foster the development of such views and encourage the emergence of a shared plan of action. Nevertheless, an agreement on rules only provides a framework; it is not enough on its own to change the pattern of industrial relations. And there is the risk that it will deteriorate unless filled with new contents. By 'common views on economic development and its priorities' we do not mean the old trade-off between employment and productivity; we refer instead to a conception of national competitiveness which gives rise to a joint effort for the full development of human resources. Despite the importance of recent developments, relationships between employers, unions and the state in Italy are still a long way from accomplishing this goal.

## NOTES

1. For a discussion of this phenomenon see Marino Regini, *Uncertain Boundaries. The Social and Political Construction of European Economies* (Cambridge UP 1995) pp.111–25.
2. The discussion will now focus on the latter two, and most important, aspects of the revival of concertation (incomes policy and pensions), while the first (laws on civil service) will be examined in the next section.
3. Jonas Pontusson and Peter Swenson, 'Labor Markets, Production Strategies and Wage Bargaining Institutions: the Swedish Employer Offensive in Comparative Perspective', *Comparative Political Studies* 29 (1996) pp.223–50 ; Torben Iversen, 'Power, Flexibility and the Breakdown of Centralised Wage Bargaining: The Cases of Denmark and Sweden in Comparative Perspective', *Comparative Politics* 28 (1996) pp.399–436.
4. The 'Clean Hands' investigation conducted by the Milan prosecutor's office against political corruption.
5. Stefano Patriarca and Fulvio Pellegrini, 'Contrattazione interconfederale', in CESOS (eds.) *Le relazioni sindacali in Italia. Rapporto 1993/94* (Rome: Edizioni Lavoro 1995) p.100.
6. According to figures issued by the OECD and the European Commission, quoted in *La Repubblica Affari & Finanza* XI, 15 (22 April 1966) pp.1–3, in 1993 overall social spending excluding education in Italy was 25.8 per cent of GDP compared with the 28.5 per cent average in the European Union (12 countries). However, spending on pensions amounted to a high 15.4 per cent of GDP compared with the average of 11.9 per cent in the 12 countries of the EU.
7. See on this point Peter Lange and Marino Regini (eds.) *State, Market and Social Regulation. New Perspectives on Italy* (Cambridge UP 1989) pp.249–72.
8. Gianprimo Cella, 'Criteria of Regulation in Italian Industrial relations: A Case of Weak Institutions', in Lange and Regini, *supra*, pp.167–85; Ida Regalia and Marino Regini, 'Between Voluntarism and Institutionalization: Industrial Relations and Human Resources Practices in Italy', in Richard Locke, Thomas Kochan and Michael Piore (eds.)

*Employment Relations in a Changing World Economy* (Cambridge, MA: MIT Press 1995) pp.131–63.

9.  However, enrolments by pensioners rose in the same period, so that the overall result was an increase in union membership from 9,006,000 to 10,144,000. See Enrico Giacinto, 'La sindicalizzazione', in CESOS (note 5) pp.83–4.

10. According to the comparative data available, in 1980 rates of unionisation in the main European countries were as follows: UK 51 per cent, German Federal Republic 37 per cent, France 19 per cent, Italy 49 per cent. In 1989 they were: UK 42 per cent, German Federal Republic 34 per cent, France 12 per cent, Italy 40 per cent. See Jelle Visser, 'The Strength of Union Movements in Advanced Capital Democracies: Social and Organizational Variations', in Marino Regini (ed.) *The Future of Labour Movements* (London: Sage 1992) p.19.

11. In fact, there had been various attempts to introduce a single representative body in the 1970s, with limited success. For a general discussion of the problem see Ida Regalia, 'Italy: The Costs and Benefits of Informality' in Joel Rogers and Wolfgang Streeck (eds.) *Works Councils, Consultation, Representation, and Cooperation in Industrial Relations* (U. of Chicago Press 1995) pp.217–41; Mimmo Carrieri, *L'incerta rappresentanza. Sindacati e consenso negli anni '90: dal monopolio confederale alle rappresentanze sindacali unitarie* (Bologna: Il Mulino 1995).

12. For this purpose the 1993 agreement made explicit reference to the understanding reached by CGIL, CISL and UIL in March 1991, which thus obtained official recognition.

13. The figures, which refer to Feb. 1995, are quoted in Carrieri (note 11) pp.46–8.

14. Anthony Ferner and Richard Hyman, 'Italy: Between Political Exchange and Micro-Corporatism', in idem (eds.) *Industrial Relations in the New Europe* (Oxford: Basil Blackwell 1992) pp.524–600.

15. Confindustria is the principal organisation for privately-owned enterprises. It has an extremely heterogeneous base in which small firms exert increasing influence. Intersind and Asap are much more homogeneous and comprise state-owned industrial – and mainly large – enterprises.

16. Significantly, Intersind defended itself against the charge of free riding by explaining – in a statement by its chairman – that its 'logic is that of a large company because [its] associates are large', and that there is no doubt that 'the large private companies understand very well indeed'. See Intersind, 'La posizione dell'Intersind sulla questione della scala mobile', *Panorama sindacale* 6 (1990) pp.8–9.

17. On the difficulties of this period see Massimo Mascini, 'Le organizzazioni imprenditoriali', in CESOS (note 5) pp.199–207.

18. Marco Barbieri, 'Le politiche contrattuali dopo il Protocollo di luglio: continuità e discontinuità degli assetti contrattuali nel pubblico impiego', in CESOS (note 5) pp.295–307. See also Mario Giovanni Garofalo, 'Legislazione e contrattazione collettiva nel 1992', *Giornale di diritto del lavoro e di relazioni industriali* XVII, 61 (1994) pp.163–95.

19. See Franco Carinci, 'L'attività della commissione di garanzia (L.N. 146/1990)', ibid. XIV, 55 (1992) pp.435–59.

20. See Lorenzo Bordogna, 'La conflittualità', in CESOS (note 5) pp.75–81. See also Lorenzo Bordogna, *Pluralismo senza mercato* (Milan: Franco Angeli 1994).

21. Tiziano Treu, 'Procedures and Institutions of Income Policies in Italy', in Ronald Dore, Robert Boyer and Zoë Mars (eds.) *The Return to Incomes Policy* (London: Pinter 1994) p.172; Lauralba Bellardi, 'La contrattazione collettiva nel 1993', *Giornale del diritto del lavoro e di relazioni industriali* XVII, 65 (1995) p.164.

22. Richard Locke and Lucio Baccaro, 'Learning from Past Mistakes? Recent Reforms in Italian Industrial Relations', *Industrial Relations Journal* 27/4 (1996) pp.289–303. See also Carrieri, *L'incerta rappresentanza* (note 11).

23. Michele Salvati, 'The Crisis of Government in Italy', *New Left Review* 213 (Sept./Oct. 1995) p.84. See also Bellardi (note 22) pp.162–3.

24. Cella (note 8) pp.167–85; Regalia and Regini (note 8) pp.131–63.

# The Uncertain Future of the Italian Welfare State

## MAURIZIO FERRERA

*The Italian model of welfare is characterised by numerous imbalances, including an uneven distribution of protection and costs, and a chronic deficit between contributions and outlays. There is also a widespread abuse of the rules governing contributions and benefits and a persisting inefficiency in public services. The failure to resolve this crisis has contributed to the erosion of Italy's social and political consensus, producing a 'tax-welfare' backlash and a new territorial cleavage in welfare politics.*

### LOW SPENDER, HIGH TAXER

In comparative perspective, the size of the Italian welfare system is slightly below average European standards. Current social expenditure amounted to 25.8 per cent of GDP in 1993: this percentage was the sixth lowest in the EU (which had an average of 27.7 per cent), while in the same year Italy's GDP per head was the fourth highest.[1] Thus, Italy can hardly be considered a big spender: on the contrary, this country could arguably afford to devote a larger share of its national income to welfare programmes. Yet in domestic public debates the *stato sociale* (welfare state) is commonly indicted as the main culprit for the country's severe financial problems and, more generally, for its serious politico-institutional predicament. Why this paradox?

There are at least three objective reasons which can explain it. The first and foremost is the huge size of Italy's public debt (123.8 per cent of GDP in 1995), whose servicing (around 10 per cent of GDP) has been exerting increasingly voracious claims on the state budget. In 1995, the budget deficit amounted to 7.3 per cent of GDP and was entirely due to interest payment on the debt. The pressing need to reduce this burden – also with a view to meeting the EMU convergence criteria by the established deadlines – has fostered a climate of permanent financial emergency around all public (and especially social) programmes and an almost frantic search for as many targets for austerity measures as possible. The second reason is the very narrow margin of manoeuvre left for tax increases. Public revenues have been growing very rapidly since the early 1980s, turning Italy into a relatively high taxer by international standards.[2] In 1995 and 1996 the level and distribution of taxation have started to provoke clear symptoms of a tax revolt, especially among northern taxpayers. In such a climate, expenditure cutbacks are the only viable strategy for containing public deficits and debt: and despite their relatively modest aggregate size, social benefits still constitute the largest item of total governmental outlays. Finally, the widespread perceptions of a welfare crisis are connected with the internal problems and contradictions of the Italian model of welfare. In qualitative terms, there can be little doubt on the distance which separates Italy's welfare state from most of its European counterparts. Welfare programmes are markedly uneven across social groups and regions; their efficiency is very low; the system is laden with fraud and abuses on both the financing and the benefit side.

Surrounded and partly aggravated by increasing fiscal pressures, these elements do indeed create serious negative effects in economic and social terms, which objectively justify much of the 'negativism' against welfare in public debates and thus offer a potential source of legitimation to the government's policy of rigour. The Italian state does not spend 'too much' for social purposes, but definitely spends badly. The combination of peculiarly intense fiscal constraints and of qualitative internal contradictions makes the crisis of the welfare system very acute: and certainly it will not be easy for the new Olive Tree coalition government to square the circle of opposing pressures and interests.

THE ITALIAN MODEL OF WELFARE

Italy has a mixed model of welfare. Income maintenance benefits are provided by occupationally fragmented social insurance funds, while health care is provided by a universal national health service. At the risk of oversimplification, it can be said that the malfunctioning of this model is the combined effect of three distributional imbalances and two defects in performance.

The first imbalance is the marked dualism of protection which exists between the core sectors of the labour force and the more peripheral sectors. On the one hand, the various categories of workers which are located in the institutional or regular labour market are entitled to extremely generous social guarantees and benefits. In the case of unemployment, for example, these workers have access to a scheme (the *Cassa Integrazione* – wages guarantee fund) which may cover up to 90 per cent of net earnings for many years.[3] When they retire, the same workers get a standard pension replacing 80 per cent of previous earnings and (until the 1995 reform) they could claim a pension equal to 70 per cent of the previous wage after 35 years of contributions *with no age threshold*.[4] On the other hand, workers located in the irregular or non-institutional labour market – the fairly extended 'grey' or 'black' economy – only get weak subsidies (if anything at all) to meet standard risks.[5] Basic unemployment benefits amount to a modest 30 per cent of previous earnings for six months and can be claimed only after periods of regular employment; in Italy there is no unemployment assistance scheme nor a means-tested minimum income. Moreover, social and minimum pensions for those who have no entitlement to contributory, earnings-related benefits are also very low. This wide gap between over-protected and under-protected categories is well known and well documented in comparative perspective.[6]

The second imbalance has to do with the distribution of protection across the standard risks and, more generally, the various functions of social policy. With respect to its European counterparts, the Italian welfare state provides disproportionate benefits for old age, invalidity, survivors, temporary/partial unemployment and short-term sickness, while it grants little protection to the risks connected with a large family, total lack of work or resources, long-term sickness or 'physical dependence' and housing problems. Italy definitely has a demographically biased welfare system. According to some recent OECD estimates, benefits for the aged (basically pensions) absorbed in 1991 as much as 15.3 per cent of GDP, as against an EU average of 9.2 per cent; the benefits for the non-aged (including family allowances and services) only amounted to 3.2 per cent, as against an EU average of 7.7 per cent. In conjunction with the first, this second imbalance creates a highly polarised social distribution which, given the geography of Italy's labour markets, also has a strong territorial component. The ultimate losers of such distribution seem to be large families with young unemployed spouses in the South.[7]

The third imbalance relates to finances. Italy's welfare state is largely funded through social security contributions. The rates of these contributions differ widely across occupational categories and economic sectors, with private employees paying the higher rates. It is true that this category also draws quite substantial benefits from social insurance. Over time, however, the contributions of private employees have *de facto* subsidised (quite heavily in some cases) the schemes of other categories, especially the pension schemes of the self-employed. This distortion has also had a demographic component. Private employees have always paid substantial contributions to the family allowance fund. However, these contributions have not been used for upgrading the amounts of family benefits (which, as mentioned, are very low by international standards) but for covering the deficits of pension schemes.[8] This contributory distortion has played some part in creating the overall 'demographic bias' of Italy's welfare model.

However, the imbalance of the model on the financing side has another aspect: a chronic aggregate deficit between contributory revenues and social outlays. It is true that, to some extent, this deficit is only a matter of incorrect accounting: social outlays also include non-contributory benefits and services (such as social pensions or hospital care) and it is therefore misleading to count as 'deficit' the transfer of general revenues which the *Istituto Nazionale della Previdenza Sociale* (INPS – national social insurance institute) or the *Servizio Sanitario Nazionale* (SSN – national health service) require to finance them. But there is also a quite substantial real deficit – that is, a gap between contributory revenues and outlays for contributory benefits – especially in the field of pensions. Moreover, in healthcare the chronic gap between allocated funds and actual expenditures has produced a large (and partly hidden) debt.[9]

The two performance defects have to do with legality and efficiency. First, within the welfare arena, in some sectors there is a low degree of compliance with the rules which discipline access to benefits and the payment of contributions: a neglect which obviously affects the 'clients' of welfare schemes, but which is systematically tolerated, if not overtly encouraged, by public authorities. The widespread abuses of invalidity pensions, the false declarations made in order to get income-tested benefits or avoid medical co-payments, the deliberate delays with which many employers and the self-employed meet their contributory obligations – not to mention outright tax evasion and even overt episodes of tax disobedience – are all well known (and partly documented) phenomena of the national tax-welfare scene. They attest to the presence of a serious deficit of legality – a deficit with both a cultural and an administrative dimension.

The second defect is the high and persisting inefficiency of public services, largely connected with the system of incentives and the organisational framework of Italy's administrative apparatus. Within the welfare state, this problem is particularly acute in the case of health care. The 1978 reform establishing the SSN introduced many perverse incentives from a financial and organisational point of view. As a matter of fact, the institutional design of the 1978 reform was largely responsible for the chaotic developments and growing financial strains experienced by this sector throughout the 1980s. Starting from 1992, steps have been taken to reform the SSN: but the challenge of efficiency has still largely to be met, as shown by the high levels of user dissatisfaction revealed by opinion surveys.[10]

These five shortcomings of the Italian welfare model are partly the result of specific policy choices (or non-choices) made in the formative years of social policy (1950–70): choices that in their turn reflected quite closely the overall 'political logic' of the 'First Republic'. This is especially true for the aforementioned distributional imbalances: the development of a 'pension-heavy' welfare system, financially distorted and inclined towards particularistic-clientelistic manipulations, was highly congruent, for example, with the competitive mechanics of Italy's polarised pluralism and, more particularly, with the interests of its three major parties – the Christian Democrats (DC), the Communist Party (PCI) and the Socialists (PSI). The emphasis on pensions as 'deferred wages' and the neglect of family policy mirrored, in fact, the social doctrines of both Marxism and catholicism. More crucially, the expansion of a highly fragmented pension system offered ample opportunities for distributing differentiated entitlements to selected party clienteles. The maintenance of an extremely variegated contributory framework, giving rise to various hidden transfers of resources across social groups, served in its turn similar objectives of 'distributive politics'. It must be not be forgotten, however, that to some extent the distinctive elements of *welfare all'italiana* – to use a well-known metaphor in the national debate[11] – find their roots in broader historical features of Italian society, such as the traditional 'uncivicness' of political culture, the uneven speed and character of socio-economic development, the failure to create a 'Weberian' administration, and so on.[12]

## THE SYSTEMIC CRISIS OF THE ITALIAN MODEL

However congruent with the overall complexion of post-war Italy, the malfunctioning of the welfare state has gradually worked, through time, to erode its very material and socio-political foundations, that is, its resources and consensus. The crucial decade in this respect was the 1980s. It was during this period that the distributional and organisational contradictions of the model began to create a real systemic crisis, which has contributed, in a sort of backlash effect, to the demise of the 'First Republic' and still casts heavy shadows over Italy's welfare future. In order to illustrate how problems snowballed into crisis, it may be useful to separate its 'functional' from its 'socio-political' aspects.

The second half of the 1970s marked the apex of the long phase of welfare expansion which had started in the 1950s. In 1975, the generous pension reform approved in 1969 entered in full operation while in 1978 a sweeping law introduced the SSN, which universalised coverage to the whole resident population. Towards the end of the 1970s, however, a new preoccupation emerged to shatter the general state of complacency concerning these social achievements: the country's parlous public finances, which had increasingly serious consequences in terms of inflation, interest rates and debt formation. To some extent the deficit problem was connected with exogenous developments of the international economy (in particular the two oil shocks) which hit Italy even more severely than her European partners. But to a larger extent the problem was directly linked with the much celebrated accomplishments in the social policy field. A major cause of the original 'hole' in the country's public finances had in fact been the financial disequilibria of the social insurance sector. Already in the second half of the 1960s, many pension schemes had started to display substantial gaps between benefits and contributions. The health funds had begun in their turn to accumulate mounting debts *vis-à-vis* hospitals – a syndrome which was further aggravated by an irresponsible reform on hospital financing passed in 1968.[13] In the first half of the 1980s the preoccupation with the state of public finances rapidly turned into real alarm and the new *pentapartito* (five-party) alliance – DC, PSI, Social Democrats (PSDI), Republicans (PRI) and Liberals (PLI) –which in 1979 replaced the National Solidarity coalition (extended to the PCI) was forced to make the *risanamento* (the restoration to health) of the public budget one of its top priorities – at least in symbolic terms.

The 1980s were a Janus-like and fairly tormented period for Italy's welfare state: a decade of both continued expansion and creeping (or better, chaotic) retrenchment. Between 1980 and 1990, total social expenditure passed from 19.4 per cent to 24.1 per cent of GDP, with an annual percentage change in real terms of 5.5 per cent.[14] The most dynamic component of change was, not surprisingly, pensions, with an annual real growth of 6.3 per cent. Also health care expenditure witnessed a remarkable growth in both relative and absolute terms, especially in the second half of the decade. The increase in social outlays was partly the effect of 'inertial' factors – most notably ageing and system maturation. But it was also the result of new provisions. For instance, in the late 1980s the pension formula of the self-employed was significantly improved and throughout the decade a very liberal use was made of the so-called *ammortizzatori sociali* (social shock absorbers) such as the *Cassa Integrazione*. Moreover, the 1980s witnessed the persistence – and in some cases or areas, a real exacerbation – of numerous traditional 'particularistic-clientelistic' practices. This was especially true for invalidity pensions, which continued to be used as a surrogate for unemployment benefits in the southern regions as well as privileged currency for the *voto di scambio* (the exchange of preference votes for semilegal or outright illegal concessions of benefits or other 'favours'). Finally, the whole welfare system, but especially the national health service, provided fertile ground for the various forms of political corruption which started to be unveiled by the magistrates during the *Tangentopoli* investigation of the early 1990s.

Despite their unremitting lip service to the exigencies of the *risanamento*, the various *pentapartito* coalition governments in office during the 1980s did not accomplish much in terms of structural measures. Since the beginning of the decade, proposals for a new pension reform had been discussed in Parliament and were included in the agenda of the different cabinets. All of these proposals went in the same austerity direction: rationalising the system, raising the age of retirement and trimming benefit formulae in order to restore financial equilibria in the medium and long terms. The financial and organisational problems raised by the newly established SSN prompted, in turn, an articulated debate on how to 'reform the reform'. The proposals in this field included changes in the overall (and highly defective) chain of command from central government down to the regions and local health units; the limitation of the power and responsibilities of partisan organs at the local level; the exclusion from coverage of higher-income categories; the enactment of stricter controls over providers; and (later in the decade) the introduction of quasi-market relationships between public purchasers and providers. Neither the pension reform nor the 'reform of the health reform' made much progress until the early 1990s. The 1980s did, however, witness some initial 'cuts' in both sectors: relatively peripheral and not very effective cuts in the case of pensions, more substantial ones in the case of health.

In the pension field, after 1983 measures were taken which aimed to subordinate some entitlements to the actual income conditions of recipients and to control abuses. Income ceilings were established for maintaining the right to minimum pensions and to multiple benefits (e.g. an old age and a survivor pension). The rules concerning invalidity pensions were completely revised, tightening medical criteria and introducing periodical reviews of the physical conditions of beneficiaries.

Though important in symbolic terms, these steps in the direction of a greater 'targeting' of Italy's social insurance were only modestly effective in financial terms. Not only were they programmatically limited to the margins, so to speak, of the system, but they also activated some counter-developments which largely neutralised their positive impact on costs. The ascertainment of the income requisites for minimum pensions and multiple benefits was entrusted to the INPS, the social insurance agency. But this authority lacked both the technical instruments and the formal powers to implement accurate controls. Consequently, the introduction of income testing produced an enormous organisational chaos, many injustices (unwarranted withdrawals and, much more often, unwarranted confirmations of benefits based on false income declarations by beneficiaries) and a massive increase in litigation between recipients and the social security administration, which had to be cleared with a general amnesty at the end of the decade. The most absurd epilogue to the 1983 targeting provisions came in 1993/94, when the Constitutional Court ruled that they were only partly legal, forcing the government to pay arrears of several trillions of lire. Cuts in invalidity pensions were also largely circumvented, in this case not through legal action, but by switching to a parallel channel. The new discipline introduced in 1984 only concerned invalidity benefits paid by the INPS on the basis of contributions, while leaving the non-contributory benefits paid by the Ministry of the Interior unaffected. The second half of the 1980s witnessed a huge increase precisely of the latter benefits, which almost completely offset the restrictive impact of the new INPS regulations.[15]

Cutbacks were more substantial and more effective, as already mentioned, in the field of healthcare. Alarmed by post-reform expenditure increases, and aware that a new 'reform of the reform' would take its time, the pentapartito government inaugurated a policy of 'financial management' of the SSN aimed at curbing the demand for services by imposing expenditure ceilings to the regions and by making users pay in part for services. The annual budget bill became the instrument *par excellence* for running the healthcare system from the centre. Allocations were set on the basis of available public funds, to be shared out among the regions. The savings deemed necessary to remain in line with the ceiling were produced through co-payments and other cuts (reduction of facilities, staff, investments, etc.).[16]

Co-payments (or *'tickets'*, as they are referred to in Italy) were, and still are, without doubt the most visible and the most unpopular instrument used by the government in the healthcare sector during the 1980s. As in the field of pensions, the turning point was 1983. Alarmed at the worrying increase in healthcare costs (especially for medicines) in the previous two years, the government decided to change the co-payment from a modest fixed fee to a percentage, making consumers pay 15 per cent of the drugs. This percentage was then raised on several occasions in later years, reaching 30 per cent in 1989.[17] The *'ticket'* was also extended from drugs to diagnostic tests and specialist consultations. Though heavily criticised, the co-payment policy generally achieved its aims, which were primarily financial. Besides bringing revenue into the state coffers, co-payments did stabilise healthcare consumption, especially of pharmaceuticals. As noted in the pension sector, health care 'targeting' through user charges did, however, have several perverse and counter-productive effects. To mitigate the social impact of such charges, a detailed legislation on exemptions was passed during the decade, combining different criteria (income, type of illness, family and work status, age, etc.). But Italian patients soon learned how to exploit the loopholes in this legislation. Moreover, just like the INPS, the SSN bureaucracy lacked the organisational capacity to administer the norms in force. The result was a rapid increase, through time, of the proportion of exempted consumers, which reached the impressive figure of 25 per cent in 1989, accounting for 75 per cent of total pharmaceutical expenditure. Only a part of this increase can be attributed to the gradual relaxation of co-payment norms. To a large extent, it must be attributed to a growth in fraud and abuses, in the form of false declarations (of income status by users or of health conditions by physicians, or both) and free-riding on exemption cards by non-exempt users.

If on the expenditure side the 1980s were definitely an ambiguous decade (combining continuing expansion with chaotic retrenchment), on the revenue side the dominant trend was much clearer: embitterment on all fronts. Contributory rates were repeatedly increased, especially for self-employed categories. In aggregate real terms, the revenue from contributions paid by both employers and protected persons rose by 48 per cent between 1980 and 1990, passing from 16.2 per cent of GDP to 17.4 per cent; the real size of contributions from the self-employed almost doubled in the same period.[18] Also the total tax take of general government grew extremely rapidly during the decade, increasing from 30.2 per cent to 40 per cent of GDP between 1980 and 1990. According to some recent EU calculations, the actual average tax rate on the incomes of employees rose by 11.4 percentage points (from 31.8 per cent to 43.2 per cent) in 1980–1993, as against an average EU increase of 6.2 percentage points. The actual average rate on incomes from self-employment rose, in turn, by as much as 18.8 per cent in the same period (from 21.7 per cent to 40.5 per cent), as against an average *decline* of 6.4 percentage points in the EU.[19]

Through this rapid and intense increase in taxation, Italy fully caught up during the 1980s with her European partners, covering the distance created by the 'flat decade' of 1965–75 during which Italy's public receipts remained virtually stagnant at around 30 per cent of national income.[20] But this remarkable tax adjustment did not cure the structural imbalance in the national accounts. As a matter of fact, throughout the decade this imbalance grew steadily worse: from 9 per cent in 1980, the public sector deficit grew to more than 12 per cent in 1984 and was still slightly above 10 per cent in 1990, while public sector debt increased from 57.7 per cent in 1980 to 97.8 per cent in 1990. To a large extent this deterioration was due to the self-sustaining dynamic of the 'debt spiral' in an unfavourable international conjuncture. But the internal imbalances of the welfare system (especially pensions) played an important part. In spite of the huge increase in contributions, transfers from central government to finance social protection rose by 76 per cent in real terms between 1980 and 1990, passing from 5.0 per cent of GDP to 7.1 per cent.[21]

The day of reckoning for Italy's 'historic' public sector profligacy came all of a sudden in 1992. As is well known, in the summer of that year, with an impending referendum in France, the international financial markets became quite nervous about the ratification of the Maastricht Treaty. The credibility of Italy's government in ever achieving the *risanamento* was put into serious question: how could the scandal-ridden politicians of Rome be trusted in the event that France (and, therefore, Europe) rejected the project on economic and monetary union, which, hopefully, would also include Italy? Despite the 'blood and tears' fiscal package introduced by Giuliano Amato in July 1992 (including a forced levy on all bank accounts), the lira suffered a violent speculative attack and was compelled to leave the Exchange Rate Mechanism (ERM) in early September, substantially devaluing against the Deutschemark and the other main currencies.

It would be certainly exaggerated to put the blame for such a dramatic crisis entirely on the welfare state. As already occurred in the second half of the 1970s, exogenous developments and endogenous factors other than welfare costs played an important role in triggering the crisis. But it would be equally misleading to neglect the 'historical' responsibility of a fiscally imbalanced pattern of welfare expansion in forming Italy's public debt. The failures of 'chaotic retrenchment' in the 1980s, as well as the social and political blocks to structural reforms in pensions and healthcare, also played a role in undermining the credibility of Italy's capacity for budgetary adjustment, during an especially turbulent international economic conjuncture.

The acute fiscal crisis of the summer of 1992 (with ordinary savers rushing to their banks in order to cash in their government bonds) offered a window of opportunity for pushing through sweeping policy changes with the autumn budget bill. The major provisions regarded, not surprisingly, pensions and health care:[22] after years of sterile debate, the Italian Parliament finally approved the much awaited and much needed pension reform and the 'reform of the health reform', thus making a significant breakthrough on the road towards a new model of welfare.

THE STRUCTURAL REFORMS OF THE 1990S

While maintaining the overall architecture of the system established in 1969 (occupational schemes and earnings-related formulae) the 1992 pension reform introduced a number of significant restrictive innovations after decades of expansion. The main provisions of the reform can be summarised as follows:

- An increase in the retirement age from 55 to 60 for females and from 60 to 65 for males (private employees), to be phased in by the year 2002;
- A gradual increase in the minimum contribution requirement for old-age benefits from 10 to 20 years;

- A gradual extension of the reference period for pensionable earnings from the last five years to the last ten years (and to the whole career for new entrants in the labour market);
- A gradual increase of the contribution requirement for seniority (early retirement) pensions to 36 years for all workers (including civil servants, who enjoyed a much lower requirement of 20 years);
- A new increase in contribution rates.

As a follow up to the reform, in 1993 new provisions for supplementary pensions were introduced. This 'second pillar' had been traditionally underdeveloped in Italy, due to the presence of a highly generous first pillar and of generous rules regarding end-of-career payments. The new provisions introduced a co-ordinated legal framework and fiscal incentives for the establishment of occupational supplementary funds. The Ciampi government decided, in turn, to introduce new restrictions on seniority pensions as well as controls on the beneficiaries of disability benefits, in an attempt to contain fraud.

However, the persisting crisis of public finances, the upward trend in pension expenditure (despite the cuts) and pressure from international agencies such as the IMF, the OECD and EU institutions combined to convince the government in the course of 1993/1994 that a more incisive reform was needed. In the autumn of 1994 the Berlusconi government tried to introduce new and severe cuts, but was only able to enact a more rapid schedule for the phasing in of the new retirement age as well as a freeze on all seniority benefits. The trade unions agreed, however, to negotiate with the government a new broad reform by the first semester of 1995. In May 1995, the Dini government succeeded in striking an agreement with the trade unions, which was approved by Parliament in the following August. The main points of this new reform were:

- The shift from the old earnings-related formula to a new contribution-related formula, to be phased in by 2013;[23]
- The introduction of a flexible retirement age (57–65);
- The introduction of an age threshold for seniority pensions (57 years) for all workers, to be phased in by 2008;
- The standardisation of rules for public and private employees;
- The graduation of survivor benefits according to income;
- Stricter rules on the cumulative receipt of disability benefits and incomes from work, as well as tighter controls on beneficiaries.

The autumn of 1992 also marked an important turning point for health care: the 'reform of the reform' was in fact finally approved. This transformed the local health units (the USLs – the basic structures of the SSN) into 'public enterprises' with ample organisational autonomy and responsibility. Henceforth, the USLs were no longer to be run by political committees, but rather, in each case, by a general manager appointed by the respective region, with professional qualifications and a private contract, renewable after five years if performance is satisfactory. Larger hospitals, formerly acting as branches of the USLs, can now establish themselves as independent public hospital agencies, with autonomous organisations and administrations. These public hospital agencies must operate within balanced budgets. Budgetary surpluses can be used for investments and staff incentives, and unjustified deficits will jeopardise their autonomy. The reform also brought changes in financing regulations. The central government maintains overall planning responsibilities, that is it pays for a standard set of services that must be guaranteed to each citizen in each region. In this way, each region will continue to receive a predetermined amount of resources from the center, in accordance with its own population (with some corrections). However, whatever remains to be paid in each region in addition to its standard yearly endowment must be covered with regional resources (higher co-payments or taxes). The regions and the USL managers will thus be encouraged to participate actively in containing costs and promoting an efficient use of resources within their jurisdictions. The implementation of the 1992 reform started in 1994 and is still under way. It must be added that rather severe restrictions were introduced in 1993 and 1994 regarding co-payment regulations and the system of exemptions, also with a view to discouraging fraud and abuses by both patients and physicians.

As noted above, the 1992–95 reforms represented major breakthroughs with respect to the institutional legacies of the past. Whether they will also be effective in defusing what we have earlier called the 'functional crisis' of Italy's welfare system is, however, another question. Two factors warn against an optimistic prognosis. In the first place, there are increasing doubts about the actual financial impact of the changes introduced by the Amato, Ciampi and Dini administrations. This is especially true for Dini's pension reform: many authoritative analysts believe that the latter is not going to be effective in restoring the long-term financial equilibria of the system.[24] Moreover, this reform has done little to redress the main distributional imbalances of Italy's welfare model. Further structural measures for the *risanamento* are therefore likely to be required in the future, owing also to the approaching EMU deadlines. The second factor has to do with Italy's new tax and welfare politics in the midst of a rather turbulent regime transition. Developments in this realm are rather crucial for assessing the prospects of the welfare state and thus deserve closer examination.

## AN INCREASINGLY UNRULY SOCIAL POLITICS

The unbalanced evolution of Italy's welfare system has not only contributed, since the late 1960s, to undermining its own material foundations (basically, the availability of financial resources within a relatively 'sound' state budget), but has also worked to erode, as noted above, a second important pre-requisite, – social and political consensus.

As is well known, in the last two decades the comparative debate has paid growing attention to the 'tax-welfare backlash' syndrome, that is the potential emergence of social coalitions calling for lower taxes and a containment of social spending. In the early phases of the debate, the main empirical referents were the Scandinavian countries (where anti-tax parties suddenly made their appearance at the beginning of the 1970s), Reagan's United States and Thatcherite Britain. Until the early 1980s, few would have bet on the plausibility of a 'backlash' scenario in the Italian case. Indeed, in the first comparative investigations of this issue, Italy displayed the lowest scores of 'tax-welfare backlash potential'.[25] But things have been changing very rapidly in the last 15 years. Public opinion surveys show that support for the welfare state has been declining quite sharply, while protest against the incidence and distribution of taxes has risen even more sharply. On the center-right of the political spectrum a new formation has emerged (the Freedom Alliance) which openly advocates a substantial withdrawal of the state from social welfare, while the Lega Nord has made the tax issue a major target of its strategy: it openly denounces 'wasteful' social spending in the South and calls for substantial curbs in inter-regional solidarity and a large reduction in the number of public employees. All these symptoms are clearly associated with the functional developments illustrated in the previous sections. But how exactly have these developments unfolded?

Despite all its imbalances and defects, at least until the early 1980s the Italian model of welfare was indeed supported by highly consensual politics. All those categories in need of social protection (and even some who did not need it) could get at least some form of subsidy, not infrequently through clientelist channels. The high degree of evasion tolerated by the tax system, and the massive recourse to deficit spending, contributed, in turn, to keeping explicit costs as low as possible. Both the 'patronage system' and the 'plague of evasion' were periodically the object of public reprobation; but neither politicians nor voters had a real interest in putting an end to them. The policy of *risanamento* inaugurated after the mid-1980s gradually altered, however, this constellation of interests. The first cuts and sharp tax increases started to make the costs of welfare much more explicit and painful for a number of categories, in particular active workers. And despite its failures, the fight against fraud and abuses contributed, in turn, to undermining the legitimacy of the social transfer system, especially among the so-called, *tartassati*.[26] Thus the 'grand coalition' of social groups supporting the traditional tax-welfare status quo started to grow smaller, while a 'backlash' constituency gained increasing ground.

This process is neatly revealed by survey data. As Table 1 shows, in 1986 almost two-thirds of citizens were in favour of the traditional model of the welfare state. Already in 1992 things had clearly changed.[27] In 1996, the situation appears to be the inverse of 1986: the supporters of a 'lean' welfare state, limited to only essential benefits and services, have reached the impressive percentage of 67 per cent of the total sample. The degree of welfare minimalism is more widespread among central age groups, the self-employed (75.3 per cent), center-right (78.6 per cent) and right wingers (75.6 per cent) as well as people living in the north-eastern regions of the country (71.9 per cent). As Table 2 shows, popular dissatisfaction with respect to the level and fairness of taxation is also impressively high. No fewer than 47.4 per cent of the respondents to the 1996 survey (the absolute majority, excluding non responses) declared that taxes are too high with respect to the benefits received. If we include also those respondents who have declared that taxes are 'rather high', the percentage of dissatisfied taxpayers reaches a total of 85.4 per cent. In 1986 the corresponding figure was 'only' 73.3 per cent: in ten years there has been an increase of 12 per-centage points. And it must be noted that the increase regarded especially the first category of responses (taxes are too high): the tax protest has thus been increasing not only in terms of its level, but also in terms of intensity. Again, this protest is more marked in the central age groups, among the employed and in the medium-high income strata, that is, those categories which have actually suffered the above-mentioned 'tax harassment' of the past decade. In particular, tax protest is very closely associated with self-employment, residence in the north-eastern regions and support for the Lega Nord. Table 2 also indicates that there is a widespread perception of tax unfairness: 85.2 per cent of the 1996 respondents thinks that taxes are unjustly distributed. In this case it is possible to make a comparison with 1967. Already at that time the perception of unfairness was quite high (65 per cent). There was also, however, a high number of 'Don't knows'. The massive decrease in this type of response in 1986 and 1996 shows that the visibility of the tax question has been significantly increasing in the last three decades.[28]

If it can be said that austerity measures bear the major responsibility for mobilising anti-tax, anti-welfare and, more generally anti-bureaucratic sentiments, it must not be forgotten that since the late 1980s the impact of these measures has been clearly exacerbated by a second factor: European integration. The completion of the internal market has in fact posed two

TABLE 1

THE ROLE OF THE STATE IN THE WELFARE SPHERE (% OF AGREEMENT)

|        | 1    | 2    |
|--------|------|------|
| 1986   | 61.1 | 38.8 |
| 1992   | 54.7 | 45.2 |
| 1996   | 33.0 | 67.0 |

Percentage in agreement with the following statements: (1) 'the government must continue to provide everyone with a broad range of social security benefits even if it means increasing taxes and contributions'; (2) 'the government should provide everyone only with a limited number of essential benefits and encourage people to provide for themselves in other respects'.

*Sources*: DOXA 1985, Eurobarometer 1992, ISPO 1996.

TABLE 2

ATTITUDES TOWARDS TAXATION (% OF AGREEMENT)

Considering all the advantages you receive (healthcare, pensions, education etc.) do you think that taxes are:

|                      | *1985* | *1996* |
|----------------------|--------|--------|
| Too high             | 30.4   | 47.4   |
| Rather high          | 42.9   | 38.0   |
| Neither high nor low | 24.5   | 6.0    |
| Rather low           | 1.6    | 0.4    |
| Very low             | 0.2    | 1.0    |
| Don't know           | 0.4    | 7.3    |

Do you think that in Italy taxes are justly or unjustly distributed among the citizens?

|            | *1967* | *1985* | *1996* |
|------------|--------|--------|--------|
| Justly     | 7.0    | 8.2    | 2.7    |
| Unjustly   | 65.0   | 87.0   | 85.2   |
| Don't know | 28.0   | 5.0    | 12.1   |

*Sources*: Daviter 1967, DOXA 1985, ISPO 1996.

additional challenges to all those categories whose wealth hinges upon foreign exports: stronger competitive pressures and higher costs (e.g. owing to more stringent health and safety or environmental regulations on businesses). The 1992 devaluation greatly helped to attenuate both challenges. But the establishment of EMU will soon rule out a similar option for the future. These categories (mainly concentrated in the North) have thus developed an interest in demanding lower taxes and better public services. And some of them have come to believe that this can only be achieved by 'dumping the South' – even at the price of outright secession.

It would be obviously too simplistic to interpret the Lega Nord phenomenon in socio-economic terms alone: there is more to it than just a 'tax-welfare backlash'. However the relevance of the factors described above (austerity measures, rapid tax increases, stronger foreign competition, etc.) cannot be neglected in the explanation of the emergence and the persistent success of this new political movement. More importantly, it would be a terrible mistake to underestimate the weight which the Lega Nord and its underlying social coalition is exerting and will continue to exert on the evolution of Italy's welfare state. A new and powerful territorial cleavage has emerged in the country's welfare politics, which is destined to condition most future social policy choices.

Again, the seriousness of the situation may be captured with the help of attitudinal evidence. The above mentioned 1996 survey asked its sample whether they agreed on the desirability of more regional autonomy in taxes and public services. As Table 3 shows, the vast majority of respondents (especially in the North) expressed a high degree of consensus on this option. However, the most alarming indications stem from Table 4. The survey asked all respondents who were in favour of more regional autonomy whether poorer regions should continue to get development aid from the government or the more prosperous regions. 36.6 per cent of northern 'autonomists' (i.e. 28.7 per cent of the whole northern sample) answered *negatively*. In the North-East, a relative majority of 42 per cent of the autonomists (33.6 per cent of the whole sample for this area) gave a negative answer. Among supporters of the Lega Nord, almost two-thirds of respondents (63 per cent) declared themselves against territorial redistribution. Not all these 'anti-solidaristic autonomists' would be prepared to subscribe to Umberto Bossi's 1996 demands for a secession of the area he refers to as 'Padania'. But certainly these data do signal that the new North–South conflict around the public sector budget has far-reaching roots in Italy's new political culture of the 1990s. The issue of tax and welfare federalism – largely cross-cutting the more traditional distributive issues – has acquired a structural prominence which is not likely to subside without major institutional reforms.

TABLE 3

ATTITUDES TOWARDS REGIONAL AUTONOMY (% OF AGREEMENT)

Today people often speak about attributing to the regions greater autonomy also as regards taxes and public services. Do you agree?

|  | Italy | North-West | North-East | Centre | South |
|---|---|---|---|---|---|
| Strongly agree | 24.2 | 0.1 | 35.4 | 18.4 | 16.7 |
| Agree | 42.1 | 48.2 | 44.5 | 40.9 | 36.6 |
| Disagree | 13.1 | 9.9 | 10.3 | 11.8 | 18.0 |
| Strongly disagree | 4.6 | 2.4 | 1.6 | 6.4 | 6.8 |
| Don't know | 6.0 | 9.4 | 8.2 | 22.5 | 21.9 |

TABLE 4

ATTITUDES TOWARDS TERRITORIAL SOLIDARITY (% OF AGREEMENT)

In your opinion, should poorer regions continue to receive financial aid from the government or more prosperous regions in order to develop?

|            | Italy | North-West | North-East | Centre | South |
|------------|-------|------------|------------|--------|-------|
| Yes        | 54.6  | 44.3       | 35.1       | 52.1   | 84.0  |
| No         | 27.0  | 32.3       | 42.0       | 27.9   | 8.2   |
| Don't know | 18.3  | 23.3       | 22.9       | 20.0   | 7.8   |

N.B. This question was posed only to those respondents who had said they were in favour of more regional autonomy (see Table 3).

CONCLUSION

As noted at the beginning of this article, it will not be easy for the new Olive Tree coalition government to respond effectively to the many challenges which currently confront the Italian model of welfare. The debt legacy, external economic and monetary constraints as well as in-built growth pressures (such as ageing, healthcare prices, system maturation, etc.) will keep cost containment at the top of the policy agenda for many years to come. Given the high potential of a tax revolt, the room for new revenue-raising measures is extremely narrow. On the other hand, further structural reforms of pension or healthcare entitlements are bound to meet the firm resistance of entrenched interests and expectations, while, in turn, the fight against welfare fraud and abuses is constrained by the persistent unavailability of an efficient tax system and administration. Thus the distributional re-balancing of the model and the correction of its historical defects does not appear within easy reach. All European countries are facing difficulties in paying their welfare bills in an increasingly unified European economy and in the wider context of globalisation. In Italy, two additional problems make this task even more difficult. In the first place, there is still an outstanding negative balance for all the free lunches of the past. Second, Signore Prodi and his team have to convince their northern and richer voters (and not only the Lega hard-liners) that this debt repayment must remain the collective business of the entire nation, with no viable (or permissible) separatist short cut. Olive trees are known to grow rich fruit even on impervious terrain. It remains to be seen whether the first centre-left government of Italy will be able to fulfil the promises of the symbol which it wisely chose for its election campaign.

NOTES

1. Commission of the European Communities, *Social Protection in Europe* (Luxemburg 1995).
2. In 1992 total tax revenues amounted to 42.4 per cent of GDP, as against an EU average of 41.4 per cent.
3. There is a statutory limit of two years, which can however be extended *de facto* through discretionary measures.
4. In the public sector the contributory requirement used to be much lower: only 20 years. These privileges were phased out by the Dini reform in 1995, but with a very gradual schedule.
5. According to some recent estimates, irregular workers represent 25 per cent of all active workers. ISTAT, *Collana d'Informazione,* Rome, No.2 (1994).
6. M. Ferrera 'The Southern Model of Welfare in Social Europe, in *Journal of European Social Policy* 6/1 (1996) pp.17–37.
7. For a more detailed discussion of the demographic imbalance of the Italian and, more generally Southern European welfare state, see F. Castles and M. Ferrera, 'Home Ownership and the Welfare State: is Southern Europe Different?', *Southern European Society and Politics* 1/2 (1996) pp.163–85. On poverty and social exclusion in Italy, see N. Negri and C. Saraceno, *La lotta contro la povertà* (Bologna: Il Mulino 1996).
8. M. Ferrera, 'Italy', in P. Flora (ed.), *Growth to Limits The European Welfare States since World War Two* (Berlin/NY: De Gruyter 1986) pp.385–482.
9. G. France, *Constrained Governance and the Evolution of the Italian National Health Service Since 1980,* paper presented at the ECPR Workshop on 'Beyond the Health Care State', Oslo, 29 March–3 April 1996.
10. M. Ferrera, *EC Citizens and Social Protection* (Brussels: Commission of the European Communities 1993).
11. U. Ascoli (ed.) *Welfare state all'italiana* (Bari: Laterza 1984).
12. For a detailed reconstruction of the politics of welfare expansion in Italy, see Ferrera, 'Italy' (note 8), and *Modelli di Solidarietà* (Bologna: Il Mulino 1993).
13. F. Gerelli and A. Majocchi (eds.) *Il deficit pubblico: origine e problemi* (Milan: Franco Angeli 1994).
14. Commission of the European Communities, *Social Protection in Europe.*
15. Ferrera, 'Southern Model' (note 6).
16. A more detailed outline of developments in the healthcare sector is contained in M. Ferrera, 'The Rise and Fall of Democratic Universalism', *Journal of Health Politics Policy and Law* 20/3 (1995), pp.275–302.
17. By 1996 the percentage had increased to 50 per cent, one of the highest in Europe.
18. Own calculations based on Eurostat, *Social Protection Expenditures and Receipts 1980–1993* (Luxemburg 1995)..
19. These figures have been drawn from the newspaper *Il Sole-24 Ore*, 21 March 1996.
20. Gerelli and Majocchi, *Il deficit pubblico* (note 13).
21. See note 9.
22. Other important measures were passed on the financing of local government and the functioning of the civil service.
23. According to the new rules the basis of calculation of benefits will no longer be related to earnings but to past contributions. The total amount of contributions paid during working life will be divided by a 'conversion coefficient' ranging from 4.719 per cent (at the age of 57) to 6.13 per cent (at 65). This coefficient will be reviewed every ten years and potentially adjusted in line with demographic and economic development. The rate of contribution payable will be reviewed annually on the basis of changes in GDP. The pension itself will be inflation-proofed and a state-financed social allowance will continue to be paid to those not eligible for a contributory benefit. The system will remain pay-as-you-go but actuarial criteria will in the future govern the determination of benefits.
24. For a critical review of the effects of the 1995 pension reform see F. Padoa Schioppa Kostoris, *Pensioni e risanamento della finanza pubblica* (Bologna: Il Mulino 1996).

25. See for instance the pioneering research by H. Wilensky, *The New Corporatism: Centralization and The Welfare State* (London: Sage 1976) and R. M. Coughlin, *Ideology Public Opinion and Welfare Policy* (Berkeley, CA: Inst. of Int. Studies 1980).

26. *Tartassati* is another popular metaphor which started to circulate during the 1980s and which can be translated as 'the tax harassed'. It refers to all those categories which, for various reasons (including the technical impossibility of evading taxes on their incomes), the tax burden is especially heavy.

27. The data for 1992 are drawn from a comprehensive Eurobarometer survey on social protection. According to this survey, the degree of welfare 'minimalism' tended to be significantly higher in Italy than in the other EC countries (Ferrera, *EC Citizens and Social Protection*, note 10). With respect to the original source, the data included in Table 1 are slightly different: some statistical corrections have been made to neutralise differences in definitions.

28. For a more detailed illustration of the data mentioned in this section, see M. Ferrera and A. Piazzini, 'Una rivolta fiscale alle porte?', *Political Trend*, 6 (April 1996) pp.15–25.

# About the Contributors

**Stefano Bartolini** is Professor of Political Science at the European University Institute, Florence, Italy.

**Martin Bull** is Senior Lecturer in Politics and Contemporary History, University of Salford, United Kingdom and, in 1996–1997, visiting Fellow in Political Science at the European University Institute, Florence, Italy.

**Roberto D'Alimonte** is Professor of Political Science at the University of Florence, Italy.

**Giacinto della Cananea** is Researcher in Administrative Law, University of Rome ('La Sapienza'), Italy.

**Vincent della Sala** is Assistant Professor of Political Science at Carleton University, Canada.

**Maurizio Ferrera** is Professor of Public Administration at the University of Pavia, Italy.

**Carlo Guarnieri** is Professor of Political Science at the University of Bologna, Italy.

**James Newell** is Lecturer in Politics and Contemporary History, University of Salford, United Kingdom.

**Gianfranco Pasquino** is Professor of Political Science at the University of Bologna and at the Bologna Centre of the Johns Hopkins University, Italy.

**Luca Ricolfi** is Professor of Social Science at the University of Turin, Italy.

**Ida Regalia** is Associate Professor of Economic Sociology at the University of Turin.

**Marino Regini** is Professor of Industrial Relations, University of Milan, Italy.

**Martin Rhodes** is Senior Research Fellow in the Robert Schuman Centre, European University Institute, Florence, Italy.

# Index

www.ingramcontent.com/pod-product-compliance
Ingram Content Group UK Ltd.
Pitfield, Milton Keynes, MK11 3LW, UK
UKHW041840280225
455677UK00010B/269

9 780714 643663